ANTIQUES
ROADSHOW

ANTIQUES
ROADSHOW

YOUR GUIDE TO ANTIQUES BY
THE BBC TEAM OF EXPERTS

BCA
LONDON · NEW YORK · SYDNEY · TORONTO

CONTENTS

A Marshall Edition

This edition published in 1991 by BCA by arrangement with BBC Books, a division of BBC Enterprises Ltd

CN4457

Edited and designed by Marshall Editions 170 Piccadilly London W1V 9DD

Editor	Mary Devine
Assistant Editor	Mary Pickles
General Editor	Mike Crossman
Sub Editor	Tim Richardson
Editorial Assistant	Simon Beecroft
Art Editor	Mike Rose
Designers	Micky Pledge
	Paul Tilby
Design Assistant	Helen O'Connor
Illustrator	Janos Marfy
Production	Barry Baker
	Janice Storr
Index	Kathy Gill

PHOTOGRAPHER   CLIVE CORLESS

Originated by Imago Publishing Ltd
Type film by Dorchester Typesetting Group
Printed and bound by Mohndruck Graphische Betriebe GmbH

Valuation is an imprecise art and prices vary for many reasons. The valuations given are estimated auction prices from 1991. As auctions take place in the public arena, this is considered to be the fairest value.

The *Antiques Roadshow* book is based on the *Antiques Roadshow Collection*, conceived by Wallington, Irving, Jackson Ltd, edited and designed by Marshall Editions Developments Ltd, and published for BBC Enterprises by Eaglemoss Publications Ltd

POTTERY, PORCELAIN & GLASS 96

CLOCKS, WATCHES & PRECISION INSTRUMENTS *132*

SILVER, GOLD & JEWELLERY *144*

ARMS & MILITARIA *176*

FOREWORD

HUGH SCULLY

In an old curiosity shop, some 30 years ago, I bought my first antique. It was an early 19th century coloured print, a rather grotesque caricature of John Bull and Napoleon Bonaparte. I carried the picture home, carefully wrapped in brown paper, little knowing that I had unlocked a Pandora's Box of interest, enchantment and sheer fun. Still less did I realize that the simple pleasure of collecting antiques would one day develop into a close professional association with programmes such as *Talking Antiques*, *Collector's World* and, for the past decade, *Antiques Roadshow*. Having started out with a modest collection of toys, I have now been given the keys to the toyshop.

During our travels around Britain I never cease to be amazed by the extraordinary range and quality of the things we see, and I am delighted that so many of Britain's hidden treasures have been brought together in this one fabulous volume. It will give endless hours of pleasure and interest, and provide a permanent source of reference. It will also remind me of the many hundreds of people whose cherished possessions have so greatly enriched the *Antiques Roadshow*. Who could forget Norah Ambrose, the charming lady from Liverpool whose 18th century punch pot was identified on the programme and subsequently sold at auction for enough money to buy the council house she had rented for 35 years? Equally unforgettable was the couple in Barnstaple who, although they did not realize it, were the owners of a long lost watercolour by the Victorian painter, Richard Dadd. To this day I have not forgotten their delight and astonishment on being told that the picture they thought worthless was valued at £100,000. They now have the money to ease their retirement, and the British Museum has acquired a national treasure. Also remembered is the taxi driver from Islington who discovered what appeared to be a charm bracelet left in the back of his cab. After it had spent three months in the hackney carriage office without being claimed, the driver and his wife became the lawful owners. What they had thought were merely charms turned out to be miniature Fabergé eggs. Then there was the lady with the extremely valuable Japanese plate who told David Battie that she had twenty more like it at home. To all of them our warmest thanks for making Sunday afternoons such a regular delight. It is their charm, good humour and, sometimes, mild eccentricity that is so essential a part of the programme's enormous success.

The expertise of my colleagues always appears so effortless, yet I know how many years of study and experience have gone into their vast fonts of knowledge. Now, that invaluable knowledge and experience have been brought together in these pages, along with Clive Corless's superb photography, to create a unique record of one year in the life of the *Antiques Roadshow*. I have no hesitation in promising that you will enjoy reading it every bit as much as I have.

INTRODUCTION
CHRISTOPHER LEWIS

Christopher Lewis, executive producer of BBC Television's Antiques Roadshow, *looks back at the programme's thirteenth year on the road.*

I can't remember a better series for really memorable discoveries than our thirteenth, broadcast in 1991. You will find all the particularly outstanding pieces described later in these pages, together with many more objects which I hope you, the reader, will recognize and value through your own association with similar pieces, whether at home, or through friends or visits to museums and so on.

In a countrywide circuit to places as diverse as Islington in north London, Whitehaven on the Cumbrian coast and Valletta, capital of Malta, we were shown paintings of astonishing beauty and worth – jewellery, furniture, porcelain and silver, watercolours, drawings and prints, books and musical boxes, dolls, medals and guns, scientific instruments, even an entire vintage car – such is the variety of material dusted down and brought to the *Antiques Roadshow*.

My own selection of the best of the year has as much to do with the owners as the objects. Being a television producer rather than an antiques expert, that is my personal slant on proceedings. I fondly remember the lady with the chocolate Easter egg modelled as a gruesome severed head, which had survived, after a fashion, since 1940. I wouldn't actually want to own it, but the delight of the lady showing it to our expert remains with me. I remember too the strange flower-like head on a wooden staff which baffled our experts, though Bill Harriman eventually decided it was a ceremonial club of Polynesian origin. After the programme, viewers' letters with all manner of suggestions as to its identity flooded in. Some of these made me wince, but most people had spotted an article which had appeared in a Sunday colour supplement, by coincidence, at about the same time. The answer was indeed a Fijian war club or 'totokia', most effective for piercing the skulls of one's enemies, and now fortunately passed down for ceremonial use only.

Other items of apparently little intrinsic value brought a response in the postbag. For example, there was a book of working sketches of the Morris Minor and the Mini, drawn in ballpoint by Alex Issigonis and signed and dated 1945 – 47. This showed how a Mini would have looked with full-sized wheels, but one could see how much habitable room would have been lost as a result. On seeing the programme, several students of the history of the motor car wrote asking if they could talk to the owner, but alas we had no record of his address.

I also particularly liked the Roman amphora that Henry Sandon dredged up in Malta. The father of the owner – not Henry – had caught it in his fishing net at St Paul's Bay, precisely where St Paul is said to have been shipwrecked. 'Interesting to think', said Henry, 'that this amphora, used for carrying wine or olive oil in Roman times, is contemporary with St Paul himself.' It makes you think.

Of the items that we know have been sold since the programmes were recorded, none has given us greater pleasure than the silver-gilt salt cellars by Paul Storr which we were shown at the Salisbury Roadshow. This is as good an example as any of the vigilance of the programme's experts. Penny Brittain was conducting the preliminary inspection of items before sending them to the specialist experts and was shown just one

Christopher Lewis and the BBC team in the control room.

of the salts. 'They've been kept under the stairs,' said the owner, 'I think they're brass'. 'So you've got more than one?' said Penny with mounting excitement. She promptly advised him to fetch the other three, and later at the silver table Brand Inglis valued them at £30,000 to £40,000. When I saw them sold in London a few months later, they were bought by the Salters' Company for £66,000.

Another outstanding and unexpectedly valuable item, later sold, was the rarest of rare wrist watches, made in the '30s for Gubelin of Lucerne, with a slim white gold case and rectangular dial. What makes it so special is that it is a minute repeater – at the press of a button it counts the minutes on tiny chimes. The watch was subsequently sold in Geneva for approximately £67,000.

Nymphenburg plate, 1760 – 65.

A Dublin cab driver in the 1930s, by Jack Yeats.

A porcelain plate kept hanging on the wall amongst several other (less valuable) plates was identified as having been made by the Nymphenburg factory and valued at £8,000. It was later sold in London for £11,000. An 18th century Chinese armorial dinner service attracted a considerable response from distant members of the Vaughan family, for whom the service had been made originally, including several family members who owned pieces from the very service shown. This time the service was not for sale, but we were responsible for quite a reunion.

Another of my favourites is the seven-barrelled flintlock volley gun made by Henry Nock and shown to militaria expert Roy Butler. Roy is as fascinated by military history as he is by the weapons themselves, so you can imagine his immense delight at finding an inscription on the butt plate detailing the capture of the weapon from a British man o' war by a French ship, which was itself captured a few months later and the weapon recovered. Fearsome as seven barrels at once must have been, Nelson, we are told, did not allow them to be fired from the crow's nest for fear of setting fire to the rigging, a not uncommon event.

The sweetest-looking wooden doll with original clothes, from around 1750, much treasured and kept in a drawer for most of her life, turned up at the Stowmarket

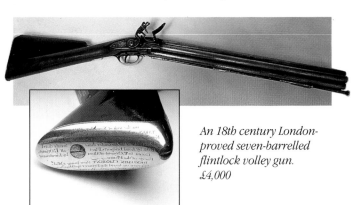

An 18th century London-proved seven-barrelled flintlock volley gun. £4,000

Roadshow. Mother and small daughter were dumbfounded when dolls and teddies expert Bunny Campione valued it at £10,000. Another doll, which boldly announced *'Je Marche'*, did just that for its surprised owner in Bunny's experienced hands. In fact it needed a lot of help, but its head swivelled charmingly with each step.

My favourite painting of the series is the Jack Yeats from the Cyfarthfa Castle Museum at Merthyr Tydfil. We don't usually see museum objects, but in this case the new curator had found it in his vault and had had a hunch about it. How right he was! The painting is a fine example of the artist's work and was valued at tens of thousand of pounds.

Similarly, ever since the Salisbury Roadshow we'd been following up several hunches about a painting of Broadstairs sent in by former Prime Minister Edward Heath, who wanted to know if we could identify the artist. Following a viewer's suggestion, Sir Robert Ponsonby Staples was confirmed as the painter.

So, what images remain after twelve so incredibly varied Roadshows? A curious assortment of the valuable and the not-so-valuable, the cherished and the unrecognized, the

Expert Brand Inglis examines a set of four 'Merman' silver salts by Paul Storr, three of which date from 1813 and one from 1811.

very old and the really quite recent – even objects from my own childhood. Somehow, this wonderful array has survived life's fitful fevers, to re-emerge at the *Antiques Roadshow*. As one woman gasped when told her battered pot was worth £3,000: 'It's survived eight house moves, decorating, boisterous children...' And another, explaining the delapidated condition of her early Nicole Frères music box: 'It's been played with by my five children and their friends. It's given a lot of pleasure to a lot of children'.

Giving pleasure over a long period of time is surely something common to all antiques and works of art, and I hope that this book will also give a great deal of pleasure.

Christopher Lewis

Wooden doll, 1760. £10,000

FURNITURE

JOHN BLY

I made my first appearance on the *Antiques Roadshow* during the 1980 series. I came to the attention of the programme makers because they had seen me presenting a very successful television programme called *Heirloom*. As well as presenting that show, I was also involved in the East Anglian county shows. Visitors would bring along their antiques and collectables, and I would examine and discuss them. All of this went on while the band of the Grenadier Guards played full blast outside the marquee where the show was being held, or the airforce put on a display right overhead.

The *Antiques Roadshow* came to Ely, I remember, looking for someone who worked in the area but didn't actually do business there. I was flattered to be asked and went along quite mystified by the whole thing. Even though the show had nothing like the momentum it has today, I can recall being amazed by the crowds that turned up and the pressure to find something worthwhile to talk about. When I first started I used to go along the queue before the doors opened looking for items of interest. Although I no longer find it necessary to do this, I still like to walk the length of the queue before the show begins to say 'good morning' to everyone.

I started on the 'Miscellaneous' table. The furniture was very much the domain of Arthur Negus, a very clever man who had a terrific appreciation of honesty and did not take at all kindly to people who weren't 'true'. I first knew Arthur when he was an auctioneer's clerk, and would arrange a 'private' view of the sale for me. In those days there were only eight programmes per series and the experts only ever did a maximum of five. The two exceptions were Bernard Price and Arthur Negus, who did them all.

I was delighted to be invited back to the Roadshow the following year to do some more shows. Gradually, Arthur began to ask me to do a few pieces of furniture with him. Our friendship really began when he asked me to be his guest on *Arthus Negus Enjoys*. He then approached the director of the Roadshow to ask if I could do some of the furniture. That was a real compliment. It is nice to be able to talk about other areas, especially silver, but furniture is my first love and, I think, the most rewarding area for the antiques collector.

A chair, for example, can be enjoyed in a complete way. You can look at it and sit in it. It doesn't have to be taken out or put away, and you don't have to spend a fortune to collect usable furniture. If you want a fine drinking glass for your wine, it is of no use

Teapoy. 1870; 29in high. £2,000 – £2,500

if it is cracked. A vase, too, is useless for holding flowers if it is broken, although the decoration can still be appreciated, but faults in a piece of furniture do not render it useless – they can even add to its charm if you can accept them.

Before collecting you must decide what sort of atmosphere you require in a room, or a whole house. Then set out to create it by choosing furniture of a particular quality, according to your pocket. If you live in a cottage, it would be rather pointless to buy a fine marquetry commode, for instance, but if you like, you can create a grand little room, an inner sanctum. If space is limited, one or two attractive pieces are all you need, providing they are of the right quality for the house and have sufficient visual interest. One good piece of primitive furniture, for example, can look dramatic in a modern bungalow. This is where the Americans are so clever and have taught us quite a lot about displaying single items, rather than arranging rooms full of Georgian furniture. Of course,

Parquetry table being examined in Malta. £2,500

you can create a 1740s-style room, but it is beyond the means of most people. Why not buy one single lovely piece for the landing or hall, and have it to look at? That is a very satisfactory way to start out and may even form the basis of a collection.

The most important criterion is that you should pick on the first thing that catches your eye. The piece must appeal to you. If your companion is rather dismissive of the later Victorian dining table you admire, don't be swayed. What really matters is that what you are being sold is genuine. You can then start reading about the period that appeals to you, and build up some knowledge.

I think that furniture, more than any other type of antique, embodies the character of people at any time in history. I am absolutely fascinated by social history but not studious by nature, so I find that the study of English furniture is the best way for me to appreciate social development. I have ended up as a historian, but I most certainly didn't start out as one – it took me years to remember which King George ruled when.

I prefer the 18th century because it is sufficiently far removed from our life today to make it interesting, whereas by the late 19th century most of the things that we know and take for granted, such as machinery and communications systems, had been invented. People in the 18th century had a wonderful appreciation of the arts and education, and designed things brilliantly. The grand houses aside, 18th century homes were furnished by the same means as today. People either inherited furniture or bought new or second-hand pieces. Those pieces bought second-hand were often of finer quality than the newer items.

If a squire was selling his estate, only a farmer or someone of a lower social order would attend the sale, never her Ladyship from the manor. That is why the Roadshow works so well – in a cottage, you can often find furniture that was made for a castle. By the 1790s, when the average yearly wage was about £5, a young aristocrat aged 20 would have had an annual disposable income of about £50,000. This meant that there was a very small section of the population with a vast amount of money to spend on the arts, and that, of course, included the commissioning of beautiful pieces of furniture.

Hall letterbox. 1860.
£1,500 – £2,000

Carver chair with cabriole legs.
Mid 18th century. £4,000

MY FAVOURITE ITEMS

The range of furniture that comes into the Roadshow is always intriguing, and the 1991 series was no exception. The globes brought to the Darlington show were particularly memorable, and it is always rewarding to see superb pieces of early craftsmanship such as the oak side table from Stafford. Trips abroad with the Roadshow usually produce some fine pieces, and the marquetry commode from Malta made the trip particularly worthwhile for me.

▽ *This wonderful pair of globes came up at Darlington. They were standard globes, 24 inches in diameter, one terrestrial and the other celestial, suspended in simple but elegant frames. They were made of pâpier maché applied over a mould. This was then covered with plaster and, when it was cheese-hard, run with a guide like a half circle of timber and spun round to smooth off the rough edges. Inside, a little bag of lead shot rolls around so that if the axis is off the vertical, the globe will always stay where it is put. I am sometimes criticised for placing too high a value on pieces, but a similar pair came up at the Grosvenor House fair which were valued at over £50,000, so my estimate of £30,000 seems conservative by comparison.*

△*My favourite piece from the series turned up at the Stafford Roadshow. It was the simplest little late 17th century English oak side table with turned legs, a single drawer to the frieze and an overhanging top. I fervently believe that furniture comes alive if you talk to it and touch it. I spotted this little chap across the hall. Only a corner of it was visible from where I was standing and it was absolutely speaking and waving to me. Every bit of turning was the colour of honey, and the only things that had happened to it in its entire life were waxing, polishing and dusting. This piece was unimportant in its time but has become significant because of its superb condition. I really fell in love with it. 1670s; 29in high. £4,500*

▷ *This 18th century Maltese commode is decorated with panels of fine marquetry in well-figured veneers. The sheer quality of this piece is apparent at first glance, but closer inspection reveals further delights. Even the feet bear the same marquetry stringing and decoration, confirming not only that they are original, but also the high pedigree of the commode. This extremely rare piece was bought first at auction, then through a dealer, and now rests, highly prized, as an important part of a private collection. It is 3ft 6in wide, and valued in excess of £20,000.*

DINING TABLES

In medieval and early Tudor times dining tables were no more than long planks of wood resting on trestles. Such simple structures could be quickly and easily dismantled when moving house or clearing a hall or dining room for after dinner dancing and revelries.

Elizabethan society was more settled, and furniture, made primarily of oak, became correspondingly heavier and more cumbersome. Dining tables were still required to be adaptable, however, and were made so by means of draw leaves in exactly the same way as modern extending tables. A leaf under each end of the table top could be pulled out and balanced by a cantilever action on two extended supports, or 'lopers'.

As the numbers of smaller houses increased in the late 17th century, so the need grew for more adaptable furniture. Folding tables, including gate-leg and drop-leaf tables, became fashionable, and versions of these in many different sizes were used in all but the grandest houses.

◁ *Oak Gate-Leg Table This typical oval gate-leg table (shown folded above) is the forerunner of the drop-leaf table. As methods of construction grew more sophisticated and tables became simpler, such elaborate constructions became obsolete. In the 19th century gate-leg tables were often trimmed around the edge, making them more convenient for use in the new smaller houses. 1700; 4ft 2in wide.* **£2,500**

▷ *Drop-Leaf Table By the 1730s drop-leaf dining tables had become fashionable, replacing the gate-leg framework. This table shows how the folding leaves are supported by legs which swing out from the main body of the table. It is made of oak and has cabriole legs and pad feet. 1745; 4ft wide.* **£3,000**

By the mid Georgian period, dining tables in which additional leaves could be inserted to extend the length were supported on central pedestals with three or four feet. An alternative was the rectangular table with legs around the edge. Both tables continued to be made in a variety of styles throughout the 19th century. The only true innovation was the introduction in the 1850s of a mechanical action for extending the frames of both round and rectangular tables. In rectangular tables a winding mechanism moved one end outward from the centre, while in round tables the segments were pushed apart, leaving spaces into which extra leaves could be inserted. The extending round table has always been much sought after, but the 'wind-up' dining table has only recently been regarded seriously as a collector's item as well as a most useful piece of furniture.

△ *THREE-PEDESTAL TABLE An early George III-style mahogany dining table. It has the traditional four-splay pedestal in the centre and the tripod form at both ends. Additional pedestals can be added to this type of table, as it was originally fitted with extra leaves. 1790; 10ft long.* **£70,000**

▽ *MAHOGANY EXTENDING DINING TABLE supported on tapering legs, with additional leaves. This type of dining table was an alternative to the pedestal table; the designs ran concurrently from the 1760s. 1790; 10ft long.* **£8,000 – £10,000**

▷ *GOTHIC REFECTORY TABLE The Gothic style of this oak table was very popular with the Victorians. Mid 19th century; 10ft long.* **£6,000 – £8,000**

▽ *WIND-UP DINING TABLE An archetypal late Victorian dining table, as used in the days of the great Victorian households when huge dinner parties were held in upper middle-class homes. It has a wind-up mechanism and six extra leaves which extend it from 5 to 17 feet. The wind-up mechanism establishes its date; the first designs for such tables were published in the mid 19th century. The huge bulges on the legs, known as cabochons, are typical of the period after 1860. This table still has its original castors. 1875. £15,000*

DINING TABLE STYLES

1 Pre-Elizabethan dining table with early style standard ends. Pre-1560.

2 Elizabethan oak table, often made to extend, and varying in length from four to ten feet. 1590.

3 Late 17th century oak gate-leg table.

4 George II period oval drop-leaf table with cabriole legs and claw and ball feet. 1750.

5 Early George III mahogany drop-leaf extending dining table. 1770 – 1810.

6 Classic three-pedestal dining table, originally with extending leaves. 1775.

7 Victorian mahogany table which could be extended up to 20 feet. After 1850 such tables often had a mechanical winding device to extend the length.

OCCASIONAL TABLES

T he great age of occasional furniture dates from the 1750s. Society was stable with firm economic growth, and this produced a rapidly growing class of nouveau riche artisans and professionals all requiring the trappings of an earlier and grander age and class but condensed into smaller houses. Much of the furniture designed for smaller-scale living comes under the broad heading of occasional furniture. In the 18th century furniture was moved around to suit the activities of the household. A tilt-top circular table would have been used as a tea table or supper table, then pushed out of the way against the wall. The drop-leaf table is another good example of occasional furniture, since it took up comparatively little space when not in use.

△ *EARLY GEORGIAN MAHOGANY TABLE in typically plain style with drop-top. 1750; 2ft 7in wide.* **£650 – £1,200**

▷ *VICTORIAN SUTHERLAND TABLE A table of this size was ideally suited to the smaller rooms of the 19th century. It could be brought out for guests, then stored discreetly away. A better quality model would have been made from walnut. 1860; 3ft wide.* **£550**

△ *MAHOGANY TABLE The ornate imitation Georgian carving was added some considerable time after this table was made. Mid 18th century; 2ft 7in wide.* **£750**

▷ *OVAL TILT-TOP TABLE The feet and columns of this rare mahogany tripod table are carved, while the top is inlaid with contrasting veneer and marquetry. The mahogany supporting block for the top is furnished with gilt metal mounts. The overall style is in the manner of Chippendale and Haig. 1780 – 90; 2ft 6in wide.* **£20,000**

◁ *SHERATON TABLE The alterations to this table, including the addition of a new drawer, have halved its value. 1775; 2ft 4in high.* **£350**

PEDESTAL TABLES

The earliest pedestal tables, measuring little over 30 inches across, were made in the second quarter of the 18th century. Known as 'supping' tables, they were generally used by one or two people, and the tilt-tops enabled them to be placed discreetly against a wall out of the way when not in use. The finest tables were made of mahogany, with intricately carved pedestals and legs in the latest styles. By the middle of the 18th century much simpler, more affordable tables were produced with legs that ended in a plain pad foot or a claw and ball foot.

Pedestal tables increased in size by the 1750s and some were made specially for games such as poker. During the 1780s a more classic style appeared, with a splay or sweeping leg, and the central column also changed shape and design according to fashion.

Oval pedestal tables from the late 18th century are the most desirable, and this is reflected in the price of genuine pieces. However, care must be taken when buying such tables, since it is relatively easy to convert the top of a rectangular table of the period into an oval shape.

▷ *MID VICTORIAN CIRCULAR TILT-TOP TABLE, veneered with highly figured mahogany and supported on a turned and carved column with four scrolling legs. 1870; 4ft 5in wide.* **£2,250**

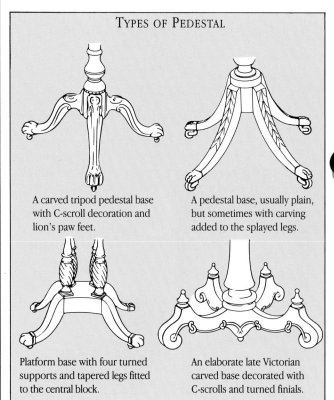

TYPES OF PEDESTAL

A carved tripod pedestal base with C-scroll decoration and lion's paw feet.

A pedestal base, usually plain, but sometimes with carving added to the splayed legs.

Platform base with four turned supports and tapered legs fitted to the central block.

An elaborate late Victorian carved base decorated with C-scrolls and turned finials.

▷ *Rosewood Dining Table* This exemplary late Regency table has rounded corners banded by satinwood and tulipwood and inlaid with brass lines. The octagonal pedestal stands on a quatrefoil base with scrolled brackets; the base is finished with elaborate ormolu lion's paw feet. 1830; 5ft 3in long. **£5,500 – £6,000**

▽ *Rosewood Tilt-Top Breakfast Table* Every well-to-do home of the time would have owned such a table. This one seats six; an eight-seater would be worth twice as much. 1840; 4ft wide. **£2,000**

△ *William IV-Period Rosewood Table* with a nulled top edge. It is supported on a substantial turned and lobed column on a quatrefoil base with heavy scrolled feet. 1830; 4ft 6in wide. **£3,500**

◁ *Walnut Pedestal Table* inlaid with intricate, though now rather faded, marquetry flowers. The octagonal table seats eight, and stands on an elaborately carved base. 1860; 4ft 6in wide. **£3,000**

WORK TABLES

The idea of making a specific piece of furniture for storing needlework accessories was inspired in the late 17th century by the special boxes used to hold lace. Measuring between 12 and 24 inches long, these boxes were fitted with compartments and were often covered in oyster wood veneer. It was a small step to place such a box on a stand and transform it into a work table.

The great age of the work table for the lady of leisure began in the 1760s, and by the 1780s innumerable varieties were available. The classical style as interpreted by Robert Adam and Thomas Sheraton was fashionable,

and the straight, tapering legs and pleasing proportions of this design convey a feeling of great elegance. By the 1830s designs had become more varied, and later still the Victorians borrowed many styles from earlier periods.

Work table interiors were covered in brightly coloured lining paper, while the undersides of the table lids were generally lined with silk or fitted with a deep silk bag.

Early examples command the highest prices, but Victorian pieces have recently become more popular. This is because plenty of tables from this period can be found today and Victorian designs are being re-appraised.

◁ WORK TABLE IN SATINWOOD, *typical of the decorative furniture made in the late 18th century. The Victorians copied this style of table in the late 19th century. 1790; 14in wide.*
£1,500 – £2,000

△ ROSEWOOD WORK TABLE *Most upper middle-class families would have owned a table such as this. Although typical of its period, it is of better than average quality. 1830s; 2ft 6in high.*
£2,500

△ ANGLO-INDIAN WORK TABLE *This pierced and elaborately carved table was made in India to the order of an Englishman. It doubled as a sewing table and writing desk. 1830s – 60s; 20in long.* **£1,500**

▽ ROSEWOOD WORK TABLE *The reverse side of the sliding top is a backgammon board, and when raised the top forms a lectern. Below the drawers, which have delicate ivory knobs, there is a pull-out needlework bag lined with silk. Early 19th century; 3ft 6in long.* **£4,000 – £6,000**

◁ PAPIER MACHE SEWING TABLE AND DESK *The great era of papier mâché was from about 1820 – 40. Its popularity had waned by the time this piece was made, and by the 1880s papier mâché furniture had virtually disappeared. This decorative work table is nonetheless typical of its period, both in shape and decoration. Its value is increased by its exceptionally good condition. 1865; 2ft long.* **£2,500**

◁ CONICAL WORK TABLE *This rosewood work table on a walnut base is of good quality, although some of the marquetry is missing. Tables of this type are prone to woodworm: if the base of such a table is found to be damaged, it is often mounted on a block of wood. Late 19th century; 3ft high.* **£350**

▷ MAHOGANY NEEDLEWORK TABLE *with three shallow drawers. The glazed top covers a cut-felt picture of flowers, and the table stands on a tapering square column and quatrefoil base with turned bun feet. 1835; 20in long.* **£3,250**

GAMES TABLES

As far back as pre-Tudor times board games were popular. There were boards for backgammon, boards for chess, and even coffer lids inlaid with games boards. Tables made specially for cards and games emerged only after the restoration of Charles II in 1660, the end of the Puritan Commonwealth. Although it was some time before card and games tables were in widespread use, by the early 18th century most upper class families would have owned one.

Tables usually had a rectangular top and a flap that opened out to form a square playing surface. Originally the flap was supported by a single swing-out leg hinged to the frame, but after the 1730s two supporting legs were more common, making the table more stable. Such structural changes in tables are a good indication of their quality, and in turn affect their present day value.

Since games tables are both decorative and compact in size – a table can be folded and left propped against a wall when not in use – they have remained popular over the generations and are still much sought after today. Luckily, the Victorians revived many earlier styles and there are plenty of tables available.

◁ *AMERICAN MAHOGANY CARD TABLE The shape of this table is English Regency, but the detail is much fussier and somewhat Germanic. The design, known as 'debasement classical', is the final phase of the classical style in America, with a hint of the rococo styles that followed. Two rare features are the stencilled baize in a mixture of Regency and rococo styles, and the wooden castors: in an English piece they would have been made of brass and porcelain. 1840s – 50s; 2ft wide.* **£1,000 – £1,500**

▽ *ROSEWOOD CHESS TABLE with brass inlay and 'demi-lune' (half-moon) ends. Lyre-shaped end supports such as these were fashionable in the early 19th century. The curved and moulded legs finish in cast brass claws set on castors. 1829; 2ft 10in wide.* **£5,000 – £6,000**

▷ *BURR WALNUT GAMES AND WORK TABLE*, typical of the multi-purpose tables that were produced in vast numbers at the end of the 19th century. The swivel top opens out to reveal boards for cribbage, backgammon and chess; the sliding box below was probably for needlework accessories. 1860s; 2ft wide.
£1,500 – £2,000

▽ *FOLD-OVER CARD TABLE* In the late 18th century the grain to the frieze was usually laid horizontally, so this thick, hand-cut veneer with a vertical grain indicates a date no later than the 1750s. A concertina action pulls out to support the opened leaf. 1745; 2ft 6in long. **£2,500**

▷ *MAHOGANY GAMES AND WRITING TABLE* The top of this Sheraton period table turns over to reveal a backgammon board. There is also a writing drawer with a pull-out ink compartment on the side and candle slides. 1795; 20in wide. **£8,500**

HALL CHAIRS

In general hall chairs are easy to recognize. Although some early examples have shaped seats, most seats are solid and unshaped. Hall chairs were positioned around the large entrance halls and along the wide corridors of great houses to be used by visitors waiting to see the master. They were also used for resting on during breaks from dancing and revelries. Since such chairs were destined for large houses, they were usually made in sets of up to 24, often containing matching two-seater benches. Over the years many great sets have been broken up, and this accounts for the substantial number of pairs and groups of four that are frequently brought to Roadshows and which regularly turn up at sales.

The most common hall chairs date from the 1850s. The best examples are those decorated with architectural carving in the style of pilasters or formalized drapery. Some examples, particularly those from the mid 18th century, display the curving lines that were popular at the time to an almost whimsical degree. Some fine early 18th century hall chairs decorated with black, and occasionally red, lacquer can also be found.

In common with all Victorian furniture, hall chairs were made from different woods in a variety of styles. However, since hall chairs were destined for the wealthiest households they were made from only the finest quality timbers. For anyone wishing to purchase a superb example of 18th century craftsmanship, a hall chair will represent it faithfully, without costing a great deal. Since these chairs can be rather uncomfortable, there is not a great demand for singles and pairs today, although sets of hall chairs are always much sought after.

▷ *LATE 17TH CENTURY CHAIR of fine mid-coloured oak. It was probably used by a wealthy farming family as a hall chair or, with a cushion, for dining. The long raised panel in the centre gives the back a slender appearance. The two little pegs standing proud on either side at the top are a good indication of age. They stick out because the wood has shrunk over the years; the pegs on a reproduction piece might be flush. 1670 – 1700; 3ft 6in high.* **£1,800**

▽ *MID VICTORIAN MAHOGANY CHAIR in French baroque style. This style, unique to the 19th century, was a pastiche of several earlier styles. 1860s; 2ft 6in high.* **£150**

△ *WALNUT CHAIR with lozenge-shaped back and cabriole legs. The chair is made of fine quality solid walnut. 1865; 2ft 6in high.* **£150**

COUNTRY CHAIRS

Simple country chairs can provide the keen collector with the opportunity to acquire fine examples of 17th and 18th century furniture at reasonable prices. Local timbers such as elm, ash, beech and yew, were used to make country chairs in hamlets and villages throughout the country, but there were great variations in the quality of the timber used and the skill of the maker. Indeed, many such chairs have deteriorated beyond redemption, so those that have survived must have been of the highest quality when made.

Many single country chairs are fairly inexpensive to buy, although sets costs more – a set being worth more than the sum of its parts – and chairs with arms are more expensive than those without.

The Windsor chair is the most popular and sought after style of country chair. Originally they were made of beech from the Chiltern Hills which was floated down the Thames to High Wycombe, once the centre of the furniture

trade. Chairs were frequently assembled from components made by several different craftsmen. The legs and spindels were turned by one man, the steam bent members were crafted by another, and the sawn components by yet another. The completed chairs were then taken to be sold in Windsor. As well being the name of a town, 'Windsor' also describes a style, and chairs in this style were made in other towns such as Grantham, Lincolnshire. Windsor chairs have remained popular for several reasons: they have a distinctive design; they were cheap to buy for many years, and, in spite of their wooden seats, they are extrememly comfortable. Many 18th century chairs were painted dark green, and traces of this paint may be found around the joins.

Early country chairs, which were originally made as rockers, are highly collectable, but potential purchasers should be somewhat wary as many ordinary chairs have been converted to rockers over the centuries.

△ *NORTH COUNTRY CHAIR made of stained ash, with a rush seat. The back is composed of three rows of simple turned spindles. 1820; 3ft 9in high.* **£300 – £400**

▽ *ROCKING CHAIR This chair is unusual in that it is made of yew rather than the more usual beech or elm. The rather flat turning indicates a provincial manufacturer and is a clue to the date of the chair. Although such rocking chairs are attractive, they are surprisingly difficult to sell. Early 19th century; 4ft high.* **£1,500**

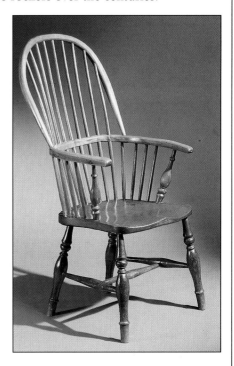

△ *WINDSOR-TYPE CHAIR A chair in Windsor design; the arms and back are in a hoop construction known as comb-back. It has a plain 'H' stretcher. 1830; 3ft high.* **£1,000**

DINING CHAIRS

The earliest type of dining chair evolved from the back stool in the late 16th century. Until this date, rather grand chairs with backs and arms were used only by the master and mistress of the household, while guests and servants made do with simple stools, having to lean back against the dining room wall if support was required. By extending the two rear legs of an ordinary stool upward, and filling in the space between, back stools were produced. These were rather uncomfortable to sit on without a cushion, however, and few ordinary people had cushions to use.

It was not until after the Restoration in 1660 that woven cane imported from the East was used for chair backs and seats. Upholstery also became popular, and by the beginning of the 18th century the dining chair, much as we know it today, had developed.

There were two different types of seat – the stuffed-over,

▷ *WALNUT DINING CHAIR combining the characteristics of the Queen Anne period – solid splat backs and turned back legs – with the outswept top rail and shaped uprights of early Chippendale. The beautiful needlework seat, embroidered by the present owner, is exactly in keeping with the original. 1700 – 50; 17in wide.* Set of six **£10,000**

◁ *ROSEWOOD CHAIR made of finely figured rosewood and retaining the formal back shape inspired by Regency design. The style of the legs and seat is of a later period. 1845; 16in wide.* **£400**

▷ *REGENCY DINING CHAIR with large crozier arms, sabre legs and a drop-in seat. The central splat is formed by two lyres flanking an entablature decorated with brass wire inlay. 1810 – 20; 17in wide.* **£1,000 – £1,250**

or fully upholstered seat, and the drop-in seat, which was a loose seat within the chair frame. In common with dining tables and cabinet furniture, early chair legs were connected by a stretcher, or strengthening bar. These became unpopular during the first quarter of the 18th century but came back into fashion from time to time.

The great age of the English dining chair was from 1760 onward, when sets of 12 or more chairs were specially made for wealthy households. Sets contained single chairs and a pair of carver, or open-arm, chairs. In the grandest houses every dining chair was a carver. Because fewer carver chairs were made than singles, they are much sought after today.

Possibly the most appealing aspect of the dining chair is that a single chair, which faithfully represents the style and fashion of society in any given historical period, can generally be bought for a reasonable price. Even chairs attributable to the Chippendale period and style, which would cost a fortune in a set, can be bought for a fairly modest sum if single. The Victorian balloon-back chair is an attractive all-purpose piece, and individual examples can be purchased for well under £100.

▷ *DUTCH WALNUT AND INLAID DINING CHAIR*
Continental furniture from the early 18th century is attractive and often greatly underrated. This Dutch chair provides an attractive alternative to an English version. A set of six or more such chairs would fetch several thousand pounds. 1730; 17in wide. **£200 – £300**

CHAIR BACK STYLES

Every chair back tells a tale, and the shape, the material used and the means of manufacture all provide important clues as to a chair's age. These basic chair back styles are typical examples from different periods.

Overhung back rail in entablature style.
1800 – 80

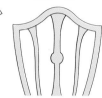

Typical curvilinear back with solid splat.
1710 – 30

Upswept top rail with pierced and carved splat.
1735 – 60

Shield shaped or 'camel' back.
1775 – 1800

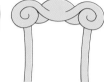
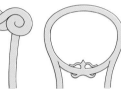

Inset rail, often with veneer or brass inlay.
1800 – 80

Curved overhung rail with neo-classical scrolling. 1815 – 45

Victorian balloon-back, open or upholstered.
1850 – 1900

LEG STYLES

1 Square chamfered, or bevelled edge leg, dating from 1750.
2 Square tapering leg; the vogue for classicism in the 1770s led to the development of this elegant style.
3 Turned leg; this more decorative style came into fashion after 1800.

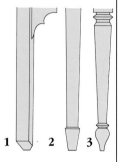

1   **2**   **3**

UPHOLSTERY STYLES

As well as providing comfort, the function of upholstery in the 18th century was to emphasize the lines of a chair and to display the covering fabric.

Prior to the development of the coiled spring in the 1820s, webbing (blue) was stretched over the chair frame. After this date, to accommodate the springs, webbing was stretched under the chair frame.

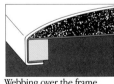

Webbing over the frame.

Webbing under the frame.

STUFFED CHAIRS

Until the mid 18th century few families could afford brand-new upholstered chairs and only wealthy households boasted comfortable furniture such as winged or 'cheeked' chairs. In the second half of the century general affluence increased and this, together with a growing interest in style, led to a greater demand for upholstered chairs. By the Victorian period a suite of stuffed furniture comprising two easy chairs and a settee was considered a necessity. This rapid advancement followed the development of the coiled spring in the 1820s. Before this, upholstery had been overstrung and the supporting webbing fixed across the top of the seat rail. With the coiled spring, the webbing was fixed below the seat rail, allowing ample space for the springs. Traditionally, the best material to use for stuffing furniture was finest sorted horsehair. By the 1880s, however, some disreputable manufacturers had resorted to using imitation straw, paper and old cloth for stuffing, in an effort to cut their costs. As a result, many brand-new pieces of furniture were sold infested with lice or woodworm.

Most 18th century furniture coverings were of high quality, and many sofas and chairs from this period still have their original coverings. Although there are also many fine examples of Victorian coverings, they were not generally of as high a standard as 18th century examples. One reason for this is that the materials used were cheaper.

◁ *MID-VICTORIAN CHAIRS, which would originally have been part of a salon suite comprising a settee or chaise longue and a set of four to six side chairs. Good-quality carving is important in such chairs; the carving here is rather poor. Properly upholstered, each chair would be worth* **£850**

▽ *GEORGE III LIBRARY ARMCHAIR, known as a 'Gainsborough chair', possibly because the artist's models were seated in such chairs. The upholstery and castors are not original. 18th century.* **£2,500**

◁ *DRAWING ROOM CHAIR with a walnut frame. Because the seats were so low such chairs were labelled 'nursing' chairs. This is a misnomer; it is far too grand a chair for such a purpose. 1870.* **£350**

◁ *IMITATION LOUIS XV-STYLE ARMCHAIR,
which is part of a salon suite. The
rosewood frame is fairly unusual, and
a more expensive example would have
been gilded. 1900.* **£1,000**

△ *SALON CHAIR The design embodies
an attractive mixture of styles, from
rococo and Adam to classical. Early
20th century.* **£400**

▷ *'GRANDFATHER' CHAIR made of walnut.
It would have formed part of an eight-
piece set which would also have included
a 'Grandmother' chair. The original
Victorian upholstery was probably brightly
patterned. This style of salon chair remains
popular today. 1860s.* **£700**

▷ *NURSING CHAIR with original
upholstery in good condition.
The beadwork squirrel on a
branch is an unusual subject.
The chair is made of ebonized
wood in which the design
has been incised and gilded:
the castors are porcelain.
1870s.* **£500**

△ *BOUDOIR CHAIR in the flamboyant style
of 'tous les Louis'. The cabriole legs are
decorated with rococo scrolls and foliage.
Although the upholstery is not original,
such pieces are fashionable and much
sought after today. 1880s or '90s;
3ft 6in wide.* **£1,000**

CHESTS & COFFERS

One of the earliest pieces of household furniture was the coffer, or chest, which dates back to a primitive age when a hollowed-out log was used for storing household items. A rough-hewn lid was soon added, converting it to a keepsafe. By the 17th century chests were widely used for storing family goods. A coffer, which is similar to a chest, was fitted with a lock because it was used for storing money and valuables.

There are two basic types of chest: the earliest was simply six boards nailed together or joined with rough-cut dovetails. The second type, made of wainscot panelling, was often constructed by the craftsman employed to make the panelled rooms and ceilings of grand houses. In common with other domestic furniture of the period, chests were made from native and local woods, although until the end of the 17th century the timber used for the finest chests was primarily oak.

Most chests contained a small tray with a lift-up top.

△ OAK TROUSSEAU BOX *Brides-to-be used such boxes for storing clothing and linen. Resembling a miniature chest, this box is finely coloured and has original carving throughout. Inside there are slots for partitions that form a candlebox, and in each corner are holes for the pins of a lift-up lid. It is quite rare to find the original lock and key together (shown right). Early 17th century; 8in high x 21in long.* **£6,000 – £8,000**

◁ RENAISSANCE-STYLE CARVED CHEST *The lid of this walnut chest is carved with 15th century scenes. King Ferdinand of Spain, who had just defeated the Moors, is shown handing the keys of Granada to his consort, Queen Isabella. The chest is probably Spanish and the design is a combination of ecclesiastical and secular styles. It was made during a period of revived interest in 'chivalry'. 1870; 4ft long.* **£3,500**

The tray was used for storing candles made of tallow so foul-smelling that it kept moths away from the linen inside. In the 17th century drawers were added below the lift-up top. These hybrid chests were known as 'mule chests' and they remained popular throughout the 18th century, particularly in the north of England.

As cabinet-making techniques improved and pieces became less expensive to produce, the more sophisticated chest of drawers became widely available and chests went out of fashion. They did not disappear, however, but remained popular as items of furniture to use for storage in bedrooms, cottages and churches.

▽ *PANELLED OAK CHEST* *The architectural mouldings are typical of those commonly used in the early 17th century. In the last 100 years the chest has been converted into a cupboard; what was the front is now a pair of doors. The castors were fitted later. Mid 17th century; 4ft long.* **£800 – £1,200**

▷ *ARMADA CHEST* *This is an iron strong box with a huge, complex lock on the underside of the lid. Decorative straps further strengthen the chest, which would have been bolted to the deck of a captain's cabin. Mid 1500s; 2ft 6in long.* **£2,000 – £3,000**

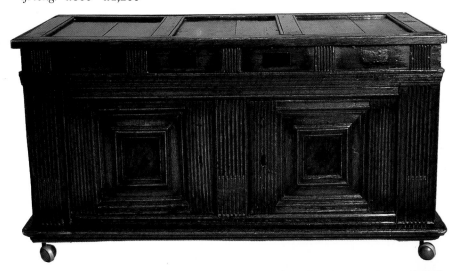

△ *DOWER CHEST* *made of iron and steel, which would have contained a bride's dowry. It has a complex locking device in the lid and the outside panels are painted. 17th century; 7in long.* **£850**

▷ *CHIP CARVED PANELLED CHEST* *The chest displays good chip carving which, although primitive, is quite precise and intricate. It was made using a round punch and half-round chisel with the aid of a rule and compasses. Such designs, using basic tools, are typical of the time. This chest still has the original iron hinges. It would probably have been placed at the end of a bed and used for storing bed linen. 17th century; 4ft long.* **£1,500**

CHESTS OF DRAWERS

The chest of drawers is one of the most successful types of furniture and from the mid 17th century could be seen in virtually every room of the well-to-do home. Because so many chests of drawers were produced, they make up a large proportion of the antique furniture around today, mostly dating from the mid 18th to the mid 19th century. The majority were made of mahogany and followed a basic pattern of either four long drawers or two short drawers at the top, and three long drawers below.

The earliest chest of drawers looked like a traditional chest, but it was in fact a set of drawers with cupboard doors in front. The doors gradually disappeared, and by the late 17th century the drawer fronts themselves had become the decorative feature. Early chests of drawers took many forms, from small to large, from three or four drawers, to five or six. Eventually the design returned to the traditional format of shallow drawers at the top,

becoming deeper towards the bottom. Initially, only the privileged owned chests of drawers, but these pieces gradually percolated down through society. Until around 1850 less well-off people bought their furniture second hand. This resulted in the 'castle to cottage' syndrome – an exquisite piece of furniture, underestimated in its time by his lordship, was bought by people of lower social standing and passed down through society over the generations.

Early chests of drawers were of framed or joined construction, but the advent of cabinet-making, using sophisticated dovetail joints, encouraged the making of better furniture. With more craftsmen specializing, much furniture became cheaper to buy, bringing new furniture within the financial reach of ordinary people. This process was hastened by the Industrial Revolution and the arrival of mass production, and today there can hardly be a household in Britain that does not own a chest of drawers.

▽ *Semainier Chest This elegant chest of drawers, probably used for storing small items of linen, is in the style of 'tous les Louis' – a mixture of 18th century French styles. Late 19th century; 2ft 6in high.* **£700**

△ *William and Mary Laburnum Chest made of veneered laburnum 'oysters'. The feet are replacements; the originals would have looked less clumsy. The handles, too, were changed in the past, but have been replaced with replicas of the originals. Late 17th century; 3ft 4in wide.* **£12,000 – £15,000**

△ KILMARNOCK CHEST OF DRAWERS This large mahogany piece is made in traditional northern style. Across the top is a slim, cushion-moulded drawer. Below, free-standing columns flank an arrangement of two deep and two shallow top drawers, with three deep, full-width drawers underneath. Mid 19th century; 4ft high. **£400**

△ DUTCH CHEST OF DRAWERS A 4-drawer 'bombe' shaped chest fitted with new handles, escutcheons and locks. It has also been repolished. Unrestored, it would be worth twice as much. 1770; 3ft wide. **£2,000**

◁ GEORGE I CHEST OF DRAWERS, made of walnut. It has the traditional combination of two short drawers and three long, below an overhanging caddy-moulded top. It stands on four shaped bracket feet. Early 18th century; 2ft 4in wide. **£7,000**

▽ WALNUT CHEST OF DRAWERS This traditional piece has been 'Victorianized'. The feet were added in the 19th century and the original drop handles have been replaced with turned wooden ones. Had it not been updated it would be about three times more valuable. Early 18th century; 3ft 2in wide. **£1,500**

CABINETS & BOOKCASES

The cabinet was one of the earliest pieces of furniture in the well-to-do household. Dating from the 15th and 16th centuries, it may well have been inspired by the large caskets brought back to England by explorers and adventurers returning from the East. Like Eastern caskets, the best cabinets were fitted with many small drawers and compartments in which the owner could store valuables and precious keepsakes. Early pieces had solid wooden 'blind' doors, but when glass manufacturing improved towards the end of the 17th century cabinet designs became more sophisticated and glazed doors were introduced, which meant that objects could be displayed. Glazed doors became even more common as the mania for collecting and displaying Oriental porcelain grew. The new door frames were more complex than the earlier ones, and had to be accurately made. As a result, a new breed of highly skilled and trained craftsman, the cabinet-maker, emerged.

By the early 18th century literacy had increased among the middle and upper middle classes, and this led to the reading and collecting of books becoming fashionable. Consequently the cabinet became a dual-purpose piece that was used for storing and displaying books as well as precious items and decorative objects.

◁ *CHIPPENDALE MAHOGANY REVIVAL CABINET The ornate carving and generous curves make this cabinet a superb example of its type. Despite its massive bulk, it would probably have been bought for a modestly sized room in an ordinary terraced house. 1905; 6ft wide.* **£2,500**

△ *ROSEWOOD DISPLAY CABINET in typically late Victorian or Edwardian style, with classical style marquetry panels and a serpentine front. A good quality mass-produced piece. 6ft 6in high.* **£700**

△ MAHOGANY SECRETAIRE-BOOKCASE *The plain and simple style of this piece indicates that it was made in the transitional Georgian–early Victorian period. The recessed cupboards are an unusual feature and give extra knee room when the 'drawer' front is let down to make a writing surface. 1835; 6ft 6in high.* **£3,000 – £4,000**

△ ITALIAN CABINET WITH EBONY AND IVORY INLAY *This massive, superb piece was brought to the Malta Roadshow and had obviously been specially made for an immensely rich family. Two of the panels may be older than the cabinet itself, dating perhaps from the 18th century. Mid 19th century; 7ft high.* **£50,000**

▷ ITALIAN CABINET *with ebony veneers and ivory marquetry. The two central panels are engraved with classical scenes in the renaissance manner. Attractive pieces such as this are most fashionable today. 19th century; 5ft 6in high.* **£2,000 – £3,000**

▷ 'SECRET' CABINET *A one-off piece, this elaborately carved Victorian renaissance cabinet displays a mixture of styles. It has a hinged roof and many secret drawers and doors. At one time the term 'cabinet' also described a secret room in a house where friends of the master gathered to view his objets d'art. 1850; 2ft 7in high.* **£2,000 – £3,000**

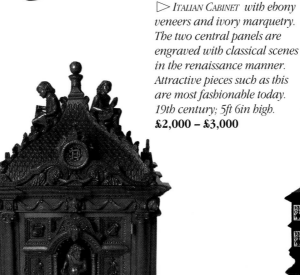

SIDEBOARDS

There are two basic types of sideboard; an oak dresser, with or without shelves in the upper part, and a mahogany sideboard with napery and cellaret drawers.

The term 'dresser' originates from the piece of furniture that was used by servants when preparing, or 'dressing', a dish of food before bedtime, in case the master of the household required a midnight snack. The style of the dresser-type sideboard changed very little after the 17th century: its features included a serving board, three or four drawers and, below these, cupboards or a large open space with a shelf, or 'pot board', at the bottom where pans were kept.

The second type of sideboard, made from mahogany, was situated in the dining room and incorporates napery and cellaret drawers. Up to the 1750s it was no more than a simple serving table flanked by cupboards or pedestals, with compartments for hot plates and cold drinks. On top of these stood a pair of large, often decorative, urns, one of which usually contained hot water for rinsing cutlery and the other iced water.

As dining rooms became smaller in size, end pedestals were built in to the serving table. The resulting sideboard displayed deep drawers or cupboards at each end, or a drawer at one end and a cupboard at the other, as well as a shallow drawer in the centre for cutlery. Sideboards also usually contained a lead-lined drawer for storing ice to keep wine cool. This type of sideboard generally has six tapering legs, either square or, later, turned.

At the beginning of the 19th century, the end cupboards in sideboards were extended to the floor to give even more storage space. These sideboards are known as 'pedestal sideboards' and they are generally associated with the late Regency and Victorian periods. As the 19th century went on, sideboards became more elaborately decorated.

SHERATON STYLE

The term 'Sheraton style' describes classically-inspired furniture of elegant, light proportions, with much use of stringing and crossbanding.

Along with most other 18th century styles, those of Thomas Sheraton were much admired and copied during the late 19th and early 20th centuries. Although this style is often referred to as 'Edwardian Sheraton' (its heyday was from 1900 to 1910), furniture in this style was in fact made both before and after that period.

Not only was contemporary furniture made in this style, plain furniture from the 18th century or earlier was updated and made more fashionable by the addition of stringing and panels of inlay and marquetry.

▽ *EDWARDIAN SHERATON-REVIVAL SIDEBOARD* The proportions reveal that this is a copy. The legs are too thin and the cross-banded decoration too narrow for this piece to be genuine. Made in large quantities, such pieces are a popular alternative to genuine Sheraton furniture which can cost between £10,000 and £15,000. Early 20th century; 4ft 6in long. **£600 – £800**

▽ *SHERATON-STYLE CABINET* A good example of a glass-fronted cabinet. Typical of a popular 1930s style of furniture from firms such as Waring & Gillow and Maples. Later dismissed as worthless, this style is now back in favour. Early 20th century; 5ft 4in long. **£2,500**

△ *GEORGE III MAHOGANY SIDEBOARD* The bowed top is cross-banded with tulip-wood and the centre drawer is flanked by two deep drawers. It has tapering square legs and spade feet. 1790; 4ft 2in long. **£3,000 – £5,000**

▷ ROBINSON CRUSOE SIDEBOARD
A magnificent carved oak
sideboard by Gerard Robinson
of Newcastle. Together with
another cabinet-maker,
Thomas Tweedy, Robinson
had a wood-carving business
in Newcastle's Grainger Street.
Both craftsmen specialized in
large, carved oak pieces and
their work is comparable to
that of the makers now
known as the Warwick School
of carving. Warwick favoured
game as a subject, while
Tweedy and Robinson carved
episodes from English history,
scenes from Shakespeare and,
as here, scenes from Robinson
Crusoe. The panel (inset)
displays the high relief carving
that was so popular in the
Victorian era. It could be
created by hand or machine;
these carvings were probably
machine-made. 1872; 7ft 2in
high x 9ft 1in wide. **£10,000**

▷ SATIN BIRCH SIDEBOARD
Although commercially
made, the workmanship
of this Arts & Crafts
Movement piece is quite
beautiful. The poker-
work panels would not
have been included
when the piece was
manufactured, but
created and stained by
hand shortly after it had
left the factory. 1890;
4ft 6in long. **£800**

△ REGENCY PEDESTAL SIDEBOARD
One of a pair of mahogany
sideboards. It has 'S' scrolling
on the moulded back, and a
panelled board. The centre
drawer is flanked by two
drawers either side above
tapering panelled cupboards
on ribbed bun feet. 1835;
3ft 10in long. **£3,000 – £5,000**

▷ SYCAMORE SIDEBOARD by
Jacques Adnet, a well known
French designer. This Art Deco
variation of the pedestal
sideboard employs the grain
of the wood as the main
decorative feature. It is
banded in stainless steel and
still has the original glass
panels on the top. 1925 – 30;
7ft long. **£5,000**

DESKS & BUREAUX

The writing desk and bureau developed from the French escritoire – a sloped writing desk with legs which was popular in the late 17th century. Unlike escritoires and bureaux, however, most desks do not have a fold-down flap. Desks were made either in table form or with a 'kneehole' space flanked by two drawers to accommodate the user's knees. Since the latter, known as a 'partner's desk', was frequently situated in the centre of an office, it was decorated all the way round. At the other end of the scale, in terms of size, were the portable desk and the bonheur du jour. Portable desks, either on a stand or of the box type, were taken to the countryside and used for painting or writing. The bonheur du jour, a French writing desk for ladies, was a daintier piece of furniture, complete with a fold-over writing surface, drawers for inkwells and small cupboards and bookshelves.

Early bureaux were often made in two parts, one on top of the other. The writing part, with sloping, fold-down panel concealing drawers and small compartments, sat on a base section of drawers with a retaining moulding around the top. By the 1720s the two parts were joined, and the moulding was sometimes kept as decoration. The sloping front style was partially superseded in the 1800s by a secretaire fitment; this is a false top drawer, the front of which pulls forwards and opens flat to provide a writing surface.

◁ *WALNUT BUREAU The moulded edges of the carcase and the waist moulding help to date this piece. The blank area above the top drawers and below the sloping fall is another early feature. Inside, there is a 'well' compartment for secret papers. 1730; 2ft 11in wide.* **£2,000 – £3,000**

△ *EARLY GEORGE II WALNUT BUREAU with original handles and escutcheons. The rich gold wood is a marvellous colour, much sought after by collectors of walnut furniture. The restored feet are the only flaws. 1730; 2ft 8in wide.* **£10,000 – £12,000**

MARRYING A BOOKCASE AND A BUREAU

The joining of a bureau and a bookcase may originally have been to create a more practical piece of furniture or to increase the commercial value of the individual items. For a bureau bookcase to be authentic, the wood and the style of both parts must be identical. There should be no veneer where the bookcase rests on the bureau, and it is always preferable for the retaining moulding at the junction of the two pieces to belong to the bureau, not the bookcase.

▷ *Mahogany Secretaire-Bookcase*
A fine Sheraton period piece with a glazed cabinet for books and display items, a deep drawer which folds down to make a writing desk, three ordinary drawers and 'French' splay bracket feet. The base was stripped and repolished 50 years ago, and boxwood lines have been added around the doors. 1800; 3ft wide. **£15,000**

◁ *Lady's Cylinder Bureau made of rosewood. The basic style is Sheraton, with Edwardian influence. The cabinet, sealed by a glass door, was used for displaying porcelain which was reflected in the rear mirror. 1890; 4ft 11in high.* **£1,000 – £1,500**

◁ *Lady's Writing Table Furniture from a lady's boudoir and drawing room was far lighter and more decorative than that found in a gentleman's room. From 1830 to the end of the century there was a revival of interest in French styles. Furniture from this period is known today as 'tous les Louis' because it embodies a mixture of 19th century French design characteristics. This bonheur du jour is made of burr walnut with kingwood cross-banding and gilt metal mounts. The porcelain plaque adds to its appeal. 1860; 3ft 5in wide.* **£2,500**

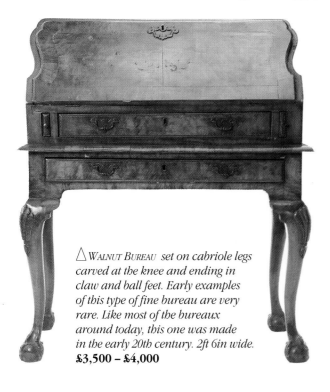

△ *Walnut Bureau set on cabriole legs carved at the knee and ending in claw and ball feet. Early examples of this type of fine bureau are very rare. Like most of the bureaux around today, this one was made in the early 20th century. 2ft 6in wide.*
£3,500 – £4,000

◁ BONHEUR DU JOUR A Continental desk with a
tulipwood and South American kingwood veneer
applied diagonally in four sections using a technique
called 'quartering'. The tapering legs are enhanced
by gilt metal mounts. 1880; 2ft 8in wide. **£2,250**

▷ READING OR WRITING TABLE This beautiful
mahogany piece is a variation of the
architect's table. The top flap lifts to form an
angled surface for drawing or reading, and
the drawer pulls out to provide a flat writing
surface lined with green baize. This, in turn,
opens to reveal a series of boxes marked with
the letters of the alphabet. The design was
inspired by the French neo-classical style.
1790; 3ft 8in wide. **£4,000 – £6,000**

◁ ROLL-TOP DESK An enormous
cylinder-fall desk that may
have once stood in a sizeable
salon or library. It is made
of mahogany and has three
drawers and two cupboards.
The top part contains small
drawers and compartments
for papers and writing
equipment. 19th century;
6ft 4in wide. **£4,000**

DAVENPORTS

The Davenport is a small writing desk with a sliding or extending writing slope, side opening drawers, and sometimes a rising compartment at the top. Legend has it that a certain Captain Davenport commissioned the first such desk in the late 18th century.

The earliest Davenports were plain and box-like in shape, in naval or military style, while later examples had recessed cases and front supports. By the 1820s the Davenport had become one of the most popular pieces of furniture in fashionable homes and styles began to vary. The scrolling piano tops and lift-up compartments of many Davenports demonstrate the Victorian capacity for ingenious design. Rosewood and mahogany were the most popular timbers to use, but by the 1850s highly patterned walnut veneer had also become fashionable. At the end of the 19th century practically every conceivable style of Davenport had been made and production waned. Early examples are always in demand because they are both decorative and functional, but in the last few years Victorian pieces have also become much sought after.

△ *ROSEWOOD DAVENPORT with turned column, classical style supports, a pierced brass gallery and small side drawer. Early Victorian; 2ft wide.* **£2,500**

◁ *BURR WALNUT DAVENPORT with a counter-balanced rising top compartment for stationery, and a sideways sliding writing surface. The scrolling supports have fret-pierced panels and the piece is decorated throughout with split column moulding. Mid Victorian; 2ft wide.* **£2,500**

△ *BURR WALNUT DAVENPORT of piano top design. The top rises to reveal a stationery compartment. 1870; 2ft wide.* **£3,500**

IDENTIFYING WOODS

It is not always easy to decide which type of wood a piece of furniture is made from, particularly since there has long been a tradition of making cheaper materials look like more prized varieties. Finish can also make a great difference. In furniture that has been restored insensitively the wood may be stained the wrong colour or even obscured by dark varnish.

When inspecting furniture, try to examine the parts where the natural, unfinished wood is visible, but do remember that components which are normally unseen are frequently made from a variety of different materials. For example, the drawer sides of a piece may be made of oak or pine, regardless of the timber used elsewhere.

Oak was the earliest wood used for furniture: strong and long-lasting, it was made into chests, chairs and tables which were usually of a simple, solid design. The oak was imported, however, since the native variety was used for building ships and houses. In the 17th century oak was gradually displaced by walnut, imported from France, and this heralded the 'Age of Walnut'. The most attractive pieces of walnut – the burrs and curls – were taken from the weakest part of the tree and so were employed mainly as decorative veneers. Mahogany was not used extensively for furniture until well into the 18th century following a reduction in import taxes and the loss of many French walnut trees to frost.

FURNITURE PERIODS IN GREAT BRITAIN

STYLE	U.K. PERIOD	DATE	WOOD
Gothic	Elizabethan	1558 – 1603	Oak period (up to 1670)
	Jacobean	1603 – 25	
Baroque	Carolean	1625 – 49	
	Cromwellian	1649 – 60	
	Restoration	1660 – 89	Walnut period (1670 – 1735)
	William & Mary	1689 – 94	
Rococo	William III	1694 – 1702	
	Queen Anne	1702 – 14	
	Early Georgian	1714 – 60	Mahogany period (1735 – 70)
Neo-classical	Late Georgian	1760 – 1811	Late Mahogany period (1770 – 1810)
Regency	Regency	1811 – 30	

FINISHES AND POLISHES

Special finishes were applied to furniture to protect the work of the craftsman. The earliest standard finish was either oil polish or a combination of beeswax and turpentine. Oxidization darkened wood finished with oil, while beeswax sealed it.

Later, in the 17th century, shellac-based finishes were applied, and in the 1820s French polishing became common. Many early pieces of furniture have been stripped and then French polished.

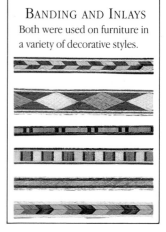

BANDING ON BUREAUX

From the early 18th century it was customary to apply banding to bureaux, with the grain of the wood running either vertically or horizontally. Banding is often used as a guide to the age of a piece, but because both types of application were used at the same time, other dating factors should also be taken into account.

Herringbone banding (**1**), created by applying two bands of veneer at an angle to each other, dates from the early 18th century, before 1710.

It is generally considered that vertical graining (**2**) may be earlier (after 1710) than horizontal graining (**3**) which dates from after 1740.

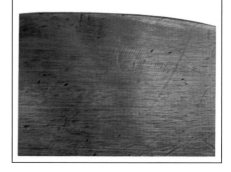

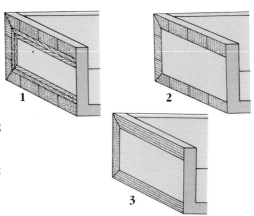

BANDING AND INLAYS

Both were used on furniture in a variety of decorative styles.

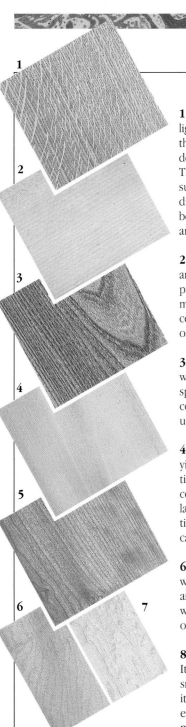

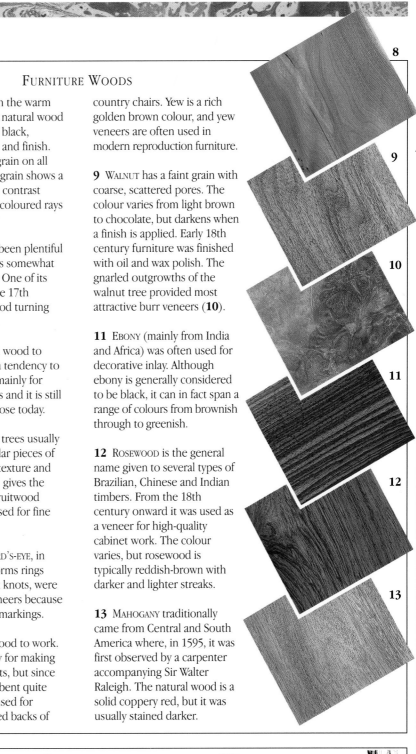

FURNITURE WOODS

1 OAK ranges from the warm light brown of the natural wood through to almost black, depending on age and finish. There is a strong grain on all surfaces. The end grain shows a distinct criss-cross contrast between the light coloured rays and darker rings.

2 BEECH has long been plentiful and cheap, but it is somewhat prone to warping. One of its main uses from the 17th century was in wood turning on country chairs.

3 ELM is a difficult wood to work since it has a tendency to split. It was used mainly for country chair seats and it is still used for this purpose today.

4 PEAR Fruitwood trees usually yield small, irregular pieces of timber with even texture and colour. CHERRY (**5**) gives the largest pieces of fruitwood timber, and was used for fine cabinet work.

6 MAPLE and **7** BIRD'S-EYE, in which the grain forms rings around small dark knots, were widely used as veneers because of their attractive markings.

8 YEW is a hard wood to work. It was used mainly for making small wooden parts, but since it could be steam bent quite easily it was also used for making the hooped backs of country chairs. Yew is a rich golden brown colour, and yew veneers are often used in modern reproduction furniture.

9 WALNUT has a faint grain with coarse, scattered pores. The colour varies from light brown to chocolate, but darkens when a finish is applied. Early 18th century furniture was finished with oil and wax polish. The gnarled outgrowths of the walnut tree provided most attractive burr veneers (**10**).

11 EBONY (mainly from India and Africa) was often used for decorative inlay. Although ebony is generally considered to be black, it can in fact span a range of colours from brownish through to greenish.

12 ROSEWOOD is the general name given to several types of Brazilian, Chinese and Indian timbers. From the 18th century onward it was used as a veneer for high-quality cabinet work. The colour varies, but rosewood is typically reddish-brown with darker and lighter streaks.

13 MAHOGANY traditionally came from Central and South America where, in 1595, it was first observed by a carpenter accompanying Sir Walter Raleigh. The natural wood is a solid coppery red, but it was usually stained darker.

RECOGNIZING GRAIN PATTERNS

1 Quarter sawn boards give straight line patterns.
2 Flat sawn timber produces a classic contour pattern.
3 Irregular patterns are produced by the growth patterns of branches and angle cutting of the timber.
4 Curl patterns are cut from the 'Y' between the trunk and a main branch.
5 Beautiful veneers can be cut from outgrowths on the main trunk.

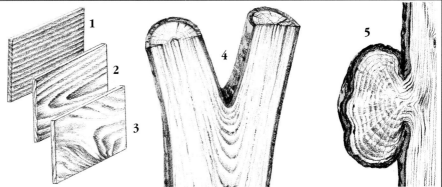

DATING CABINETRY

There are many clues that can help to date cabinetry, but before examining a piece closely with a view to buying, stand back and look at it as a whole. Note the overall shape, decoration and proportions to establish its general style and where in the home it would have been used. If a piece was made for a bedroom, for example, it will frequently be simple and unadorned, but if it was intended for a drawing room it is more likely to be ornate and lavishly decorated.

Having established the 'feel' of a piece, further information about its age can be gleaned from the materials used, the construction, the shape and, if applicable, the drawer handles and feet. Handles are not always a reliable guide to age, however, since they are easy to change and may even have been altered several times during the lifetime of a piece. If so, there will probably be indentations on the drawer front and the wood may be of a different colour.

A good indicator of age in cabinetry is the style of moulding at the top edge of a piece. The differences are subtle, however, and may only be obvious to the expert eye (see 'Moulding Profiles', below). The grain pattern of the wood used in the moulding may offer another useful clue. In pieces made before the 1730s the grain pattern is vertical, but after the 1740s it is usually horizontal.

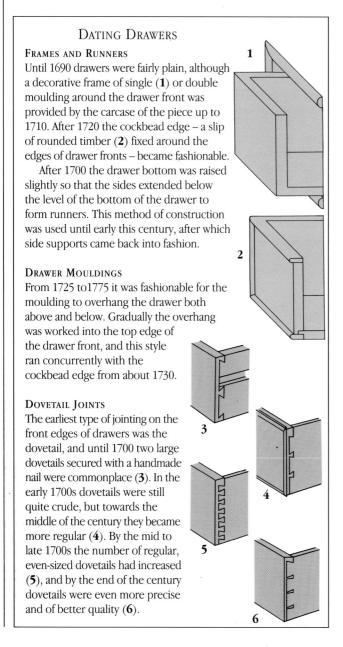

DATING DRAWERS

FRAMES AND RUNNERS
Until 1690 drawers were fairly plain, although a decorative frame of single (**1**) or double moulding around the drawer front was provided by the carcase of the piece up to 1710. After 1720 the cockbead edge – a slip of rounded timber (**2**) fixed around the edges of drawer fronts – became fashionable.

After 1700 the drawer bottom was raised slightly so that the sides extended below the level of the bottom of the drawer to form runners. This method of construction was used until early this century, after which side supports came back into fashion.

DRAWER MOULDINGS
From 1725 to 1775 it was fashionable for the moulding to overhang the drawer both above and below. Gradually the overhang was worked into the top edge of the drawer front, and this style ran concurrently with the cockbead edge from about 1730.

DOVETAIL JOINTS
The earliest type of jointing on the front edges of drawers was the dovetail, and until 1700 two large dovetails secured with a handmade nail were commonplace (**3**). In the early 1700s dovetails were still quite crude, but towards the middle of the century they became more regular (**4**). By the mid to late 1700s the number of regular, even-sized dovetails had increased (**5**), and by the end of the century dovetails were even more precise and of better quality (**6**).

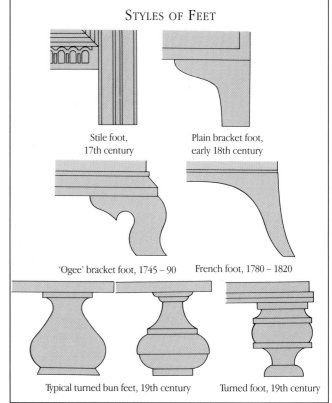

STYLES OF FEET

Stile foot, 17th century

Plain bracket foot, early 18th century

'Ogee' bracket foot, 1745 – 90

French foot, 1780 – 1820

Typical turned bun feet, 19th century

Turned foot, 19th century

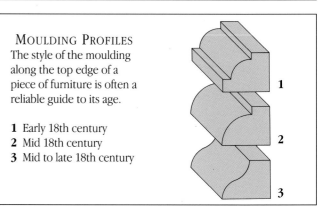

MOULDING PROFILES
The style of the moulding along the top edge of a piece of furniture is often a reliable guide to its age.

1 Early 18th century
2 Mid 18th century
3 Mid to late 18th century

HANDLES

The style of carrying handles and drawer pulls followed the fashion of the time. A popular way of updating a piece of furniture was to replace the handles with more fashionable ones – many pieces lost their original handles this way.

The earliest handles were made of iron; steel was used next, and then brass, of which the best quality was gilded. Traces of gilt can be found even on fairly plain late 18th century handles, and if the original metal mounts are to be preserved, it is important not to overclean them. From around 1850 a much wider variety of machine-made handles became available.

Since popular styles were revived over and over again, the illustrations here serve only as a general dating guide.

Iron inverted heart-shaped drop handle, early 17th century

Brass pendant handles, early 18th century

Cast brass loop handle with engraved backplate, early 18th century

Cast brass loop handle, early 18th century

Cast brass loop handle, early 18th century

Cast brass loop handle with pierced backplate, second half 18th century

Cast brass loop handle with octagonal roses, French style, second half 18th century

Decoratively cast and chased loop handle with roses, late 18th century

Loop or swan neck handle of cast brass, second half 18th century

Loop handle with stamped sheet brass backplate, late 18th century

Stamped brass knob, late 18th century

Two drop handles, cast in brass, 1750 – 75; 1775 – 1800

Regency period star knob

Turned wood knobs were popular in Victorian times. They were made of ebony, walnut, rosewood or mahogany, and were often decorated

HINGES

Hinges provide a useful guide to the age of a piece of furniture.

 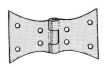

Iron split-pin hinge; found on coffers from the Middle Ages

Butterfly hinge, 17th century

Gilt metal hinge, late 17th century

Cross-section of basic wood-pin hinge, 12th and 13th centuries

  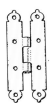

Miniaturized door hinge in iron, 16th century

Pin and butt hinge, early 18th century

'H' hinge, popular by the 1720s

DEVELOPMENT OF THE DECORATIVE ESCUTCHEON

Two main types of escutcheon developed from the external lock. One is the decorative cover, the other the lining to the actual keyhole. Confusingly, they are both known as escutcheons.

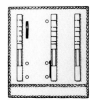

An early example of an external lock with a decorative escutcheon on the left which moves over to conceal the keyhole

Early 18th century decorative escutcheons

Decorative escutcheon with swan neck handle, late 18th century

Stamped brass escutcheon with decoratively cast swan neck handle with roses, early 19th century

Distinctive patterns from the late 19th century

DATING WOOD SCREWS

A handmade screw (right) has an uncentred driver slot, a filed top and uneven, hand-cut thread (1720 – 1830s). A machine-made screw (left) has a precisely centred driver slot, a lathe-finished top and milled thread (from mid 1800s).

BRAMAH LOCK

This lock was patented in 1784 by Joseph Bramah, a British locksmith who ranks with Yale and Chubb. He is best known for his furniture locks.

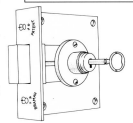

COLLECTABLES

HILARY KAY

I was invited to my first *Antiques Roadshow* in 1980, and so I cannot claim to be a founder member of the team. I had been running the Collectors' Department at Sotheby's for three years, which involved valuing and auctioning a wide variety of objects, ranging from stuffed birds to stevengraphs (paintings on silk). All of this proved to be ideal training for a typical day on the 'Miscellaneous' table at the *Antiques Roadshow*.

No-one is surprised if you collect silver, porcelain, clocks, furniture and pictures, but some connoisseurs raise their eyebrows when they discover that one has a collection of toys, typewriters, sewing machines, printed ephemera or, for that matter, any other subject drawn from the long list of 'collectables'.

Although collectables cannot be readily annexed to any of the more recognized fields of antique collecting, similar criteria are used by all collectors, regardless of their specialized subject. These are: date, rarity, quality, condition (and degree of restoration, if any), aesthetic appeal, importance in the collecting field and, perhaps most important of all, whether the collector actually likes the object.

The latter is vital, since it must be assumed that items are being purchased to form a collection rather than being acquired for no cost, and prices in the art and antiques market can move down as well as up. If prices do level for a period, the collection should continue to provide pleasure, which is impossible if the objects have only been bought as investments and hold no interest or appeal for the collector.

The decision to form a collection may be triggered by a variety of reasons. An absorbing hobby perhaps, or feelings of nostalgia for one's own early life, an interest connected with one's job, wish fulfilment, or the desire to learn about social history – these are all factors which could stimulate someone to start collecting.

For the car enthusiast, for example, there is automobilia (there are many 'ilias' or 'alias' in the collectables world, 'kitchenalia' and 'nauticalia', to name just two). Everything and anything relating to cars, other than the full-size vehicles themselves, is embraced by this wide heading, which includes car mascots, handbooks, posters for famous races and events, headlamps, horns and spares. Specialist shops and auctions have been established over the last five years, selling nothing but automobilia, and interest in the subject has been increasing gradually for some time.

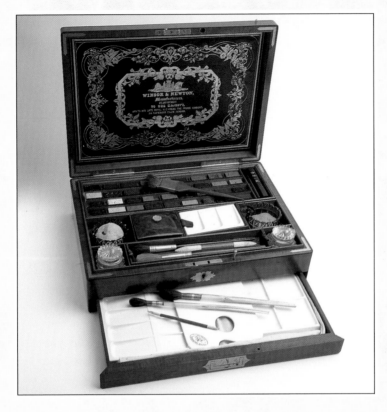

Portable paintbox, 1870s. £2,500

The accountant may be drawn to collect objects linked to his or her profession (rather than hobby), and I have been to see several fascinating collections of early items, such as adding machines, slide-rules and cheque-printing machines, belonging to collectors in the financial world. Early woodworking tools are often collected by master cabinet-makers, who buy both to admire and to use, since the quality of the early tools and their specialized nature can outstrip their modern counterparts. Ghoulish though it may sound, I have even seen several collections of frightening dental instruments from the past on display (including pliers for tooth extraction) in the waiting rooms of some dental surgeries – perhaps placed on public view to ensure that patients greet modern dental instruments with a certain degree of relief.

A child who dreamt for years of owning all the Gauge 'O' trains and accessories in a 1950s Hornby catalogue was almost certainly unable to fulfil his dreams as a child, but today, with a regular income, this can become a reality. The young woman for-bidden to wear stilettos by her parents may be older and

A rare orrery by William & Samuel Jones, 1810. £25,000 – £35,000

wiser, but she can now indulge in her passion for outrageous shoe design by forming a collection of the more sensational styles from the 1950s, which can be found in charity shops and market stalls today.

Nostalgia is an important ingredient in collecting. A particular style of telescope may remind someone of a much-loved seafaring grandfather and provide the first spark to fire a whole collection of telescopes, binoculars and opera glasses. The sound of a treadle sewing machine may bring back memories of a mother dressmaking, and stimulate someone to accumulate a collection of sewing machines of all types.

The development of society can be charted by many subjects in the collectables category. The emancipation of women can be glimpsed through their increasing employment outside the home, first as secretaries using typewriters in offices. The loss of servants, as they were enticed to other, more convivial, job opportunities, can be measured by the growth in the number of labour-saving devices used in domestic households by the end of the 19th century. The changing way in which children were regarded can be seen through their amusements and toys, particularly the concept of learning through play, illustrated by innumerable alphabet blocks, dissected maps and card games.

Whatever you choose to collect, be it Dinkys or Daimlers, microscopes or Meissen, it is important to enjoy yourself. Have fun learning about your subject, tracking down the rarities and meeting people who share your enthusiasm. Never be put off by raised eyebrows – remember, they laughed at the Impressionist painters at the time.

'The wolf shall dwell with the lamb' is a Biblical quotation which always comes to mind when I see my Roadshow colleagues, drawn from rival dealers, museums and auctioneers, sitting down to dinner on the evening before a Road-show recording, with gales of laughter erupting from all sides as antiques-world anecdotes are exchanged. Indeed, *Antiques Roadshow* provides an unusual forum in which people in highly competitive businesses can put rivalries aside and concentrate on their shared interests.

When I recorded my first item, I found that being on television isn't quite as easy as it appears. There's so much more to think about than simply telling a person about the history and value of their object. How should you hold it? How do you make sure the camera can see it? How do you encourage the owner to relax when you yourself are feeling nervous? How do you forget about the millions of people who will eventually see the programme? It is hardly surprising that the first series is a blur in my memory, and I can honestly say that I have completely forgotten the first item I recorded. All very nerve-wracking at the age of 23, but it was, and continues to be, the team of experts who encouraged me to succeed. All the specialists and the BBC crew behind the scenes help everyone to relax, have fun, and give their best possible performance in front of the cameras.

It was Arthur Negus particularly who taught me lessons in patience and stamina. Although in his seventies when I recorded my first Roadshow, Arthur would stand for three or four hours at a time talking to the public, looking at their 'treasures', encouraging them and being photographed with his fans. He is much loved and missed. We hope that all on the *Antiques Roadshow* are in some way perpetuating Arthur Negus's dedication to the subject, and providing entertaining and informative viewing.

MY FAVOURITE ITEMS

The objects I record are delightfully unpredictable, and those from the 1991 series were no exception. I recorded a rare orrery this year – the most valuable item I have ever seen at a Roadshow – as well as my favourite toy, the 'Mac' motorcycle. The 'Miscellaneous' table is always one of the busiest. In Lancashire I saw enough hob-nailed clogs to open a shop, and in Nottingham, lace sufficient to trim a closetful of frilled petticoats.

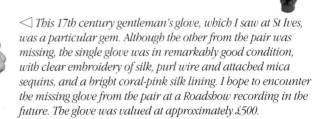

◁ *In Islington I was brought a walnut musical hall chair, well carved and decorated, with a lovely four-air melody played by a cylindrical musical movement that operates when someone sits on the seat. A great novelty, and in good original condition, it was made in the latter part of the 19th century. Today, it could be an amusing and inoffensive version of the whoopee cushion, used to surprise innocent visitors! The chair was valued at between £500 and £700.*

△ *A particular favourite has always been the 'Mac' motorcycle – a 16 inch tin plate clockwork toy made by the Arnold factory in Germany in the 1950s. Wound up and ready to go, a flick of a lever sets the motorcycle buzzing in an arc. Suddenly it stops, the clockwork motor ticks over and the rider dismounts; after a moment he clambers aboard again and continues his circular journey. A terrific action and the quality of the lithography on the toy, which shows the engine in detail, add to my enjoyment. The 'Mac' motorcycle was valued at £350.*

◁ *This 17th century gentleman's glove, which I saw at St Ives, was a particular gem. Although the other from the pair was missing, the single glove was in remarkably good condition, with clear embroidery of silk, purl wire and attached mica sequins, and a bright coral-pink silk lining. I hope to encounter the missing glove from the pair at a Roadshow recording in the future. The glove was valued at approximately £500.*

PAPER EPHEMERA & POSTCARDS

▽ *FRENCH FIGURES engraved on card. These charming hand-coloured figures in a market scene are mounted on wooden blocks. 1850s; 1½ – 3in high.* **£70 – £90**

▽ *PINWORK GREETINGS CARDS Declicate cards such as these were produced as a 'cottage industry'. The workforce, which was often made up of children, would have been issued with templates from which to work. 1815 – 20; 9in x 13in.* **£30 – £50**

The word 'ephemeral' describes something which does not last. Paper ephemera, then, are items that are made to be thrown away. The term applies to anything that is quickly updated, outmoded or made of short-life material, such as bus, train or tram tickets, calendars, royal celebration souvenirs or paper souvenirs of visits to towns or exhibitions. Cheaply produced paper or cardboard games and amusements, which were made for a limited lifespan and were cheap to buy at the time, are some of the rarer surviving paper ephemera items. Packaging and labels are also ephemera, but cards such as cigarette and tea cards are not. Most of these were produced specifically to be collected as sets. The value of paper ephemera is not governed by age or manufacturer; ephemera is judged more on its aesthetic appeal, historical significance and condition. Collectors should, therefore, try to find material that comes from a particular era. World War II, for example, could be represented by a collection of ration books, advertising leaflets and perhaps evacuation labels.

Picture postcards were a phenomenon of the 19th century. They were produced in response to the growth in tourism, improvements in colour printing and methods of photographic reproduction. Although millions of the cards sent in the last 100 years have been thrown away, luckily many thousands have survived. As a result, postcard collecting is a popular hobby, catered for by specialist fairs, auctions and enthusiasts' clubs. Although some cards may fetch hundreds of pounds, most can be bought for one pound or less, which means that a collection can be built up on a fairly modest budget. There is such a wide range of postcards available that collectors do tend to specialize. Popular collecting themes include scenic views, royalty, seaside and comic cards.

△ *UNFOLDING PANORAMA which reveals a grand procession of coaches, horse guards, soldiers and Yeomen of the Guard. It was made to celebrate Queen Victoria's coronation. The hand-coloured engravings are still bright and fresh, and it is in good condition. 1837; 4in x 7ft.* **£100 – £150**

▽ *LANES' AMUSEMENT* When extended, the card shows a three-dimensional view of the interior of the Crystal Palace, including exhibits, trees and people. 1851; 7in x 7½ in. **£150 – 200**

▷ *VICTORIAN UNFOLDING CARD* The card was folded (above) and then cut to create the pattern. The flower engravings are hand-coloured, and there are eight rhyming verses on the back. Open, 9in x 9in. **£25 – £35**

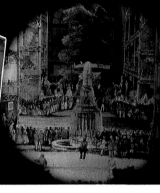

▽ *WORLD WAR I POSTCARD ALBUM* It includes cards with embroidered designs, some black and white views of London and Faversham in Kent, family portrait postcards and a set of Bamforth song cards. 1918. Individual cards £5 – £15. The album **£150 – £200**

△ *GREETINGS CARD* in unusually good condition. When lifted, the pear flap reveals a picture of Queen Victoria and Prince Albert. 3½ in x 5in. **£15**

▷ *SUFFRAGETTE CARD* This very rare postcard of a normally sweet and lovable kitten snarling its demand for the vote promoted the Suffragette cause in England. It features the colours of the movement. Early 1920s. **£15 – £20**

BOOKS

It is seldom realized that the condition of a book is all-important to its worth. With very few exceptions, missing plates or pages and a general tattiness will affect a book's value, regardless of its age.

This point is illustrated by the many Bibles that are brought to the Roadshow, especially those printed between about 1860 and 1900. Since they almost all contain plates, and the bindings may be fastened with brass clasps, these books are often so heavy that the bindings are broken. If so, they will fetch only about £5, rather than a possible £100 if in good condition.

It may come as a surprise that the quality of 17th and 18th century books was of a very high standard, since at that time paper was handmade from rags and wood pulp. The introduction of machine-made paper in the 19th century led to a general decline in the quality of books.

As with other antiques, there are fashions in book collecting. Books from the 1930s, for example, which in the past have been cheap and easy to find, are now much sought after. To maximize its value, a modern first edition must have a dustjacket in mint condition; that is, it must not be marked or damaged in any way.

△ *JOURNAL OF THE BOMBAY NATURAL HISTORY SOCIETY There are 15 volumes in all, in excellent condition and containing 145 beautiful colour plates. The few copies printed were sent to subscribers, so they are rarely seen outside private collections. 1886 – 1900; 7¼ in x 9¾ in.* **£400 – £500**

△ *BOTANICAL DRAWINGS One of a set of handmade volumes of drawings and quotations. It is in splendid condition. The drawings are copied from 'Curtis's Flower Garden Displayed'. 1789; 10in x 12in. The set* **£3,000 – £4,000**

◁ *ILLUMINATED ADDRESS Early this century, it was customary for high-ranking council officials to be presented with an illuminated 'address'. This highly ornate volume, illustrated with scenes of Merthyr Tydfil, was presented to the owner's great-grandfather in 1908. It details his achievements and council work. The binding is embossed with leeks, the Prince of Wales' feathers and a small Welsh dragon. It would have cost over £200 to produce.* **£800 – £1,200**

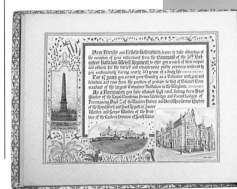

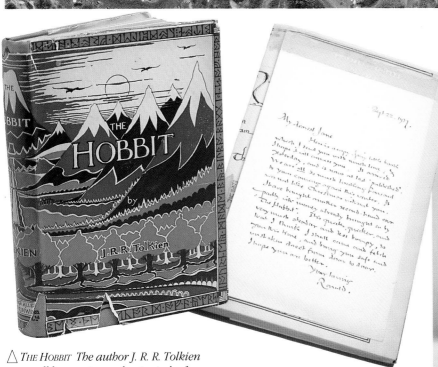

▽ THE LAND OF LONG AGO *is a typical Victorian pop-up book of English nursery rhymes. Pop-up books have been popular since the 1850s, but they are fragile, and examples in good condition are becoming increasingly rare. Late 19th century; 12in x 8in.* **£40 – £60**

△ THE HOBBIT *The author J. R. R. Tolkien was well known in academic circles for his 'Anglo-Saxon Grammar', but it was the publication in 1936 of his story 'The Hobbit' that brought him public recognition. The book did not become hugely popular until it was reprinted in 1953, to coincide with the publication of 'The Lord of the Rings'.*

In the 1960s and '70s, Tolkien became a cult figure, and collectors today pay large sums for first editions of these books, which are both extremely rare. This copy of 'The Hobbit' is particularly unusual. It has its original dustjacket, in reasonable condition, and inside there is an inscription and a letter from the author presenting the book to his aunt.

Also of interest to collectors are those copies of 'The Hobbit' which passed through Tolkien's hands; on the jacket flaps, where his work is compared with that of 'Charles Dodgeson' (Lewis Carroll), Tolkien would meticulously correct the spelling to 'Dodgson'. 1936. **£3,000 – £3,500**

▷ TOM BOBBIN'S TOY-SHOP OPENE'D OR HIS WHIMSICAL AMUSEMENTS *is a collection of humorous dialogues in Lanacashire dialects, all written phonetically. 1763; 4in x 3in.* **£50 – £80**

◁ MINIATURE BOOK *A reproduction of the first edition of a book of poems by Robert Burns, published in 1786. Printed on Indian paper, it is in excellent condition. 1900; under 1in high.* **£60**

WRITING ACCESSORIES

Many writing accessories have survived from the Victorian era and later, making this a rich and attractive field for collectors. Particularly desirable are items such as inkwells, writing cabinets, pens and pencils, paper weights, letter and note racks, pencil boxes and cases, ceramic memorandum tablets, seals and penknives.

It was not until Victorian times that inkwells, made from silver, brass, bronze and other metals, pottery, porcelain, and cut and coloured glass, reached their full decorative potential. The best glass examples have silver tops and can be dated by their hallmarks.

Inkwells were often included in desk sets or travelling writing cabinets. Popular from the early 19th century onward, the desk set usually comprised a stationery box, a blotter, an inkstand and a pen tray. Complete sets in wood, pottery, porcelain, glass, papier mâché and metal are much sought after by collectors. More elaborate, and

expensive, are travelling writing cabinets in wood or tooled leather that come complete with a writing slope and compartments for all sorts of pens and accessories.

The modern fountain pen was developed in the late 19th century, principally by three American makers – Louis Waterman, George Parker and Walter Sheaffer. In the 1920s and '30s fountain pens came into their own, and those from this period are the most collectable. Pens from the 1950s and '60s, although elegant and with aerodynamic styling, are undervalued in today's market. Old pens are generally well made and it is not difficult to restore vintage examples. Collectors would do well to seek out pens by well-known makers – Waterman, Parker, Sheaffer, Conway Stewart, Swan, Blackbird, Waverley and Onoto – but interesting examples by lesser makers should not be overlooked. Prices range from about ten pounds to several thousand pounds.

◁ *WRITING CABINET This was an important accessory for the 18th and 19th century traveller. Elegantly covered in red leather, this French cabinet is well fitted with compartments and drawers for stationery, writing equipment, sealing wax and other necessities. Early 18th century; 17in wide.* **£1,500 – £2,000**

▽ *TRAVEL INKWELL The crocodile skin-covered base contains a glass bottle with a spring-loaded clip which prevents the ink spilling out during a journey. The inkwell would probably have been used by travellers to the Continent toward the end of the 19th century. Late 1800s; 2in high.* **£30 – £40**

◁ PRESENTATION WRITING SET comprising propelling pencil, eraser, quill, inkpot and two pencils: the pieces are made of chrome-plated metal, wood and early plastics. The manufacturer was the British Basket Company Ltd. 1920; 7in long. **£30 – £40**

▷ FOUNTAIN PENS made by Conway Stewart (left) and Swan (right). With their gold nibs and decorative cases in abstract patterns, these classic pens are popular today both with serious collectors and those who want to use them as fashionable accessories. 1930s – 50s; 5 – 5¼ in long. Each **£150**

◁ LEATHER WRITING FOLDER The precursors of the modern wallet, such writing folders with compartments and pockets were common in the 19th and early 20th centuries. Late 19th century; 8in long. **£50 – £100**

▷ SILVER AND ENAMEL INKWELL The style is typical of the English Arts and Crafts movement at the turn of the century. The movement combined traditional styles with handicraft techniques. The inkwell was made at Chipping Camden by C. R. Ashbee's Guild of Handicraft. 1905; 4¼ in high. **£2,000 – £4,000**

NEEDLEWORK & WOOLWORK

In the 18th century, needlework was a popular pursuit among aristocratic ladies. They produced decorative embroidered pictures, mostly inspired by biblical, classical or mythological stories, using silk thread stitched on to silk fabric. The pictures were often oval in shape, with background details, faces and hands painted on to the fabric in watercolour.

This style of embroidery continued into the first quarter of the 19th century, after which date popular needlework changed dramatically. The growth of industry created a prosperous middle class that sought to emulate the aristocracy, and needlework became a far more widely practised pastime than ever before. Pictures in silks and wools were enormously popular, but as a result of such widespread interest designs became more repetitive and the needlework less skilled.

The stitching of samplers began even earlier than silkwork pictures; the first signed and dated pieces were made in the 1630s. They were not originally intended for display but to serve as an aide-mémoire of stitches. They took the form of narrow strips of linen sewn with random examples of stitches, patterns, letters and numbers. By the late 17th century, needlework had become an essential part of a young girl's education, and samplers became more orderly in design.

It was not until the 18th century that the typical sampler emerged, with alphabets, verses, pictorial images and later, maps and almanacs with embroidered borders. The backing was usually linen or canvas and the embroidery was done in multi-coloured silk thread in cross-stitch, eye-stitch, herringbone and outline tent-stitch, among others. Numerous such samplers were made in the late 18th and early 19th centuries, and many survive today.

Berlin woolwork (so named because originally both the designs and the dyed merino wool came from that city) became increasingly popular from the 1830s. The wools were worked to a grid pattern in plain tent-stitch or cross-stitch. Some designs were highlighted with silks or with

◁ *SATIN SKETCH of Christ with the Woman of Samaria. It is worked in wool – apart from Christ's silk halo. Such pictures were sometimes bought in kit form. This picture has faded badly. 1800; 12in high.* **£150**

△ *RELIGIOUS SAMPLER by a 10-year-old girl. The colours are still bright, so this sampler was probably kept rolled up out of the light. The frame is not in period. 1840; 18in long.* **£60**

△ SAMPLER *worked by Janet Richmond Alexander of Mauchline. Her descendants can trace their ancestors back to Robert Burns. The sampler would probably be worth more if it were sold in Scotland. 1837; 18½ in square.* **£500 – £600**

glass or metal beads, bugle beads or pearls. Popular subjects for embroidery included animals, flowers, and sentimental scenes. Biblical scenes were also stitched in woolwork, but they are not as much sought after by collectors today. So popular was this hobby that it rapidly became a craze, and photographs show Florence Nightingale working at her Berlin woolwork. Queen Victoria is also known to have indulged in this passion. Enthusiasm for Berlin woolwork declined, however, towards the end of the 19th century.

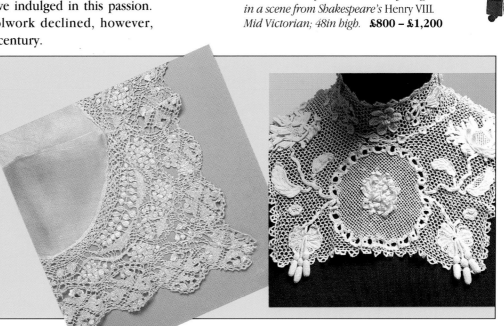

△ FIRE SCREEN *A Berlin woolwork panel mounted as a fire screen in a walnut support in the Renaissance style. The screen depicts Cardinal Wolsey and Catherine of Aragon in a scene from Shakespeare's* Henry VIII. *Mid Victorian; 48in high.* **£800 – £1,200**

LACE
Occasionally pieces of lace are brought to Roadshows for appraisal, but evaluating lace is an extremely difficult task. It is frequently critical that the expert sees the whole piece, and factors such as the condition, size and the date of manufacture are all-important. Nevertheless, the experts are always delighted to see beautiful examples of lace such as this Maltese handkerchief and Irish collar.

HOUSEHOLD ITEMS

Most of the antique domestic equipment owned by ordinary families today dates from the late 19th and early 20th centuries. At about this time the growth of female emancipation and the loss of manpower during World War I led to the invention of many labour-saving devices and gadgets for the home. This meant that middle-class and upper-class homes could be run efficiently with fewer staff than in previous generations.

Among these devices were sewing machines, washing machines and mangles, food choppers, coffee grinders, tea makers and cake mixers. Other more utilitarian domestic items included irons, lighting devices and fire extinguishers. This is a fascinating field for the collector. It provides an insight into a society that can still be remembered by older family members. Furthermore, an interesting and varied collection can be built up on a relatively modest budget.

△ *DELUXE TEA MAKER A chrome-plated copper model with three pots in recesses on top. These are kept warm by water below which is heated by a gas burner. Edwardian; 22in high.* **£100 – £150**

◁ *SILVER RIBBON PULLERS, often mistaken for candle snuffers or sugar tongs. They were in fact used to thread ribbons through babies' clothes. The design is copied from a mid 18th century German design. Late 19th century; 5in long.* **£70 – £80**

▷ *PINCUSHION PIG Of all animal designs pigs are the most popular. Items like this Birmingham-made pig (containing less than £1.50 worth of silver) are much sought after. 1909; 1½ in high.* **£60 – £80**

▷ *LANTERNS AND TORCHES*
1 *Early German bicycle lamp, 1900.*
2 *Ever Ready travelling lamp, 1920s.*
3 *Philips pump torch, 1940s.*
4 *Two Bakelite hand torches, 1930s.*
5 *Nickel-plated brass lantern, 1930s.*
6 *Ever Ready bicycle lamp with bull's eye glass lens, 1930s.*
7 *Ever Ready reading lantern, 1900.*
8 *Ever Ready oak box lamp, 1920s.*
Complete collection around **£300**

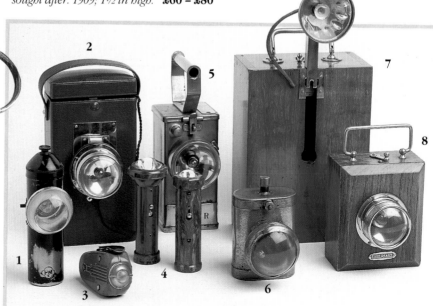

MAUCHLINEWARE

Mauchlineware is the name given to a wide range of decorative wooden boxes, keepsakes and tartanware items made in Scotland from the 1840s for the developing tourist market. The main manufacturers were A. & S. Smith of Mauchline, and Alexander Brown's Caledonia Boxworks. The most commonly used material was sycamore, and many of the boxes had integral and mechanically perfect wooden hinges, reflecting the high standard of finishing that characterizes the best pieces. The range of Mauchlineware includes snuff boxes, tea caddies, sewing, knitting and writing accessories as well as miniature jewellery.

The first tartans used in tartanware were either hand-painted or machine-woven on to paper which was applied to the item before varnishing. The revival in popularity of tartan boosted Scottish tourism, and Prince Albert himself designed a Balmoral tartan.

▽ *TARTANWARE BOX 1870;*
1½ in across. **£50 – £70**

△ *CAPSTAN for holding pins.*
1870; 2½ in high. **£50 – £70**

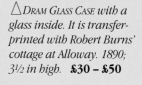

△*DRAM GLASS CASE with a glass inside. It is transfer-printed with Robert Burns' cottage at Alloway. 1890; 3½ in high.* **£30 – £50**

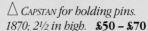

◁ *MAUCHLINEWARE PURSE showing a scene of Mont St Michel, France. 1860; 3in long.* **£20 – £25**

▷ *FIRE EXTINGUISHER This fine specimen would once have graced the corridor of a great house; there is said to be a similar one at Warwick Castle. It cost the present owner, who restored it himself, just £25. 1948; 28in high.* **£100 – £150**

△ *BRASS AND WALNUT ORNAMENTAL COAL SCUTTLE which can be dated by its gothic-style hinges, since the Arts and Crafts revival occurred at around the time it was made. 1860s; 11½ in wide x 17in deep x 11in high.* **£250 – £350**

TREEN

Treen, literally meaning 'of the tree', is the descriptive term generally used for wooden objects that are not large enough to be classed as furniture. Included in this category are items as diverse as an early trencher (a food plate) and a 1920s bell-pull. The earliest treen was made using a bow-like contraption called a pole lathe. Some of the most familiar and popular items of treen, such as cups, candlesticks and bowls, were made by this method. Other widely available items are snuff boxes of every description and betrothal tokens, such as spoons or knitting sheaths hand-carved by a young man for his beloved. Many kitchen implements, including wooden spoons, chopping boards and cream scoops, are also classified as treen. Although late examples of treen are common, pieces from the 17th century are extremely rare.

Among the most sought after treen objects are wassail bowls for spiced beer or mulled wine – the earliest of which date from the Elizabethan period – and maizers, or drinking cups, which were usually made from tree burrs.

▷ *CEREMONIAL MALLET for laying a foundation stone. It is an elaborate reproduction of a mason's tool and is made of a hardwood such as ebony or lignum vitae. The mallet may have been used by Queen Victoria, who would have tapped the stone with it as a symbolic gesture. On the underside of the ceremonial mallet (above) there is a portrait of Queen Victoria as a young woman. A decorative pattern of carved bands radiates from the portrait. 1850; 9in long.* **£100 – £150**

▽ *MAHOGANY BOX with two lids, each topped with a kingfisher, which slide out sideways to reveal two compartments. It may have been used to contain spices. Unique pieces such as this are extremely difficult to date since they are the work of local craftsmen. Early 20th century; 9in long.* **£30 – £40**

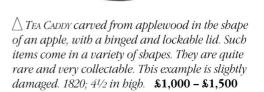

△ *TEA CADDY carved from applewood in the shape of an apple, with a hinged and lockable lid. Such items come in a variety of shapes. They are quite rare and very collectable. This example is slightly damaged. 1820; 4½ in high.* **£1,000 – £1,500**

TEA CADDIES

Tea was first introduced into English society in the early 17th century and rapidly gained a bad reputation for its hallucinogenic effects. It was not until late in the century that it achieved respectability and became regarded as something of a 'cure-all'. Samuel Pepys went so far as to describe it in his diary as being beneficial for a variety of ailments, including 'Mrs Pepys' defluxions'.

Tea arrived in Britain in containers known as 'katis' (probably the origin of the word caddy), which were made of lead or pewter and decorated in the chinoiserie style, but it was not long before British furniture-makers and silversmiths were producing decorative boxes to hold the precious leaves. By the 1770s, tea caddies came in all shapes, sizes and materials: glass, porcelain, silver, pewter,

tortoiseshell and ivory, as well as wood. All were fitted with lock and key because tea was such an expensive and valuable commodity. Since tea was considered a luxury item in the 18th century, it was usually offered to guests after dinner as an alternative to alcohol. It was only in the 19th century that the ceremony of taking tea in the afternoon began. Tea was usually boiled once for her ladyship, a second time by the servants, and a third time by the poor, who collected it at the garden gate. Tea leaves were not generally chopped into small pieces until the late 1700s. Caddies would often have inner containers with 'G' and 'B', for green and bohea (black Chinese tea), engraved on the lid to indicate the different types of tea, which would be blended in a central bowl to suit individual tastes.

▷ *TORTOISESHELL TEA CADDY This octagonal tea caddy has handles, gilt metal lion's paw feet, and a fitted interior edged with ivory. (It is slightly damaged.) Early 19th century; 8in long.* **£300 – £500**

△ *OVOID TEA CADDY, veneered in burr maple, with pressed gilt brass handles and feet. 1805; 10in long.* **£1,000 – £1,500**

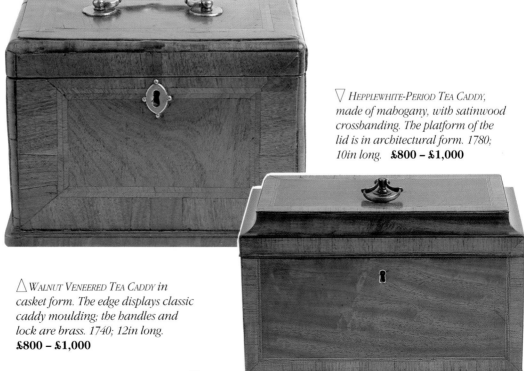

▽ *HEPPLEWHITE-PERIOD TEA CADDY, made of mahogany, with satinwood crossbanding. The platform of the lid is in architectural form. 1780; 10in long.* **£800 – £1,000**

△ *WALNUT VENEERED TEA CADDY in casket form. The edge displays classic caddy moulding; the handles and lock are brass. 1740; 12in long.* **£800 – £1,000**

SMOKERS' ITEMS

Throughout the 19th century the smoking of pipes or cigars was almost universal among men, and a smoker's cabinet was always a popular present. Pipes were made from a variety of materials that could easily be carved and had good insulating properties. Clay was the traditional material, followed by porcelain, briar and meerschaum (literally 'sea foam') – a form of magnesium silicate from the shores of the Black Sea. Eventually, briar was re-established as the standard material for pipes.

In polite 19th century society, after-dinner smoking was a strictly masculine ritual, and a selection of pipes would have been kept for this purpose, as well as a wide range of smoking accessories. These included items such as a pipe rack, tobacco jars and boxes, cigar cutters and pipe tampers, and perhaps even an opium pipe, which was quite common at this time. At the end of the 19th century cigarettes became increasingly popular, and the choice of related collectables is considerable, including cigarette holders in various materials, cigarette boxes, cases and old packs, as well as advertisements and cigarette cards.

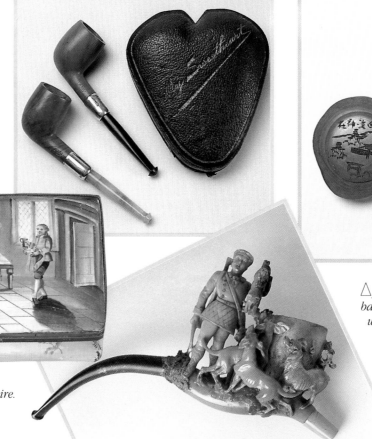

▷ *LOVE TOKEN PIPES Both pipes have silver mounts, and one has an amber mouthpiece. They come in a case clearly designed to be given by a girl to her sweetheart. 1920s; 5in long.* **£10 – £30**

△ *TOBACCO BOX from Staffordshire. It is printed and painted with figures at an inn, in the style of Teniers, the 17th century Dutch painter. 1770; 5in long.* **£800 – £1,000**

△ *JAPANESE OPIUM PIPE with bamboo case and carved wooden box (attached). Many such sets were brought back from the Far East. 1890; 8in long.* **£25 – £50**

▷ *REVOLVER PIPE Novelty pipes, mostly made of wood or meerschaum, were a phenomenon of the late 19th century and are particularly sought after today. 1890s; 5½ in long.* **£50 – £75**

△ *GERMAN MEERSCHAUM PIPE depicting a gamekeeper, his hounds and their catch. Hunting subjects are popular today, but naked ladies are the most valuable. (Slightly damaged.) 1910; 6in long.* **£100 – £120**

MATCH CASES

In Victorian times, the popularity of the match case – more commonly known as a vesta – grew rapidly, and it soon became a regular part of a gentleman's dress. Cases were made complete with tiny loops designed to hang from a watch chain. Silver and gold were the most valuable metals used, and from the 1850s novelty styles in a variety of materials including porcelain, wood, tinware and even papier mâché became fashionable.

△ SMOKER'S SET on a turned-wood plinth, designed to stand by a gentleman's armchair in his study or club. The set comprises a tobacco box and bowl, a match holder and a candlestick. Such items appeal both to collectors of smokers' items and collectors of treen. 1880; 26in high. **£100 – £150**

△ SILVER MATCH CASES The small hole in the corner of each case was used to hold a lighted match for a few moments, to melt sealing wax, for example. 1860 – 1910; 1½ – 2½ in. **Each £35 – £75**

◁ 'HIP FLASK' MATCH CASES Novelty cases shaped like hip flasks were popular with Victorian gentlemen. Made of silver and part-covered with leather, each has a ridged striker on the base. 1860 – 1910; 1½ – 2½ in. **Each £30 – £50**

△ LEATHER MATCH CASES for holding book matches. These were often made to resemble cigar cases. 1860 – 1910; 1½ – 2½ in. **Each £5 – £25**

◁ SOUVENIR MATCH CASES, three printed with views; one covered with mother-of-pearl. 1860 – 1910; 1½ – 2½ in. **Each from £10**

TRAVEL MEMORABILIA

The term 'travel memorabilia' covers a wide range of collectable items that relate to the motor car, railways and nautical vessels. (Motor car-related items are collectively known as 'automobilia', and railway-related items as 'railwayana'.)

Perhaps the most obvious types of automobilia are the spares and accessories for the actual vehicles – dashboard instruments, head and side lamps, car horns and klaxons, and car mascots. Indeed, highly desirable examples of the best car mascots can fetch many thousands of pounds at auction. Items related to the running of the car form another interesting group for collectors and include, for example, advertisements for oil and petrol, and even petrol pump globes. More widely popular are objects inspired by the design of the motor car: these include desk sets in the shape of saloon cars; pocket watches embossed with motor car motifs, and silver or nickel-plate teasets in which the teapot, hot water jug, sugar basin and milk jug are all moulded to look like streamlined limousines.

Printed items are also much sought after, including

◁ *MINERVA MASCOT in plated metal. 'Minerva' is the name of a Belgian manufacturer of luxury cars. 1925 – 37; 5½ in high.* **£250 – £350**

▷ *VAUXHALL WYVERN MASCOT on a marble base, stamped 'Joseph Fray'. 1929; 3½ in high.* **£300 – £400**

▽ *SIGNED PHOTOGRAPH OF JIM CLARK, one of the greatest racing drivers ever. He first raced in a single-seater car in 1959 and won a total of 25 Grand Prix races. 1960; 8in x 10in wide.* **£300 – £400**

▽ *SHELL PETROL PUMP GLOBE made of glass. 1950s; 15in high.* **£180 – £220**

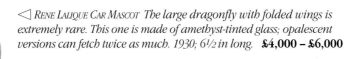

◁ *RENE LALIQUE CAR MASCOT The large dragonfly with folded wings is extremely rare. This one is made of amethyst-tinted glass; opalescent versions can fetch twice as much. 1930; 6½ in long.* **£4,000 – £6,000**

posters, race meeting programmes and photographs, and vehicle classification books. Signatures of drivers and mementoes from famous races (relatively easy to obtain decades ago) are always of interest to today's enthusiasts.

One of the leading Art Deco artists of the 1920s and '30s, René Lalique, designed 29 different types of car mascot and they are much sought after all over the world. Among Lalique's designs are animals, birds, and even a comet. Perhaps the best known car mascot is the elegant Victoire, or 'Spirit of the Wind'. These mascots could be fitted to the bonnet of any car and were sold in London by Brèves Galleries, a main retailer of Lalique glass.

'Railwayana' ranges from simple leaflets, timetables,

posters and lamps, to station waiting room furniture, signalling apparatus, official uniforms, locomotives and even the identification plaques from engine sheds. Some items were made in limited numbers, and are much sought after. Decorative station clocks, for example, are in great demand, but most desirable of all are locomotive nameplates, some of which have been sold for over £1,000.

Railway advertising posters painted by major artists were also printed in large quantities and were fairly inexpensive to buy only ten years ago. Since then, however, they have become popular with art collectors as well as railway fans, and prices have increased dramatically. A poster that would have sold for £20 ten years ago, for

△ ENAMEL ADVERTISING SIGN for Cleveland Discol petrol. 1950s; 4ft wide. **£400 – £500**

◁ BREXTON FOUR-PERSON PICNIC SET containing a Grimswades 'The Cube' ceramic tea service, a kettle and stove, and two wicker-covered bottles. Some of the more elaborate picnic sets of the time included a small primus stove, copper kettle, bone china and silver-plated cutlery among their interior fittings. These sets are much in demand today and command high prices. 1930s; 24in wide. **£1,000 – £1,500**

△ DASHBOARD SPEEDOMETER AND TIMEPIECE in matching alloy cases, made by the French company Jaeger. 1930s; 4in diameter. The pair **£250 – £300**

◁ TIN PLATE MOTORING DESKPIECE in the form of a four-door saloon, the roof of which opens to reveal a double inkwell. Under the bonnet there is a stamp compartment, and the spare tyre is an eraser. 1920; 9in long. **£100 – £150**

example, could now fetch up to £500 or more.

Antiques with nautical associations appeal to all types of collectors, from weekend yachters to those collectors who simply enjoy decorative objects whatever their origin.

Nautical memorabilia is an extremely diverse field, incorporating ships' fittings, artworks, craftworks and scale models. Ships' fittings include bells, wheels, tiller arms, lamps and portholes – these are especially interesting if their origin is known or if they are from a famous vessel. Navigational instruments, such as sextants, chronometers, telescopes and drawing and chart-ing instruments are much sought after, and ships' models made to scale are always in demand. Shellwork pictures, woolwork, scrimshaw (decora-tive items made from marine by-products, such as whalebone) and ships in bottles are just some of the nautical artworks and craftworks collected today.

△ *LNER POSTER designed by Frank Newbould. Posters are some of the most impressive items of railway memorabilia, and artists employed by the railway companies competed to produce the most stylish images. In 1980 this poster was worth around £20. 1930s; 50in x 39in.* **£400**

△ *RAILWAY LAMPS Some lamps were carried (left) and others were attached to rolling stock (right) as tail lamps. The most collectable lamps are those used before the railway mergers of 1923. Lamps bearing a company name (right) are of greater appeal than those marked with the letters BRE or BRM. Pre-1923.* Each **£80 – £100**

▷ *BLOCK INSTRUMENT One of a series of instruments which were kept in a signal box to indicate what was happening on the railway line. This item is a telegraph instrument with which signalmen could communicate with each other. (Made for Great Central Railway.) 1900; 2ft 6in high.* **£100 – £200**

△ LONDON AND NORTH EASTERN RAILWAY COMPANY SIGN Directional arrows and station names make such signs all the more desirable. 1923 – 48. **£60 – £80**

▽ REFRACTING TELESCOPES with leather-bound tubes and brass draws. Inset with prints. Mid 19th century; 30in extended. The pair **£350 – £550**

▷ BRASS SHIP'S BELL from the English ship 'Conquest'. Late 19th century; diameter at the mouth 12in. **£300 – £500**

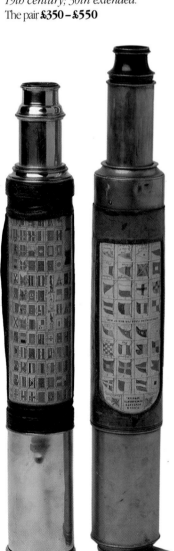

▽ TOPSAIL SCHOONER MODEL replete with all kinds of detail, including a carved figurehead, anchors and winches. It was made in England. Late 1800s; 3ft long. **£1,200 – £1,800**

SPORTING MEMORABILIA

The games of football and cricket have been of major interest for over a century, although the roots of both sports go back far further. In fact, cricket has been played locally and nationally since the 18th century.

The choice of sporting memorabilia is considerable. Among the earliest examples of football collectables, dating from the 1860s, are Staffordshire ceramic wares decorated with printed football scenes. It was after 1888, however, that the market expanded, inspired initially by the formation of the Football League, and later by the interest aroused by both domestic and international competitions. Ceramic wares remained popular, and plaques, mugs, plates and teapots decorated with football scenes were made by the thousand. Items commemorating particular games or competitions were also produced, along with busts and figurines of famous football stars, prints, postcards and cigarette cards. Boxed football games in good condition are also much sought after, and some collectors specialize in football ephemera such as old programmes and posters, souvenir books, team photographs and general fan club memorabilia.

Particularly sought-after items of cricketing memorabilia include paintings and prints depicting matches in progress, and equipment or clothing associated with famous players. Bats bearing the signatures of team members and signed prints or photographs are always desirable, as are postcards, cigarette cards, old cricket books (such as early copies of 'Wisden', cricket's annual almanac), magazines and ephemera. The ephemera category includes items from particular clubs or matches such as tickets, photographs, score cards, programmes and dinner menus.

△ FRAMED PRINT of a group of leading English football players, from 'Boy's Own' magazine. They are wearing club shirts and knee breeches. 1881; 15in x 11in. £60 – £80

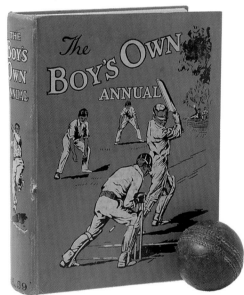

△ 'BOY'S OWN' ANNUAL Books are of value only if in good condition and if the covers are decorative, as here. 1900s; 10in high. £10 – £40

◁ FOOTBALL TEAPOT A player forms the handle, and the knob represents the FA Cup. 1930s; 6in high. £30 – £70

▷ STAFFORDSHIRE MUG, decorated with a football scene print. It is slightly damaged; if in perfect condition it would be worth £50 – £100. 1880s; 4½ in high. £20 – £30

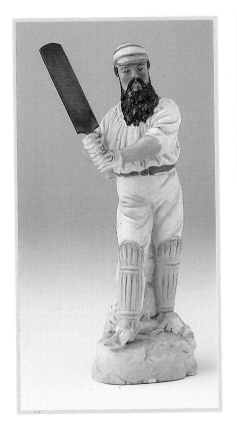

△ BISQUE FIGURE OF W. G. GRACE, the great English cricketer (1848 – 1915), wielding a wooden cricket bat which is detachable. 1900; 9in high. **£200 – £250**

◁ BISCUIT TIN A rare metal tin decorated with football scenes. On the top is a picture of Blackburn Rovers. It commemorates their three consecutive FA Cup wins – the only club ever to accomplish this feat. Mid 1880s; 7in high. **£200 – £300**

▽ ELECTROPLATED NICKEL SILVER TOAST RACK formed of cricket bats and stumps, with cricket ball feet and a belt handle. 1876 – 1910; 6in long. **£150 – £250**

△ STAFFORDSHIRE POTTERY FIGURES depicting George Ball and Julius Caesar in typical attire of the period. 1860; Ball and Caesar 10in high; wicket keeper and batsman group 5in high. Each **£200 – £600**

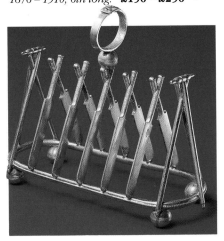

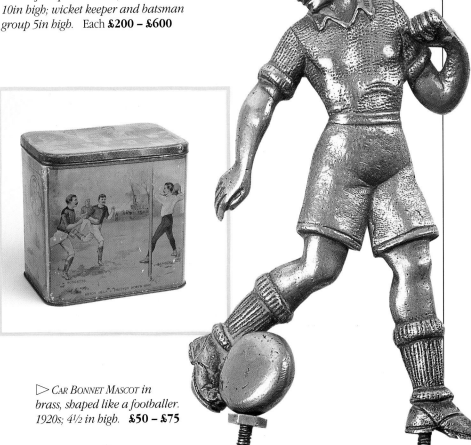

▷ CAR BONNET MASCOT in brass, shaped like a footballer. 1920s; 4½ in high. **£50 – £75**

CAMERAS

Two important occasions were celebrated in 1988 – the 150th anniversary of the invention of photography and the 100th anniversary of Kodak's first camera (Eastman had produced cameras before this date, but not under the Kodak name). The publicity surrounding these events stimulated plenty of new interest in cameras, but prices were not affected, and remain relatively low.

120mm and 350mm film for old cameras is still available, although for early plate cameras it needs to be specially cut. The fact that old cameras are usable today provides added interest for collectors and enthusiasts. There are thousands of different types of camera produced all over the world, and so the choice is exceptionally wide. Collectors may wish to specialize in box cameras, disguised cameras, folding cameras or even complete ranges from manufacturers such as Kodak, Canon or Nikon.

△ *Ticka 'Spy' Camera, disguised as a pocket watch. It was made when photography was still a novelty, and cameras were sometimes disguised to look like top hats and parcels. This chrome-plated brass model takes surprisingly good pictures. Ticka cameras were also made in solid silver. Although originally manufactured in the USA, they were also produced under licence in the UK. 1906; 2½ in high.* **£120 – £180**

△ *Plate Camera A mahogany and brass plate camera made by Thornton Picard in the early 1900s, a period when many fine cameras were produced in the UK. This model has a mahogany 'Time and Instant' shutter. Until the 1920s, all serious photographers used a plate camera such as this. It folds down to a compact size. 10in x 10in x 2in.* **£120 – £150**

△ *Stereoscopic Camera Using special 'standing' film, it could take two photographs at the same time with twin lenses set at the same distance apart as human eyes, resulting in a 3-D photograph. 1930s.* **£50 – £80**

▷ BOX CAMERAS *The Kodak models (1 and 2) were mass produced from 1900 to 1952 in an effort to bring photography to the general public. They were also made in other colours, including blue (2). Zeiss cameras (3) were made to a higher specification than Kodak, with better quality lenses, but were fairly inexpensive to buy. 1940s.* Each **£20 – £40**

▽ FOLDING CAMERAS *with bellows. As well as making the camera more compact when not in use, the bellows erected the lens to its correct focal length. The 'Carbine' (1) took postcard-sized photos. By the 1930s, Zeiss plate cameras (2) had become fairly advanced technologically. (3) is a rollfilm Zeiss, using 120mm film.* Each **£30 – £100**

△ LEICA CAMERAS *made by the German manufacturer, Leitz. Technically excellent, these are top-of-the-range cameras. Prices vary widely, but can range from £150 to several thousand pounds.* Each **£150 – £400**

DOLLS

Toys are a delightful field for collectors, but dolls in particular have a special charm – they recall a bygone era of childhood, and are of great historical interest. Many of the miniature adult-type dolls accurately reflect the latest fashions of their period, often down to the tiniest detail. Identifying and dating dolls is also of enormous interest to owners and collectors. Many clues to a doll's origin are provided by the materials from which it is made, its composition and shape, and the marks it may carry.

WOODEN, WAX AND PAPIER MACHE DOLLS

The earliest wooden dolls brought to the Roadshow dated from the 1730s. The heads and bodies were turned from one piece of wood, while the legs slotted into the bottom of the body. The head, chest, lower arms and legs of these dolls were covered with gesso, a type of plaster of Paris, painted in flesh tones. Eyes were also painted originally, but in the late 18th century black enamel was used for realism.

Machine-moulded papier mâché dolls were being made in great numbers in Germany by the 1830s and they were exported throughout Europe. Wax, too, could be easily shaped, and it was used in various ways to make dolls' heads or 'shoulder heads' (in this process the head and shoulders were cast together). The main methods used were: carving a block

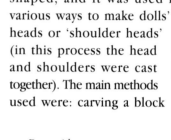

◁ *ENGLISH WOODEN DOLL with the square, jointed hips, pegged knees and blocked feet typical of the period. Also typical are the little dots for eyelashes and the single line for an eyebrow. She is carved from one piece of wood to the waist, and the layer of gesso covering the wood is painted and varnished. The doll is rare because it is in perfect condition, apart from a little 'rub' on the tip of the nose. Her expression is delightfully prim. Mid 18th century; 15in tall.* **£6,000 – £10,000**

△ *GEORGE III WOODEN DOLL made in England. She has rouged cheeks, inserted black pupil-less eyes, feathered brows and a blonde wig. Her waist is tapered to rounded hips and her legs taper to block feet. She has wooden forearms with long, bent fingers and is dressed in a pink-flowered, open cream dress, with a blue skirt and a white spotted apron. 1790; 13½ in tall.* **£500 – £700**

◁ *POURED-WAX SHOULDER HEAD DOLL, probably Italian, with a cloth body. The lower parts of the limbs are also poured wax. She has a well-moulded mouth, fixed blue glass eyes with slightly lowered lids and inserted hair. Late 19th century; on turned wooden stand, 20½ in tall.* **£350 – £400**

▷ *WAXED COMPOSITION SHOULDER HEAD DOLL, with a cloth body and wooden lower arms; made in Germany. She has an open mouth with upper and lower teeth, fixed glass eyes, and wig made of real hair. She is wearing her original clothes. 1865; 19in tall.* **£350 – £450**

◁ *PAPIER MACHE SHOULDER HEAD DOLL with a kid body, made in Germany. Her dark plaited wig conceals a black-painted head. 1850; 18½ in tall.* **£500 – £650**

▽ *PAPIER MACHE SHOULDER HEAD DOLL with a cloth body and composition limbs, made by Cuno and Otto Dressel of Germany. An unusally large doll, she has an open mouth with two moulded lower teeth, fixed blue glass eyes and a mohair wig. Late 19th century; 27in tall.* **£350 – £450**

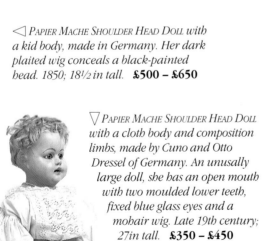

△ *WAXED PAPIER MACHE SHOULDER HEAD DOLL, made in Germany. A Motschmann-type doll, she has 'floating' joints (unfilled tubes of cloth connecting her torso to her lower arms) and wooden legs. She also has a squeaker in her stomach. 1850; 22in tall.* **£250 – £300**

of wax; pouring wax into a mould, or dipping a head made of wood or paper pulp into melted wax. Wax dolls were popular between 1830 and 1890, but they gradually lost ground to the bisque and china dolls that emerged in the late 19th century.

FRENCH AND GERMAN BISQUE DOLLS

From the mid 19th century to the mid 20th century the most popular material for dolls' heads was 'bisque' – a once-fired, unglazed porcelain made from kaolin, which gave a matt, rather than a glossy, finish. Early bisque dolls had moulded hair and fixed glass eyes, but later dolls were designed to accomodate gravity-operated sleeping eyes, and the heads were tinted in flesh tones and fitted with mohair or real hair wigs. Dolls' bodies were usually made of papier mâché, but some were made entirely of bisque; these were known as 'all-bisque' dolls.

In the 18th century, France gained a reputation for making fine-quality dolls, and several French makers began producing bisque dolls of great beauty, including Jumeau, Gaultier and Bru in 1842, 1860 and 1866 respectively. Two types of French bisque doll were commonly made: the bébé and the lady doll or 'Parisienne', whose golden age was the 1860s and '70s. These lady dolls usually had bisque shoulder heads stitched on to a kid body, with the lower legs and arms made of kid or porcelain. The high-quality bisque heads usually had blown glass eyes, a closed mouth, a real hair wig arranged in a complicated coiffure, and frequently pierced ears complete with

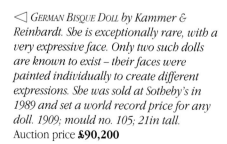

◁ *GERMAN BISQUE DOLL by Kammer & Reinhardt. She is exceptionally rare, with a very expressive face. Only two such dolls are known to exist – their faces were painted individually to create different expressions. She was sold at Sotheby's in 1989 and set a world record price for any doll. 1909; mould no. 105; 21in tall.* Auction price **£90,200**

△ *JUMEAU FASHION DOLL This swivel head bisque doll has a closed mouth, fixed blue glass eyes, pierced ears and a blonde mohair wig over a cork crown. Her body is leather and her fingers are separately stitched. She is wearing an embroidered cream on beige silk taffeta dress and matching hat, leather shoes and silk stockings. 1875; 18in tall.* **£4,000 – £6,000**

earrings. Dressed in the latest styles, these dolls were couriers of French fashion, and their large, lustrous glass eyes gave them a particularly lifelike quality.

Bisque dolls continued to be made throughout the 19th and into the 20th century, but most of those manufactured between 1870 and 1940 came from Germany. A plentiful supply of kaolin and a large but poorly paid workforce ensured that millions of cheap dolls were made and exported during this period.

If a bisque doll is conventionally pretty, the chances are she will have been produced in far greater numbers than a less attractive doll and may, surprisingly, be less rare. Desirability is dictated by the rarity of the mould number and the quality of manufacture, although the origin of the doll and her clothes are also important. Identification marks can be found either on the back of the doll's head or on the shoulder plate. These marks generally comprise a mould number, the manufacturer's initials or trademark, and the doll's size. Specialist books on doll trademarks are particularly useful when deciphering marks.

▷ *EMILE JUMEAU BÉBÉ DOLL with fixed blue glass eyes, stuck-on pierced ears, and a brown mohair wig over a cork crown. Her dress and shoes are from a later period. 1875; 23in tall.* **£2,000 – £3,000**

◁ *GERMAN BISQUE DOLL, probably made by Simon & Halbig. She has a toddler's body and her expression is known as a 'character face'. The number 914 is incised on the back of her head. 1915; 14in tall.* **£180 – £250**

▷ *EARLY BISQUE SHOULDER HEAD DOLL made by Simon and Halbig in Germany. She is wearing her original fine woollen clothes. Clothing that has survived for this long is usually full of moth-holes, but the owner kept this doll in a box containing moth balls, so the clothes are in very good condition. 1880; 16in tall.* **£600 – £700**

◁ *FRANÇOIS GAULTIER DOLL with blue glass eyes, pierced ears and a brown real hair wig over a cork crown. Her body is jointed wood and composition, and she is wearing an original maroon satin lace-edged dress, with a cream cut-silk taffeta front panel, a lace bonnet and brown lace-up boots. 1885; 36in tall.* **£4,000 – £6,000**

TEDDY BEARS

◁ *SOMERSAULTING BEAR This mechanical teddy bear was probably made by Gebrüder Bing. When his arms are wound, the bear turns somersaults (below). His fur is blond plush, and he has black boot-button eyes. 1913; 13½ in tall.* **£400 – £600**

Although soft bears on all fours were made before 1900 and the first with movable joints in 1902, it was not until 1906 that the teddy bear got its name (it was named after President Theodore 'Teddy' Roosevelt of America).

Until the 1920s, bears looked fiercer than the cuddly teddies of today, with their features closer to those of the real grizzly bears and brown bears on which they were modelled. Bears were made in many naturalistic colours, but in the 1930s they also appeared in scarlet, blue, purple and yellow. Initially bears were filled with 'Excelsior' (a trade name for fine wood straw) or a mixture of kapok and wood shavings. Later on bears were stuffed with kapok alone, and later still with foam rubber.

The German company Margarete Steiff is the best known manufacturer of teddies; these can easily be recognized by the metal button attached to the left ear. Other firms also made bears as part of their range: Merrythought, Chad Valley and Pedigree in England; Schuco, Fleischmann & Bloedal, Gebrüder Sussenguth and Bing in Germany; and the Ideal Novelty and Toy Company in the USA.

Teddy bears have become very popular with collectors in the last five years, particularly those made by Steiff. Although well-cuddled teddy bears with bodies and faces moulded into individual shapes and expressions through years of affection are often the most endearing, bears in good condition with no signs of wear and tear are the most highly prized by collectors.

△ *GOLD PLUSH TEDDY A good gold plush teddy bear made in England, probably by Merrythought. He has a plastic nose, brown and black glass eyes, pricked ears and velvet pads with stitched claws. 1930; 21in tall.* **£150 – £200**

△ *SCHUCO YES/NO TEDDY made in Germany. He is covered in gold plush, with a black stitched snout, and is stuffed with 'excelsior'. His tail is linked to his head; when it is moved the head goes from side to side, and up and down. He has lost his ears, pads and eyes. 1925; 15in tall.* **£200 – £300**

◁ STEIFF TEDDY *A gold plush teddy bear, with a photograph showing him and his original owners. Made in Germany, he has a Steiff button in his ear, a humped back, and is stuffed with 'Excelsior'. 1908; 11in tall.* **£400 – £600**

△ MUZZLED BEAR *Teddies in mint condition can fetch huge sums, particularly unusual examples such as this fine blond plush teddy with a leather muzzle. A German teddy, he has a Steiff button in his ear, a brown stitched nose, a humped back and a growler in his stomach. 1908; 22in tall.* **£5,000 – £6,000**

△ METAL IDENTIFICATION BUTTON *Some toys can be identified by a metal button (similar to the one above) or tag, usually attached to the left ear. Buttons and tags are still used by many companies today.*

◁ SCHUCO MUSICAL TEDDY *made in Germany. He has gold plush 'fur', a black stitched snout, black glass eyes, a humped back, swivel joints and a metal rod attaching his head to his body. The keywind mechanism on his back operates a musical movement inside. 1925; 22in tall.* **£400 – £600**

SOFT TOYS

Although some soft toys were made before 1890, it was only after this date that serious production of fabric animals and figures began. At this time a German company, Margarete Steiff, began manufacturing soft animals on a commercial scale. Best known for their teddy bears, Steiff produced a wide variety of animals and dolls in felt and mohair, all marked with a distinctive metal button in the left ear. The factory is still in production, making their famous teddy bears and other soft toys.

Schuco, another German toy manufacturer, began producing soft animals in the 1920s. Toys sometimes had a clockwork movement or wire linkage from the top to the tail so that the head could be moved up and down or from side to side.

Several factories in England were also involved in the making of soft toys at this time: Dean's began production in 1903; Chad Valley in the early 1920s; Nora Wellings in 1926; Merrythought in 1930 and Pedigree in 1942. Their products are marked in various ways – labels sewn on to the sole of the foot, printed or woven tags, or alternatively the name of the manufacturer was stamped or stencilled on to the fabric in ink. Soft toys were made from felt, plush, velvet, mohair, fur cloth and printed cotton, and the fillings included kapok, 'Excelsior' (thin wood shavings), granulated cork and sawdust.

Good condition is particularly important in soft toys, as they are difficult, if not impossible, to restore once stained or badly worn.

△ OSWALD THE LUCKY RABBIT, *made by Dean's Rag Book Company. This delightful toy, with a cream printed face and a toothy grin, is velvet-covered and has black button eyes. 1927; 15in to the top of his ears.* **£500 – £700**

◁ FELIX THE CAT *The felt-covered cat (left) has a pink ribbon and squeaker. The seated cat (right) is made of black and white plush and has felt ears, glass eyes and a humped back. 1920s; 12in tall (left), 14in tall (right).* Each **£400 – £600**

▷ MERRYTHOUGHT PANDA *with the original felt discs behind the eyes, giving him a melancholy but lovable air. Pandas are more unusual than teddy bears. 1935; 12in tall.* **£30 – £50**

△ FELT ELEPHANT ON WHEELS An early Steiff pull-along elephant on four metal wheels, with a press squeaker in his belly. 1897; 16in long. **£300 – £400**

▷ VELVET DOPEY with a painted face. One of the seven dwarves, he was made for the promotion of the Disney film 'Snow White and the Seven Dwarfs'. 1937; 10in high. **£300 – £400**

▽ STEIFF BULLY BULLDOG covered in orange and white plush. He has a brown leather collar with a brown-tipped hair trim. 1927; 12in tall. **£300 – £400**

△ MINNIE AND MICKEY MOUSE by Dean's Rag Book Company of London. Made of velvet and cotton, they are both missing their tails and are rather grubby. Though large and unusual, their price would have doubled if they had been in better condition. 1930s; 14in high seated. **£400 – 600**

▽ STEIFF GNOME with a pressed vinyl face, grey mohair beard and moustache, and a jointed, felt-covered body. He is wearing black felt trousers and a blue felt cape. 1950s; 12in tall. **£300 – £400**

CARVED & CAST TOYS

Toys carved from wood or cast in metal are highly collectable today, and the best examples can fetch surprisingly high prices. Carved toys, such as nativity scenes, forts and Noah's arks, are particularly popular with collectors, and the finest examples are regarded as works of art. Many of the highest quality carved toys were made in the mountainous region around Bohemia between Germany and Czechoslovakia in the 18th and 19th centuries.

Lead figures were made from the late 18th century onward, but it was not until the late 19th century that the technique was developed to produce solid-cast, realistic looking, three-dimensional figures. At the end of the 19th century hollow casting was invented and the method patented by William Britain. This enabled the production of a wide variety of figures that were fairly cheap to buy.

The first die-cast toy vehicles were made in the early 20th century by the French company Simon & Rivollet (in the die-casting process, molten metal is poured into a mould and great pressure applied). The Dowst Manufacturing Company of Chicago, who manufactured die-cast vehicles in the US from 1914, went on to produce a series which was sold under the trade name of

△ *CARVED AND PAINTED WOODEN NOAH'S ARK complete with 275 carved and painted animals. The condition is rather poor. It was made in Bavaria. 1850 – 75; 23in long.* **£400 – £600**

▽ *LEAD CAVALRY A collection of lead soldiers from various cavalry regiments, made by the English company, Britain's. 1920s; 2in high.* **£80 – £100**

'Tootsie Toys'. To most people, however, the best known die-cast toys are Dinky Toys (initially known as 'Modelled Miniatures'), which first appeared in England in 1934. They were originally made as accessories for Meccano's gauge O Hornby Trains to a scale of 1:43 – the same scale as the train sets. Other British companies quickly realized the market potential of such toys, and in 1935 Lesney Products began manufacturing the enormously popular 'Matchbox Miniatures' at a scale of 1:130.

Corgi Toys, introduced in 1956, were designed to be different from Dinky products, and from the first were known as 'the ones with windows'. Other distinctive extra features included independent suspension, jewelled headlights and tail lights, opening bonnets, detailed engines and even spare wheels.

The condition of die-cast toys is all-important. On the whole these toys are not rarities, and it is only those in perfect condition that can command high prices.

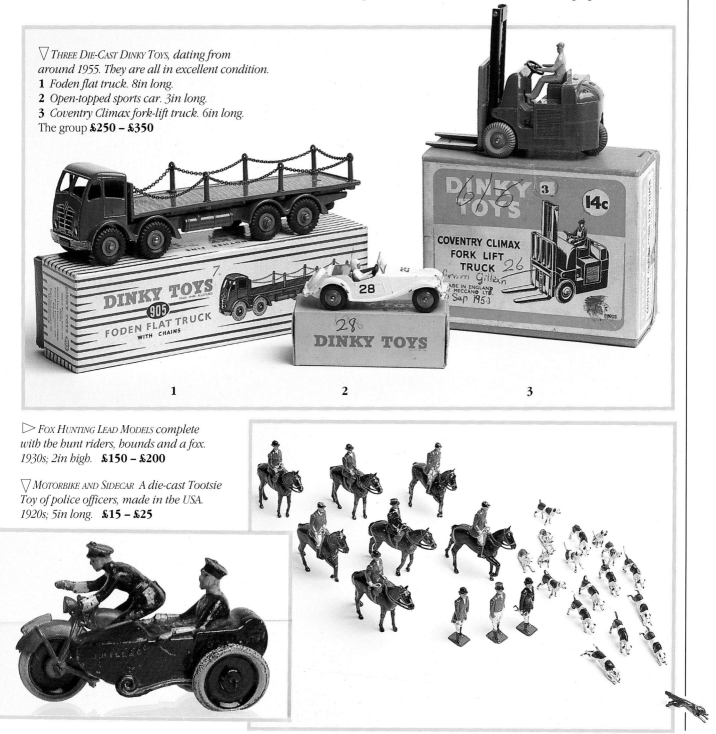

▽ THREE DIE-CAST DINKY TOYS, *dating from around 1955. They are all in excellent condition.*
1 *Foden flat truck. 8in long.*
2 *Open-topped sports car. 3in long.*
3 *Coventry Climax fork-lift truck. 6in long.*
The group **£250 – £350**

1   2   3

▷ FOX HUNTING LEAD MODELS *complete with the hunt riders, hounds and a fox. 1930s; 2in high.* **£150 – £200**

▽ MOTORBIKE AND SIDECAR *A die-cast Tootsie Toy of police officers, made in the USA. 1920s; 5in long.* **£15 – £25**

TIN PLATE TOYS

Novelty toys and tin plate vehicles were first made in Germany in the 19th century. The novelty toys ranged from imaginary figures to amusing models of figures from contemporary life, or those based on characters from films, plays, books or fables, while the tin plate vehicles included horsedrawn carriages and, later in the century, motor cars. Several makers in particular are associated with tin plate toys: Lehmann, Schuco, Adams and Stock (German), Martin (French) and Marx (American). Such toys were also produced by the toy manufacturing 'heavyweights' of Germany – Märklin, Bing, Carette, Guntherman and Plank, all of whom are best known for train and road vehicles.

Several English manufacturers also began making tin

plate vehicles after World War I. The major manufacturers will probably be familiar to many adults today: Hornby, Lines Brothers (later Tri-ang), Wells, Burnett, Walker and Chad Valley. Until the mid 20th century most toys were manufactured in Europe, but the outbreak of World War II seriously disrupted German toy production. After 1945, the Japanese entered the market, and within a short time they had become leaders in the field, mass-producing a wide range of attractive toys, such as small versions of American 'gas guzzler' cars. Space toys and robots were also popular Japanese lines, but it is the German toys that are most collectable today. Of all the German makers only Märklin has stood the test of time and remained in business.

◁ *GOOFY THE GARDENER, by Louis Marx, was made both in the United States and Britain. Toys representing Walt Disney characters are particularly sought after, and this one is in very good condition. 1935 – 40; 4in high.* **£150 – £180**

△*LEHMANN CAT AND MOUSE TOY called 'Nina'. It is made of tin which has been painted and sprayed with a type of flock. The toy is still in good working condition; it winds up underneath and scoots along. It has been kept in its original box, but it is not in very good condition. Made in Germany. 1920s; 7in long.* **£500 – £600**

▷ *TIN PLATE GYROSCOPIC BALLERINA made in Germany. A gyroscope in the dancer's body keeps her balancing on one leg. 1950; 5in tall.* **£50 – £80**

▷ GUNTHERMANN 'KAYE DON'S SILVER BULLET' RECORD CAR *This German model with a Union Jack on the tail fins is made of tin plate and lithographed in silver and blue. The car comes in the original box with the key to wind the clockwork mechanism. British racing champion Kaye Don failed to break the world land speed record in the Silver Bullet in 1930. 1930; 22in long.* **£650 – £850**

▷ EARLY GERMAN ROBOT *with the original box. (The operating key is missing.) 1955 – 60; 8in tall.* **£500 – £700**

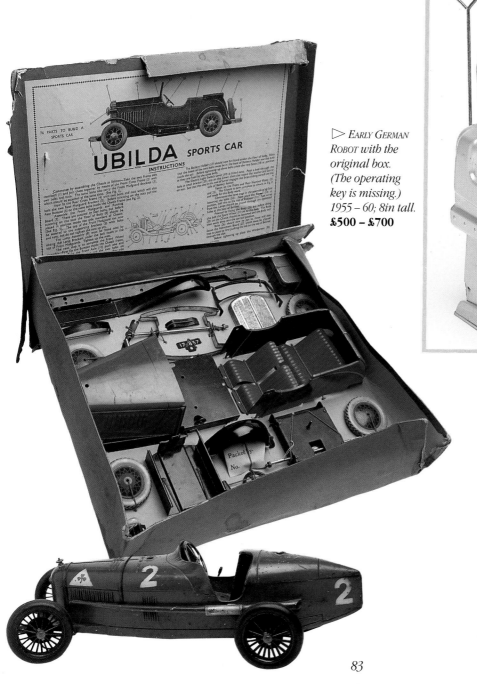

◁ BURNETT 'UBILDA' SPORTS CAR *A good, British-made model lithographed in red, black and cream. Its special features include battery-illuminated lights and a rear axle powered by clockwork. The car comes completely unconstructed and unused in the original cardboard box. 1930s; 16in long.* **£300 – £600**

◁ FRENCH ALFA ROMEO *made by C. I. J. (Compagnie Industrielle du Jouet). This model has a dark blue finish and tan seats. It features a clockwork motor, smooth rubber tyres, leather bonnet straps, a rear-wheel brake and a steering wheel that turns the front wheels. Mid 1920s; 20½ in long.* **£800 – £1,200**

MODEL TRAINS

The earliest toy trains, produced in the 1830s, were made from lead or wood. They were meant to be played with on a table top or on the floor, and it was not until later on in the century that they were specially designed to run on rails. German manufacturers were the first to make tin plate tracks that could be bought by section, enabling large layouts to be constructed. The first trains were pulled along or steam driven, but by 1900 clockwork was widely available. In 1898 a German manufacturer invented the first electric trainset, using three-railed track with a 'live' central rail. Toy train layouts quickly became popular, and many companies were associated with this type of toy manufacture. In England, the top makers were Hornby and Bassett-Lowke; in Germany,

△ *HORNBY O GAUGE TRAINSET with a four-wheeled tank locomotive, three coaches and a section of track. Bought in 1947 for £4 4s 7d, this is a fine example, still in its original box.* **£150 – £200**

▷ *ELECTRIC TRAINSET A tin plate Continental-style electric trainset made in O gauge by Märklin. This German company also made a series of corporate rolling stock with authentic logos and company colours, highly prized by enthusiasts. 1939.* **£200 – £250**

there were Märklin, Schönner, Carette, Bing and Plank; and in America the most important names were Lionel, Ives and American Flyer.

The manufacturers kept demand high by constantly introducing new locomotives, rolling stock and accessories to mirror developments as they occurred in real-life railways. Although most people today are familiar with the OO (16.5mm) and O (35mm) gauge trainsets, toy locomotives have been produced up to gauge IV (85mm).

As homes have become more modest in size over the years, however, manufacturers have increasingly tended to concentrate on the smaller gauge toys.

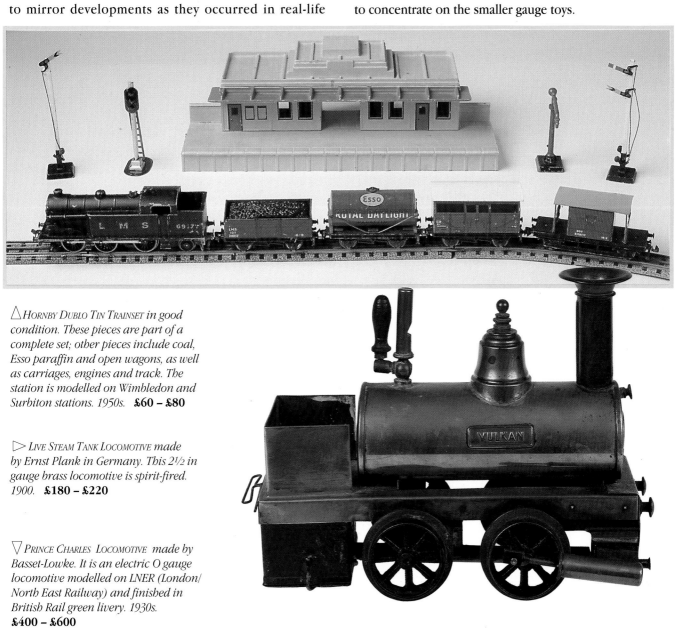

△ HORNBY DUBLO TIN TRAINSET *in good condition. These pieces are part of a complete set; other pieces include coal, Esso paraffin and open wagons, as well as carriages, engines and track. The station is modelled on Wimbledon and Surbiton stations. 1950s.* **£60 – £80**

▷ LIVE STEAM TANK LOCOMOTIVE *made by Ernst Plank in Germany. This 2½ in gauge brass locomotive is spirit-fired. 1900.* **£180 – £220**

▽ PRINCE CHARLES LOCOMOTIVE *made by Basset-Lowke. It is an electric O gauge locomotive modelled on LNER (London/North East Railway) and finished in British Rail green livery. 1930s.* **£400 – £600**

GALLERY

STEPHEN SOMERVILLE

The 1991 series is my fourth with the *Antiques Roadshow* team, although it seems considerably longer since my somewhat hesitant start. I had, of course, watched the show for many years, but it was slightly disconcerting actually to be a part of it. I am always impressed by the way the Roadshow sets give a sense of being 'at home', whether we are in a cathedral, town hall or leisure centre.

My area of expertise is in paintings, prints, drawings and watercolours, and my 30 years of experience – gathered first in the print departments at Sotheby's in London and New York in the '60s, then as a member of P & D Colnaghi, and now as a dealer with my own

company – means that I am well used used to dealing with many people and with a great number of objects. Even so, I was over-whelmed at first by the volume of people and number of items with which I was confronted at the *Antiques Roadshow*. However, after the first few shows I detected a certain pattern to events, and often saw familiar-looking items wherever we happened to be. Of course, it is the more unusual items that make the show, and it is quite extraordinary just how many turn up. I know from talking to people who have just watched a Roadshow that they are simply astounded that a particular owner has almost thrown something valuable away, or has had no idea of its artistic or commercial worth, but this is often the case.

In Dublin, I remember a charming lady brought me a portrait of a young girl by Harold Harvey. She informed me that it had been discovered in the garage and was about to be thrown out, when she rescued it because she liked it. She had been laughed at by her children for bringing it to the show, but it later sold at auction for £18,000.

I am sometimes known as 'Smasher' – not for my looks, but because of an incident in Lincoln Cathedral. At each Roadshow there is a security room (in Lincoln Cathedral this was a screened-off area). I went in and opened my briefcase on a table, but the lid fell back and struck a Chinese vase, knocking it off – I watched with horror as it smashed on to the stone floor. The noise reverberated around the cathedral and all the visitors gasped simultaneously. To make matters worse, I was due to record an item on a watercolour which belonged to the owners of the vase. I was very embarrassed, but they could not have been more charming, maintaining that they did not care for it that much anyway. However, it was one of a pair worth £1,500, and a single vase was worth only £400. They received

Dedham Church, painted, signed and dated by Frederick George Cotman, 1884. £5,000

insurance compensation and the vase was mended, so they still have the pair. Luckily it turned out quite well, but I made a note to be more careful in future.

Collecting is dependent on many criteria: knowledge, opportunity, interest, luck and, last but not least, money. However, it is fascinating to know how many collectors have been able to form collections on modest means. It would be quite impossible today to collect great paintings without spending a fortune, but if one were less ambitious and collected, for instance, 18th, 19th or 20th century British prints, one could put together a representative collection of great interest, where individual items could be purchased for a few pounds rather than several thousand.

We live in a time when so much emphasis is placed on commercial value and investment that it is easy to forget that only a decade or so ago collectors purchased pictures according to spendable income, rather than having to borrow or sell an asset to make a significant addition to their collection. Realistic collecting involves balancing desire with a fair price.

Buying a few items to decorate the home can be called collecting, but to my mind it should be a far more absorbing occupation, requiring real knowledge and a dedication verging on the obsessive. Visits to galleries, museums, collections, dealers and auctions are mandatory. Meeting fellow collectors and other people involved with the subject can be as interesting and enjoyable as collecting itself.

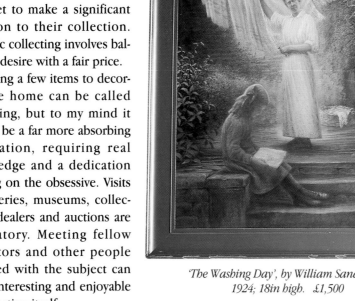

'The Washing Day', by William Sanderson.
1924; 18in high.   £1,500

Obsession can, of course, become a little overwhelming. There was once a book collector who filled his house with books to the point that he was only able to get into bed by crawling through a small gap in the stacks. How ironic the story of another obsessive who, to protect his collection of paintings, set an immense spring-trap of heavy books, which finally killed him and not a burglar!

For British collectors, I'm sure that between paintings, watercolours, drawings and prints, English watercolours would be the most popular. At the end of the 18th century there were numerous professional watercolour artists, and their work was very popular with collectors. In the 19th century, amateur artists took a great interest in the medium, and Victorian ladies (including the Queen herself) spent many hours at their landscapes and flowers, carrying sketchbooks in which to record their travels. Today there is also wide interest in and appreciation of watercolours by professional and amateur artists.

Collecting oil paintings, on the other hand, is quite different. They are more expensive and often larger than watercolours, which makes them more difficult to collect.

However, portraits dating from the 18th and 19th centuries can sometimes be purchased quite cheaply, and they are often complemented by beautiful and valuable original frames.

Print collecting is an area which offers plentiful material and modest prices. 18th century mezzotint subject and portrait prints are readily available at a fraction of the prices they realized at the beginning of this century. The works of the 'Modern British Etchers' of the 1920s could provide the basis for an excellent collection.

Always take advice when making a purchase. Dealers, auction experts and museum curators are usually quite willing to give free advice. Spend time looking, too, and compare what it is available on the market.

Condition is crucial: prints, drawings and watercolours can be overcleaned, and tears and damage invisibly mended and restored. Oil paintings are sometimes relined so heavily that all the brush strokes are flattened on to the surface of the canvas. There are, however, relatively safe ways through this minefield, and the rewards are worthwhile. Remember – do not clean paintings or works on paper yourself, take professional advice. Local museums can often advise on which restorers to use. Do not hang watercolours in direct sunlight (remember the sun moves, so you must check on the times when light strikes a wall where watercolours hang). Have watercolours, drawings and prints mounted on museum-quality boards which contain no impurities that can be absorbed into the paper.

Forming a collection can become a lifelong pastime, so remember my warning about it becoming an obsession. It is time-consuming, and becoming knowledgeable requires hard work, but with perseverance you will find it incredibly rewarding.

MY FAVOURITE ITEMS

The 1991 Roadshow was particularly productive for paintings and watercolours. I find it extraordinary that so many interesting paintings keep turning up at each location. It was difficult to select just four favourites from last year's series, but these are the pictures that I would most like to have taken home with me.

▷ *This portrait of a dog (or is it of the child?) is a wonderful, slightly primitive painting by the Colchester artist, John Vine. In fact it is a family christening portrait of George Frith Parson. (Although he is a boy, all children of this time were dressed in skirts until the boys were 'breeched'.) The artist, who is said to have painted with his feet, settled in Colchester and painted in Suffolk and Essex. I particulary like the dominant figure of the favourite pet with beautifully painted fur and a great brush of a tail.*

▽ *These charming cappriccio views, showing Dutch domestic life in summer and winter, are by the Dutch artist, Hendrick Mayer, and are signed and dated 'Mayer, 1788'. He worked in England at the end of the 18th century, and exhibited at the Royal Academy. The drawings were both painted in watercolour and gouache (an opaque colouring). They were of such quality that it seemed odd that they appeared to be unsigned. I had a feeling, though, that they might be signed on the back. The owner said that they had never been taken from their frames, so we carefully removed the drawings, and there, on the reverse of each, was a handsome signature in pen and brown ink.*

△ *This striking pastel shows elegant figures on the parade at Broadstairs. It was brought to the Salisbury Roadshow by Edward Heath's housekeeper. Judging by the artistic style and fashionable feathered hats, the date is probably early 20th century. Suggestions as to the artist's origins ranged from Scandinavia, France and Belgium to, of course, England. After the pastel was shown on television, three viewers suggested possible artists, the most interesting being the Irish artist Sir Robert Ponsonby Staples,who was later confirmed as the painter.*

PAINTING OUTDOORS

Since the early 16th century, when the German artist Dürer used watercolour to record the countryside, landscape has been a popular subject for artists. It was not until the early 17th century, however, that landscapes were featured prominently in oil paintings. The French artist Claude Lorrain painted the countryside near Rome to a formula based partly on invention and partly on observation. His atmospheric and serene classical style influenced Richard Wilson, J. M. W. Turner and John Constable, and laid the foundation for classical landscape painting in Britain. The artist Canaletto's visits to London in the 18th century increased Italian influence on landscape painting, as did the frequent trips to Italy by many British artists in the 18th and 19th centuries, most of whom painted in watercolour.

Thomas Gainsborough's early Suffolk landscapes reflect the influence of the Dutch landscape painters of the period, as do those of John Constable. However, Gainsborough's later 'fancy' landscapes were romantic inventions, painted in the studio. Constable laboured to be as accurate as possible in recording the appearance of a landscape. His technique of broken brushstrokes and use of many different shades of the same colour (especially green) were influential in France where, unlike in his own country, he was much admired.

△ *TRONGATE A Glasgow street scene by Charles James Lauder, an artist well known for his paintings of towns and architecture. The owner bought this work for 18s 6d (92p) 30 years ago in a Glasgow junk shop. 1900; 24in high.* **£12,000**

▷ *HOUGHTON MILL A watercolour by William Garden Fraser (1856 – 1921), who used a variety of signatures, including William Fraser Garden and W. F. Garden. He is the best known of a clan of Frasers, all of whom were artists in the Huntingdon and Bedfordshire areas. This small scale example is characteristic of his work. 1902; 6in wide.* **£700 – £1,000**

▷ *Kynance Cove*
An oil painting of
a beauty spot at the
Lizard, Cornwall
by E. W. Cooke, one
of the foremost
Victorian marine
artists. Painted
towards the end of
Cooke's life, this is
an unusual
example of his
work, since it is
rather subdued in
mood and colour.
1871; 12in high.
£3,000 – £4,000

△ *An Idyllic View of the
Countryside* A typical
anonymous Victorian
watercolour – probably
painted from life during
the 19th century. Hundreds
of similar works adorn
the walls of homes all
over Great Britain.

▽ *Landscape* in oil on
canvas by George
Houston. A girl is
depicted fetching water
from the river behind the
artist's house at Dalry,
near Ayr. The owner's
father was friendly
with the artist, who was
known as an Ayrshire
painter. The picture is
signed. 1890 – 1900;
30in wide. **£8,000**

◁ *Sweetwater* The artist Myles
Birkett Foster was one of the
best known Victorian
watercolourists. He worked in
London, but from the early
1860s lived at Whitley, Surrey.
This pastoral, tranquil and
superbly detailed painting is
typical of the artist's style. His
heyday was between 1860 and
1880. Highly finished Victorian
watercolours of this type are
currently very fashionable.
1860 – 70; 8in wide.
£7,000 – £8,000

▽ *Fishing Boats in a Harbour*
An amateur Victorian watercolour painting illustrating
the perennial English
fascination for all things
associated with the sea.

▷ *Pastoral
Evening Scene* A
moodily romantic
Victorian
interpretation of
the countryside
(Anonymous).

PORTRAITS

When Henry VIII broke with the Church of Rome in 1534, religious themes were banned in art. This contributed to the rise in importance of portraiture in England until it was perhaps unequalled anywhere else in Europe. Elizabeth I was the first English monarch to recognize the value of portraits that presented her as an icon of the people, adorned with the symbols of chastity, loyalty and service. Portraits of this nature were widely copied, and the image of the Queen became known throughout the country. In the 17th century, the painters Anthony Van Dyck and Peter Lely gave portraiture a great boost, and native artists began to expand their range of sitters. Early in the 18th century William Hogarth developed the 'conversation piece' painting, depicting rich merchants with all the trappings of their success, such as silver, Italian paintings and elegant clothes.

The greatest English portrait painters of the mid to late 18th century were Thomas Gainsborough and Joshua Reynolds, who worked to flatter their sitters and show their importance in society. With the onset of print-making and photography, painted portraiture became less popular, but it is still used today as the principal means of providing a formal record of people of status.

▽ *ALFRED, LORD TENNYSON This portrait of the poet was reputedly painted by James Smetham (1821 – 89), although the identity of neither the painter nor the subject has been confirmed. It is marred only by the 'craquelure', caused by the breakdown of the bituminous paint. 12in high.* **£1,000 – £1,500**

PORTRAIT MINIATURES
Portrait miniatures provided an intimate and easily portable likeness of friends or family, and were as popular as full-size formal portraits. Miniatures were often commissioned in order to portray to advantage the looks of a potential bride or groom, especially in royal betrothals to foreigners. Small likenesses were particularly advantageous in many instances since painters of miniatures could, if necessary, idealize their subjects' features. This portrait of a child, painted in the manner of Louis Marie Autissier at the end of the 18th century, is possibly French. The image here is approximately actual size. 3in high. **£250 – £350**

◁ THE NAVIGATOR This portrait of Domenico Trevisan, by an unknown artist, was discovered at the Malta Roadshow. The subject is depicted with the tools of his trade, and the inscription gives the date. The portrait is not well painted, but it is nevertheless of considerable historical interest. 1755; 3ft 6in high. **£500**

◁ PORTRAIT OF A BOY, painted by Solomon J. Solomon when he was a student at the Royal Academy. The artist was unhappy with the painting and so had discarded it in a corner, when the present owner's great-grandfather asked if he could have it. The painting is slightly damaged. 1884; 9in high. **£2,000 – £3,000**

▽ The label on the back of this pastel · portrait attributes it to Sir Thomas Lawrence; this is quite plausible as he often drew such portraits for a few pence. However, in his early days as an artist he frequently changed his style, so it is difficult to be certain of the attribution. 24in high. If by Lawrence **£2,500 – £3,500**

◁ MILITARY PORTRAIT Like many family portraits or portraits of local figures, this painting of a sergeant in the Royal Malta Regiment of Militia is of specific local interest. Portraits of a military nature are especially in demand because they are also attractive to collectors of militaria. 1900; 17in high. **£200 – £300**

◁ A DISTINGUISHED GENTLEMAN Although this portrait is painted in a style very close to that of Sir Thomas Lawrence (1769 – 1830), it is not by the artist. 34in high. **£1,500**

▷ PORTRAIT OF A YOUNG GIRL by William Huggins of Liverpool, later famous for his animal paintings. 1848; 24in high. **£1,800**

93

PRINTS & ENGRAVINGS

The term 'print' covers a wide field, from a 15th century engraving by Dürer or Mantegna to a lithograph by Picasso or a screen print by Andy Warhol. The earliest and most important print-making techniques of woodcut and metal engraving had reached a high state of excellence in Europe by the early 16th century, and at this time etching was also introduced. The relative simplicity of making prints by etching encouraged many artists who had previously been inhibited by the more exacting techniques of woodcut and engraving. Artists often made changes to their etching plates for each new printing; the changes were sometimes minute, and in other instances relatively dramatic. These plate changes are known as 'states', and the various states of certain artists' work have been recorded by collectors and experts.

In the 17th and 18th centuries, refinements in metal engraving techniques such as mezzotint, giving gradations of tone, were developed. Aquatint, which produced a shadow effect on etchings, was also developed at this time. By the end of the 18th century the art of the woodcut had largely disappeared, although in England Thomas Bewick began to produce wood engravings of great charm and skill.

In order to achieve a good market price, the condition of a print should be as near as possible to that of its first printing. There is a general agreement among connoisseurs

△ *REMBRANDT LANDSCAPE, typical of the many etchings by the 17th century master. The dark accents on the print were made using a technique called 'dry-point'.*

▽ *FOX HUNTING PRINTS One of a set of four prints on the same theme, using etching and aquatint coloured by hand. They were made after original designs by Dean Wolstenholme and Thomas Sunderland, and published as reprints by Ackermann. 20in wide.* The set **£300 – £400.**

▷ *DR THORNTON'S 'TEMPLE OF FLORA' A series of plates published 1799 – 1807. A full set contains 20 – 30 plates featuring a variety of print-making techniques, including mezzotint, aquatint and etching. Complete sets in very good condition are valued at £45,000 – £75,000. 16in high.* This single plate **£1,000**

and collectors that the amount of paper margin beyond the platemark is important when valuing a print. Many early prints have been trimmed over the years, or accidentally torn whilst being removed from picture albums.

English sporting prints are among the most common pictures brought to the *Antiques Roadshow*, and although interesting, they are generally of little commercial value. Many etchings by Muirhead Bone, D. Y. Cameron and Seymour Haydon, collectively known as the 'Modern British Etchers', are also brought along. Interestingly, they fetch much the same prices today as when they were first published in the 1920s. Contrary perhaps to general opinion, works of art do not necessarily increase in value with time.

◁ *GOING TO COVER, taken from a work by the early 18th century sporting artist James Seymour. It is one of a set of four published by Carrington Bowles. On its own this hand-coloured print is worth £500. The set uncoloured would be worth perhaps £1,500, while a single plate would fetch £300. The publisher's name and address and the title of the piece appear along the bottom edge of this print. 1775; 16in wide.* The set **£2,500**

△ *THE CHILLINGHAM BULL. This is artist Thomas Bewick's rarest wood engraving, of which only about ten perfect prints were made. After these were printed, the block was left on a window sill to dry, where it split. Other prints were made from the damaged block, and later a copperplate engraving was made after the original. An original print and the damaged block can be seen at the Bewick Birthplace Museum near Hexham. Bewick was most famous for his book illustrations.*

△ *WOODCUT OF A WOMAN, by George Buday, a Hungarian artist. It is the fourth print of a limited edition of 25.*

▷ *GIN LANE This engraving is after Hogarth's 'Modern Moral Subjects' series, in which he satirized the society of the day.*

POTTERY, PORCELAIN & GLASS

DAVID BATTIE

Back in the dim, dark days before the *Antiques Roadshow*, the major London salerooms used to send teams of experts to hotels or country houses and invite the public to bring along their works of art for valuation. Thousands of people turned up over the three or four days, and each event caused a local sensation. On one such 'Discovery Day' I was with the team on location in a hotel in Exeter when a television crew from Bristol came down to record the event for that evening's local news, and I was recorded talking to a lady about her object. The idea of a programme based on these

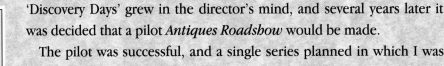

'Discovery Days' grew in the director's mind, and several years later it was decided that a pilot *Antiques Roadshow* would be made.

The pilot was successful, and a single series planned in which I was invited to take part. The rest, as they say, is history. In those days, of course, Arthur Negus was the doyen of all antiques programmes and he was the person responsible for making the whole area so popular.

His attraction lay in the disarmingly natural way in which he approached antiques, his obvious love of materials – particularly wood – and his infectious pleasure in meeting the public. I was lucky enough to make three of the *Arthur Negus Enjoys* programmes from various large country houses, and learnt a great deal from him. He is sadly missed; we all owe him a tremendous debt.

I look forward to Roadshows with mixed feelings as there is the certain knowledge that the day will be hot and very tiring. Every one of the 5,000 visitors is seen and told about their items. The series is recorded during summer, but the enormous lights required by the cameras burn all day. Although the halls sometimes have air-conditioning, it often has to be turned off because of the noise. So we melt. But this is a small complaint set against the excitement and anticipation. Am I going to unwrap the star piece of the show? Am I going to unwrap anything at all worth recording? Unless the object is outside our speciality we record on a 'finders-keepers' principle, and so days can go by without finding anything which would make a really entertaining slot in the programme.

I came to ceramics and Oriental works of art totally by accident. These subjects didn't appeal to me in any way – I collected books, and had done so since I was twelve. But when I joined Sotheby's as a porter in 1967 I was moved into a vacant job

Chinese punch bowl. 1760; 11in wide.   £1,800 – £2,000.

in the Ceramics and Glass department. Amongst the numerous jobs I had to perform was polishing and numbering the glass for Sarah Francis, who ran that department. I later became her director, and later still made her redundant! (We are still happily married.) I have to confess that it took me over a year to develop any serious interest in pottery or porcelain, but once hooked, I was hooked for good. I suspect that this is a slightly unusual way for someone to end up spending their life in one particular field.

Most would-be collectors are first tempted by something displayed in an antique shop or illustrated in a magazine, and wish that they could own it. Often their first, nervous, inexpensive purchase becomes the foundation for lifetime love. And love it is that should drive the collector, not prestige or the wish for profit. Without that all-consuming passion, the collector is unlikely to be prepared to pop into antique shops at every free moment, searching for the one object that is right for him or her. Oddly enough, buyers who set out with profit in mind very frequently make a loss when they sell. For collectors with a passion, however, antiques are one of the best investments they can make. Why?, because they are dedicated enough to spend time learning and looking. These two are irreplaceable ingredients in any collection.

The collector of ceramics and glass is spoiled for choice. While the average house may have one dining room table and a picture or two, it will surely have a kitchen

cupboard full of china and glass, while other pieces may hold pot plants, and porcelain figures and knick-knacks may cover the mantle-piece and window ledge. This is not a modern phenomenon; ceramics and glass are inexpensive materials and have been so for several centuries. Even the poorest households had a few jugs and plates. That is why the ceramics tables at the Roadshows have more experts around them and, despite this, why we feel we have to work twice as hard as anyone else!

Although apparently fragile, antique ceramics and glass have survived in larger numbers than any other type of antique. A frequently heard comment on the Roadshow is: 'It's well over a hundred years old and the colours have never faded'. And they never will. Once fired, ceramic colours, whether underglaze or overglaze, will remain unchanged until the end of time. Because of this, they do not need as much care as wood or ivory, for example. They can be washed in hot, soapy water without fear of damage, unless they have been restored, which might lead to a slight colour change. However, you should never use a dishwasher to clean good ceramics and glass.

Like all antiques, ceramics present a snapshot of the time in which they were produced. Learning to pin-point the style of an object is a worthwhile and necessary task for collectors. There are more reproductions and forgeries in ceramics than in any other field of antique collecting. The background knowledge is essential to determine whether or not a piece is 'right'.

The true collector probably has a picture in mind of what his or her collection should comprise. It will be slightly different from that of someone else collecting in the same field. For instance, we may both collect Victorian jugs; we may both collect only moulded jugs from the 1830s to 1860s, a fairly narrow field, but you may only collect parian and I stoneware. Thank heavens this is so, otherwise there would be half a dozen amazingly expensive, unobtainable objects and millions of uncollected ones. It is probably true to say that the greatest satisfaction comes from owning objects that are in pristine condition. It is also true that undamaged articles tend to increase in value faster, if this consideration is important to you. Nevertheless, considerable pleasure can be gained from simply owning a very rare and attractive object, even if it has suffered the ravages of time.

The skills of modern restorers are such that it is sometimes impossible to tell by eye alone whether a piece has been restored. Two instant tests are available. If you tap an unrestored piece of pottery or porcelain against a tooth there will be a sharp click; a restored portion gives a dull thud. Or use a pin lightly. It will run over the unrestored part easily, but will catch on the softer restoration. However, the first rule is to ask whoever is selling it: 'Has this been restored?' 'Not as far as I know' might well mean 'Yes'. Whatever happens, get a receipt and ensure that there is a full description of the piece, including a condition report. If there is a question over authenticity or condition you can then get your money back.

No collector can survive for long without being curious about the historical and social background to his or her collection, so visits to museums are a must. So too are a limited number of reference books on the specialist subject, and a good general encyclopaedia of antiques which will satisfy the collector's curiosity on related subjects.

Imari vase. 24in high; 1880.
£700 – £1,000

MY FAVOURITE ITEMS

The 1991 series of the *Antiques Roadshow* provided the usual wealth of interesting and, in some cases, valuable objects. The two are not necessarily linked, of course, and there are very many objects worth only a few pounds which are typical of their period, well-made and attractive. They could date as late as the 1970s, but they will be the antiques of the future, and as such are just as collectable as older pieces.

◁ *An armorial plate of unusual design turned up at the Islington Roadshow. Chinese porcelain painted with the armorial bearings of the English and Continental landed gentry was exported to order in the 18th century. Unlike the far more common blue and white ware, this was coloured and gilded, and as such was much more expensive. The decoration was added in Canton, and the dinner or tea service arrived back in England a year or two after the order had been sent. Today's prices are interesting: an ordinary blue and white plate from around 1760 would fetch about £80 – £100, and a chipped or cracked one about £50; £50 for 250 years of history must be cheap! This famille-verte example of around 1730 has a family crest and is worth about £300 – £500.*

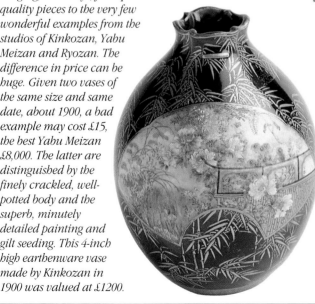

△ *The usual spread of Japanese Satsuma ware turns up at many Roadshows, ranging, as always, from poor quality pieces to the very few wonderful examples from the studios of Kinkozan, Yabu Meizan and Ryozan. The difference in price can be huge. Given two vases of the same size and same date, about 1900, a bad example may cost £15, the best Yabu Meizan £8,000. The latter are distinguished by the finely crackled, well-potted body and the superb, minutely detailed painting and gilt seeding. This 4-inch high earthenware vase made by Kinkozan in 1900 was valued at £1200.*

△ *My main interest lies in Oriental works of art, particularly Japanese. The sheer brilliance of their designs and unsurpassed technique at the turn of the 20th century I find irresistible. These works of art are not yet 'antiques' and are proof, if proof were needed, that age is not necessarily an ingredient in the value of an object. The Japanese were working at the same time as the famous French jeweller Fabergé, who was employed at the Russian court by the Tsar. The quality of the Japanese craftsmen's work was certainly equal to Fabergé's, and their designs were far more inventive. These miniature cabinets, decorated in gold on an iron ground, appeared during the 1991 series. They were made by Komai, one of the leading craftsmen of the period, and did not suffer from that common affliction of iron – rust. I valued them at £2,000 – £3,000 each, which came as a shock to the owner – particularly as she had 20 more at home!*

CHINESE PORCELAIN

The exact date at which Chinese porcelain with underglaze blue decoration was first made is uncertain. The Chinese probably began making porcelain in about the 7th century, and certainly by the mid 14th century it was in full and fairly sophisticated production.

Blue and white porcelain was made primarily for export to Persia, where there was considerable demand for big serving dishes that were used to hold rice and other foods. Curiously, the Chinese had no use for large pieces, with a few exceptions; temple vases for instance. The most famous of these is a pair, dated 1351, now in the Percival David Foundation in London.

From the 15th century, pots made for palace use were marked, by painting or stamping, with the Emperor's name and reign. This is generally six characters, but can be four. The first two marks are the dynasty name, Ming or Ching; the next two marks are the Emperor's adopted name, and the last pair read 'made in the reign of .....'.

Reign marks must be treated with some caution when dating pieces, however, because the Chinese frequently added reign marks from earlier periods to contemporary wares, to pay homage to their ancestors, or to evoke the spirit of a previous age.

Porcelain began to be exported to Europe in the 1600s, along with silks and spices, and it was an immediate success. By the 18th century millions of pieces were imported each year, many of which have survived, although usually in a damaged state. This means that a mid 18th century teapot with a chip or crack can be bought for around £80, or an imperfect tea bowl for just £1 – £2, making Chinese porcelain among the most inexpensive works of art to collect.

△ *PLATE, unusually well painted with the type of scene on which the English 'Willow Pattern' was based. Such plates were imported in huge numbers and many still survive, although they are mostly chipped or cracked because they were thinly potted. 1770; 8½ in across.* **£80**

▷ *PRUNUS PATTERN JAR AND COVER painted with flowers on a 'cracked ice' ground. Pots of this type were imported by stores such as Liberty as decorative, rather than collectors', pieces. Late 1900s; 13in high.* **£300**

$\triangledown$ *EXPORT DISH, hand-painted in a pattern that is often called a 'temple landscape'. It is part of a dinner service which would have been ordered from China, since it was cheaper to do this than to buy English porcelain. Such pieces are unmarked, and the underneath has a pleasant, slightly 'orange peel' surface. The foot rim is burnt orange-red where the iron oxide in the porcelain is exposed. (The dish is chipped.) 1770; 16in long.* **£200 – £300**

$\triangle$ *'KRAAK' DISH* This term describes the earliest type of Chinese export porcelain. These large dishes were sent to Europe in great numbers toward the end of the Ming dynasty, but of those left today, most are damaged. The design always features a wide border of panels painted with precious objects and flowers. In the centre are usually birds or flowers. If it were in perfect condition this dish would fetch £2,000. 1620; 14in. **£400**

$\triangledown$ *PORCELAIN TEAPOT, the design of which is based on an English silver example. When this teapot reached London, it was felt that it needed brightening up, so decorative gilding was added and the gilder inscribed his number on the base. 1790; 5in high.* **£500**

$\triangledown$ *RARE MING TEA BOWL* This quite ordinary looking Chinese bowl bears the mark of Emperor Yongle. It was sold in 1986 for the staggering amount below. 1403 – 24; 3¾ in across. **£363,000**

$\triangledown$ *TEAPOT in underglaze blue, painted with a flower pattern. This fairly common sort of teapot is relatively cheap to buy if it is damaged, as here. In perfect condition it would fetch around £200. Mid 1700s; 4in high.* **£70**

The Chinese first attempted to make coloured porcelain in the 14th century, using cobalt or copper under the glaze. The result was blue or red decoration, these being the only colours that could withstand high temperature firing. In the 15th century enamel colours that could be applied over the glaze were developed. Unlike blue and white ware which was made primarily for export, coloured porcelain was reserved for the Chinese court, and it was not until the reign of Emperor Kangxi (1666 – 1726) that it was traded to Europe. Most coloured porcelain had bright green enamel decoration known as famille-verte, or 'green family'. The famille-noire (black) and famille-jaune (yellow) palettes are variations of this decoration. The next important development was the use of a bright pink enamel derived from gold, famille-rose, which was produced in the early 18th century using a new technique brought from Europe to China. Decoration in the famille-rose group of colours was an immediate success when it first appeared on Chinese porcelain shipped to the West.

Most European trading nations had their own East India Company which imported the standard wares, mainly blue and white, in vast quantities. More expensive special orders were arranged privately by a man known as the 'supercargo' who dealt on his own behalf as well as working for the company. It was possible to send a drawing of a family coat-of-arms to China with a list of required items for a service – plates, tureens, sauce boats and so on – and two years later back would come the service, each piece appropriately painted.

Ordinary plates with flowers, dating from the mid 18th century, can be bought for about £150; pieces with hairline cracks can be found for as little as £40.

▽ QIANLONG VASE *The decoration of this rare, brilliantly enamelled piece incorporates peaches and bats (a red bat is visible on the left) signifying happiness and long life. The vase was made for court use, not export, and bears Emperor Qianlong's seal mark. 1736 – 96; 20in high. (Its 1986 sale price is approximate.)* **£850,000**

◁ TEA CANISTER AND COVER, *brightly decorated in the 'famille-rose' palette and with a scroll at the foot typical of the period. A fair number of such pieces – made as part of tea services for sale in Europe – have survived, but usually without covers. Mid 18th century; 5¼ in high.* **£100**

△ EXPORT PLATE *in underglaze blue and iron-red with the unusual addition of pink flowers. The unglazed edge is typically burnt orange. Mid 18th century; 8in.* **£120**

◁ *FAMILLE-VERTE VASE The style is similar to that of the dish, but the vase was made much later for export. The neck has been cut down, probably after damage. Mid 19th century; 20in high.* **£150 – £250**

▽ *FAMILLE-VERTE DISH, made in Emperor Kangxi's reign, depicting subjects bringing tributes to a mandarin and his consort. If perfect, the vase would be worth twice as much, but it has two hairline cracks. 1666 – 1722; 12in.* **£700 – £900**

△ *CADOGAN TEAPOT decorated in Canton style. Puzzle pieces such as this were popular in* the late 18th and 19th centuries. This particular type of teapot was reputedly first used by Lady Cadogan, who amazed her friends by pouring tea from a pot with no lid. In fact, the base has a hole from which a tube extends inside almost to the top. Tea is made in a separate pot, this one is turned upside down and the tea is poured in. When the pot is turned the right way up, the tea stays in. The handle has been restored, which more than halves the value of the piece. 1880; 5½ in high.
£60 – £80

▷ *ARMORIAL PLATE, well painted with a coat of arms within a spearhead border and vigorous feathery scrolls. There is too much white showing for the plate to fetch a really high price. 1740; 9in.* **£800 – £1,200**

△ *UNUSUAL CHINESE EXPORT PLATE painted in a refined style, in underglaze blue, iron-red and other enamels. The curious fan shape may have been a family crest. 1720 – 40; 10in.* **£300 – £500**

▷ *KANGXI FAMILLE-VERTE DISH in good condition. The red border successfully sets off the design of birds and flowers around a central scene of peacocks. 1730; 15in.* **£4,000**

JAPANESE CERAMICS

Much of Japan's ceramic tradition is attributable to Korea. In the late 16th century a great number of skilled Korean potters, both immigrants and captives, were brought to Japan to work in the ceramics industry.

Around 1620 the Japanese began making porcelain as well as traditional stoneware. Early pieces decorated in underglaze blue imitated imported Chinese 'ko-sometsuke'. In the mid 17th century the Dutch began to import blue and white Japanese porcelain and, later, enamelled wares. The most popular wares were of 'Imari' and 'Kakiemon' designs. Imari porcelain, named after the trading port from which it was exported, was decorated in underglaze blue, iron-red, gilding and occasionally other colours. Kakiemon ware, made at Arita, was usually decorated with skilfully applied, multi-coloured translucent enamelling, although some pieces were decorated simply in blue. Kakiemon is one of the most coveted types of Japanese porcelain, and in fact it is most sought after by the Japanese themselves.

The country's porcelain industry declined in the early 18th century and through the 19th century, but its reputation for excellence was restored in the 1880s thanks to the superb wares made at the Fukagawa factory and by the artist-potter Makuzu.

◁ *KUTANI VASE, decorated in iron-red with gilding. The shape is ideal for a lamp base but it should not be drilled. Items must be in pristine condition to fetch the best price; damaged goods may be un-sellable at any price. (The cover is missing.) Late 19th century; 14in high.* **£200 – £300**

△ *TYPICAL 'ROADSHOW' TEA SERVICE If 50 similar sets have not turned up at the Roadshow by the end of the day, there is something amiss! Millions of these poorly painted eggshell services were produced for export to Europe. 1870s – 1930s. Cup and saucer* **£2**

△*A SETO VASE There is a 'nervous' quality to Seto painting, and the vases are usually more thinly potted than those made at Arita. A pair would be worth three times as much as a single item. 1900; 10in high.* **£35**

▷ *IMARI BOWL This typical bowl is identifiable by the blue underglaze, the iron-red enamel and gilding overglaze. The decoration also includes green and yellow. The shape of the bowl is typical of export ware made in the 19th century. 1900; 10in across.* **£45**

▽ A NORITAKI CUP AND SAUCER *Examples of Noritaki porcelain are rarely of superb quality, but this cup and saucer pair is both well painted and designed. The factory mark is stamped on the base of the cup (shown inset). Early 20th century.* **£40**

◁ A KAKIEMON PLATE *depicting a man in a landscape (originally one of a set). Such plates are rare and much sought after. Surprisingly, perhaps, this type of plate is worth more sold individually than as part of a set. 1720; 8in across.* **£1,500 – £2,000**

Late 19th century Japanese ceramics manufacturers were highly accomplished and produced superb pieces with fine gilding and enamelling. They were also skilled at seeing the world through the wrong end of a telescope, and Satsuma and Kyoto pottery designs from this period are masterpieces of meticulous miniaturization.

The most easily recognizable characteristics of Satsuma ware are the cream-coloured body and the fine, even crazing of the glaze. Although this type of pottery is popularly known as Satsuma ware, much of it was in fact made at Kyoto. Helpfully, however, most pieces are marked with the maker's name. Further information is also frequently marked, such as the name of the town, the painter's name, and even the words 'bi jitsu', meaning 'beautiful art object'. Three great makers of Satsuma ware stand out: Kinkozan, the most prolific; Ryozan, and Yabu Meizan,

who is arguably the best. Their work is now extremely valuable and even a small pot can fetch thousands of pounds. These potters were building on a tradition of larger, heavily-enamelled pieces of enormous power and verve. Exactly when these earlier pieces were made is still a matter for debate, but a mid 19th century date seems most likely – probably shortly after Japan was opened up to Western trade in 1853.

At the beginning of the 20th century, the standard of Japanese pottery fell dramatically and very poor pieces flooded the European market. Almost all the pottery seen in Britain today was made for export within the last 150 years. It is interesting to note that the Japanese aesthetic eye is quite unlike that of the West and delights in happy accidents, damage and flaws, and in pieces which would be considered by some Westerners to be useless kiln-wasters.

▽ SATSUMA VASE *in which Satsuma enamelling and gilding is at its best, with large flowers and well-painted brocade borders. The cream-coloured, finely crazed, or crackled, body has been thrown in a shape that echoes those of the 17th century potter Ninsei, who supposedly introduced enamelled earthenware. 1860; 12in high.* **£3,800**

△ SATSUMA DISH, *attractively fluted and enamelled, and gilded with a gnarled prunus and chrysanthemums. The subject is typically Japanese, and the tree is possibly a bonsai. The handling is rather heavy and dense. Mid 19th century; 5½ in.* **£450**

◁ SATSUMA TEA SERVICE *which was given to the owner's parents as a wedding present in 1927. Such tea services are not uncommon, and often survive unused in their original boxes. The first impression is good, but closer inspection reveals the set to be of poor quality with brassy gilding. 1927.* **£200**

△ SATSUMA VASE *by the prolific potter, Hododa, who specialized in rather dark, ugly lohan, or 'immortals', often featuring a white dragon – the symbol of good fortune. 1890; 6in high.* **£80**

◁ SATSUMA UMBRELLA STAND *These decorative pieces were used for holding umbrellas or sticks, so the bases are often cracked. This colour scheme was often used by Taizan. 1890; 24in high.* **£500**

△ KINKOZAN EARTHENWARE VASE *with maker's marks. It is well painted with a panel of flowers on a finely seeded gilt ground. The gilt bamboo is slightly worn because it has not adhered well to the glaze. 1900; 4in high.* **£1,200**

▷ KYOTO VASES *Millions of these abysmally poor so-called Satsuma vases were exported to Europe and they survive in sizes ranging from a few inches to several feet. The crazing in the glaze is very wide, and the painting and gilding are atrocious. 1910; 12in high.* **£125**

CONTINENTAL PORCELAIN

The excitement caused by the arrival in Europe of Chinese porcelain was intense. By the 17th century the race was on to uncover the mystery of this desirable commodity – a race won by Meissen in 1708. Within a few years the secret had spread throughout the Continent.

18TH CENTURY PORCELAIN

From the 14th century until the end of the 17th century the demand for porcelain in Europe was met by Chinese imports. After this date, porcelain – albeit soft paste, or artificial, porcelain – was supplied by the newly established factory at Rouen, France. Two other French factories, St Cloud and Chantilly, were founded soon after, and all three manufacturers made porcelain to soft paste formulae with glass in the clay mix. Many of the early wares from the French factories were decorated in underglaze blue, but the Chantilly factory, whose tin glaze produced a jewel-like brilliance in the enamels, specialized in colourful designs influenced by Japanese Kakiemon ware.

Soft paste porcelain had in fact been made in the 16th century in Florence, but only a small amount was produced, of which about 60 pieces remain today. The elusive formula for hard paste, or true, porcelain was not discovered in Europe until 1708. This discovery, by Johann Böttger, a young German alchemist, led to the foundation of the famous Meissen factory at Dresden, which still produces high quality wares today.

At first, Meissen's hard paste porcelain was creamy white in colour, but the factory rapidly developed a very hard white paste which has changed little over the years. The earliest decorated pieces were greatly influenced by Oriental designs, particularly stylized Japanese flowers and birds, and idealized Chinese landscapes and figures.

Despite Meissen's attempts to keep the hard paste porcelain formula secret, Meissen workers, who were held virtually as prisoners, managed to escape and sell their expert knowledge to other porcelain manufacturers. The first factories to set up in competition with Meissen were

△ *VINCENNES ARROSOIR This watering can, or arrosoir, is very rare indeed; only five are known to exist. Madame de Pompadour is said to have sprinkled porcelain flowers with scented water, perhaps using a can of this type. 1754; 8in high. It was sold in 1984 for* **£31,000**

▽ *CAPO DI MONTE SNUFF BOX modelled by Giuseppe Gricci in the form of overlapping shells. With its gold mounts and naturalistic hand-colouring, this snuff box epitomizes rococo design. The painting on the inside of the lid is of a classical scene called 'The Education of Cupid'. Italian porcelain from this date and of this quality is rare. 1745; 3in wide.* **£15,000**

at Venice and Vienna. The Vienna factory, founded in 1719, employed ex-Meissen workers, but it was never successful financially and was sold in 1744.

The greatest French porcelain factory was Sèvres. It was founded in 1740 at the Château de Vincennes and moved to Sèvres in 1757. The factory was owned for most of its life by Louis XV and Louis XVI, and consequently it was not subjected to the same financial strictures as other factories. Sèvres porcelain, such as the much-copied unglazed biscuit figures, is of the highest quality and is greatly prized today.

After Meissen and Sèvres, the next Continental factory of note was Venice. The founder, goldsmith Francesco Vezzi, employed a worker who had previously been with the Meissen and Vienna factories to start production. The factory chose a red anchor as its mark, which was similar to Chelsea's mark but painted much larger.

Capo di Monte, notable primarily for its figure groups, is another of Italy's most famous factories. It was established in Naples in 1743, but lasted only until 1759 in its original form. Confusingly, the cups and vases decorated with coloured relief classical figures that have traditionally been attributed to the Capo di Monte factory were in fact made at the Doccia factory near Florence. 'Capo di Monte' later became the collective term for this type of ware, and the modern factory now produces these distinctively decorated pieces.

△ *FRANKENTHAL TEA BOWL AND SAUCER Like most Continental factories in the 19th century, Frankenthal favoured pseudo-Oriental designs. Small German factories such as Frankenthal have a strong following and their pieces often fetch surprisingly high prices. 1771; saucer 4¾ in.* **£3,000**

△ *RARE CHANTILLY BARREL-FORM MUG The decoration of exotic flowers and dancing cranes is inspired by Japanese Kakiemon designs. A tin glaze over the body heightens the brilliant colours of the enamels. 1730; 3in high.* **£1,800**

△ *NYMPHENBURG PLATE with magnificent gilding and luscious painted flowers and insects, decorated by Josef Zachenberger between 1760 and 1765. A service of identical design was made for the Bavarian electoral court. Since this plate is impressed with the Bavarian shield mark, it is likely to have come from that service. A similar plate was sold in 1990 in Geneva, Switzerland, for* **£8,000**

◁ VIENNA BEAKER, COVER AND SAUCER made in the Du Paquier period (1719 – 44). The attractively painted, stylized decoration is known as 'Berainesque' Bandelwerk, and the borders are decorated with lambrequins. Baroque was the predominant stylistic influence on ceramic painting at this time. 1725; beaker 4in high. **£3,000**

▽ MEISSEN TEAPOT in the shape of a cockerel. This amusing item was modelled by J. J. Kaendler in the style of a Chinese yixing (stoneware) original. Prices for such pieces can be unpredictable. 1725; 6¼ in long. **£2,400**

◁ MEISSEN TEAPOT from the Böttger period. This example, like most of the artist's early porcelain, is predominantly creamy white in colour. Many Meissen wares were sold uncoloured and were later decorated elsewhere. The gilt chinoiserie here was added at Augsberg. 1720; 4¾ in high. **£3,500**

▷ SEVRES BUTTER TUB With its floral sprays and blue and gold border, this piece displays the cheapest yet most enduring of Sèvres' patterns. The mark of the painter, Le Bel jeune, appears on the base. By the time this piece was made, the factory was in decline. 1791; 8in wide. **£350**

19TH & 20TH CENTURY PORCELAIN

In the latter half of the 19th century, factories in France, Germany and Bohemia in particular, began turning out cheap, mass-produced and often poor quality figures and wares. These flooded Britain, which could not compete because of rising wages, and by the 1880s even souvenirs commemorating Queen Victoria's Golden Jubilee could be imported more cheaply than made in Britain.

Despite this downward trend, good pieces were still made, notably by Berlin and Meissen. The latter relied heavily on its old moulds to reproduce the cupids, pretty ladies, gentlemen and animals that had been introduced a century before. Meissen ware is popularly known as Dresden ware, but this is incorrect; there are many other porcelain factories and decorating studios in Dresden besides Meissen.

Towards the end of the 19th century in Austria, the finely painted wares produced by the Vienna factory in the early 19th century were revived, many with transfer-printed decoration. The quality of painting in Vienna ware is all-important; so too is the content. Young girls were the favoured subject, preferably showing a little décolletage. These highly finished paintings on porcelain were often decorated by outside artists working on factory blanks.

Forgeries of Vienna ware abound. The factory mark of a shield – often wrongly identified as a beehive – can frequently be found on pieces made after the closure of the Royal Vienna factory in 1864.

In the late 19th century the Royal Copenhagen factory in Denmark had a revival in popularity. The factory produced many attractive figures and moulded plates, mostly in a blue and grey colour scheme inspired by Japanese wares decorated in these colours.

△ *VIENNA-STYLE CABINET PLATE painted with a portrait of a young girl within a border of rich raised gilding on a deep blue background. 1890; 9in.* **£1,300 – £1,500**

▷ *DRESDEN VASE The scene, featuring couples in a landscape alternating with flowers on a green background, was painted by Donath in 18th century style. The shape is inspired by Japanese designs. (One of a pair.) Late 19th century; 13in high.* The pair **£350**

◁ *CABINET CUP AND SAUCER in Paris porcelain, beautifully hand-painted with a view of the Palais des Tuileries, but with some damage to the saucer. 1830; saucer 5½ in, cup 3½ in high.* **£60 – £90**

CONTINENTAL FIGURES

△ *VOLKSTEDT FIGURES The Volkstedt factory produced a large number of poor to medium-quality figures. The quality of this pair is fair, but the coloration is dull. 1900; 7in high.* **£70 – £100**

Porcelain figures were among the earliest pieces made by Meissen, and the factory proved so great an influence that newly established factories often copied their designs. Some Dresden reproductions are very deceptive, and the famous Meissen crossed swords mark in underglaze blue has often been convincingly forged.

The end of the 19th century saw a craze for small French and German 'biscuit' figures. Crudely modelled in pastel pink and blue, the figures of babies were frequently used as wedding cake decorations. Many of the figures were made in pairs. The little boy and girl biscuit pairs are usually marked with a moulded factory number, which is often mistaken for a date. At this time the Austrian Royal Dux factory was making Art Nouveau-influenced figures which were usually small and rather spikily modelled. These pieces are now widely collected, and the larger they are, the greater their value.

Meissen re-issued many of its 18th century figures in the 19th century using original moulds. The quality remained high, but some of the detail in the painting was lost.

◁ *ROYAL DUX GOATHERD AND SHEPHERDESS Such figures were influenced by the Royal Worcester factory. They are very saleable because of their quality and size. Early 20th century; 18in high.*
The pair **£1,500 – £2,000**

△ *MEISSEN CUPIDS, one forcing two hearts together in a vice, the other fanning a burning heart with bellows. These allegorical images of love are part of a large series of cupid figures. 1860; 5in high.*
The pair **£800 – £1,000**

CONTINENTAL POTTERY

Throughout most of the 19th century the Staffordshire potteries dominated the world markets. Continental factories concentrated on porcelain, although here, too, Staffordshire reigned supreme, and what pottery existed was usually quite crude. Faïence or delft (tin-glazed earthenware) lingered far longer in Continental Europe than in England, where it was ousted by Wedgwood's creamware, and its imitators. This was followed by Staffordshire underglaze-blue transferred ware and ironstone ware. Despite the production of a few feeble copies of both types of pottery, Europe was swamped by British imports.

Some rural potteries in Europe continued to make decorative wares and these are now becoming sought after: for instance, colourful, naively painted pieces from Quimper in Brittany are now very fashionable.

At the end of the century Continental factories began to challenge Staffordshire porcelain, but Britain still excelled at pottery. There were, however, exceptions: the stonewares made by Mettlach are of good quality, especially the beer steins. The Germans also imitated Staffordshire majolica, but the quality never rivalled that of English pieces.

The Dutch produced much imitation 18th century delft ware for the tourist market, so be wary if intending to buy: a piece marked 'delft' may not be genuine.

△ *AUSTRIAN OR HUNGARIAN VASES made for export. Rich in baroque decoration, they are pierced and heavily gilded. 1880 – 90; 15in high.*
£80 – £120

▽ *CABBAGE TEAPOT based on a style created by Bernard Palissy in France in the 17th century. The style was revived there, and in Portugal, in later periods. Late 19th century; 7in high.* **£100**

△ *WALL PLAQUE made in Germany. It is beautifully executed, with a border of raised flowers and foliage and a classical scene in the centre. 1850; 18in across.* **£400 – £500**

▷ *ZSOLNAY JARDINIERE made of cream-coloured earthenware. A Hungarian factory in Pecs, Zsolnay specialized in elaborately pierced and gilded wares, and in designs with Oriental or Middle Eastern influences. They are good quality, but not much appreciated. 1890; 18in wide.* **£450**

ENGLISH PORCELAIN & POTTERY

△ *DERBY BASKET AND STAND for roasted chestnuts, which were eaten with port at the end of a meal. It is unusual to find such a basket complete with its stand, and Derby examples are rarer than Worcester pieces of the same date. 1760; stand 9½ in diameter.* **£2,000**

IDENTIFYING FEATURES
There are sometimes clues that help experts to establish precisely in which factory a piece of porcelain was made. This plate, for example, displays a distinctively green tinge when held to the light, and this helps to identify it as a First Period Worcester piece (1751–83). Another feature found on other Worcester pieces, such as plates, bowls and tea pots, is an unglazed line within the foot rim.

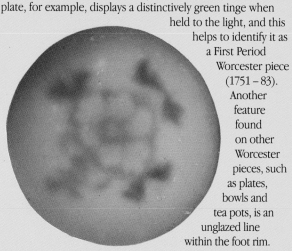

Of the European countries, England came late to making porcelain. The first factories, Chelsea and Bow, made a substitute for true porcelain – soft paste. While influenced by the Continent and China, the figures and wares they produced were characteristically English.

18TH CENTURY BLUE & WHITE WARE
Most 18th century factories made great quantities of blue and white porcelain for the general public. At first, pieces were hand-painted, but following the introduction of a new transfer-printing process (developed in Liverpool), pieces could be be mass produced with identical designs, so maintaining a constant standard. Staffordshire rapidly adopted the new printing process, and the subsequent success of Stoke-on-Trent pottery was due to underglaze blue transfers. The process involved engraving a design on a copper plate, inking it and running it through a press on to a thin tissue which was stuck to the unfired pot. When dry, the tissue was washed off, the pot fired, glazed and then fired again, fixing the pattern permanently.

The major porcelain manufacturers in the mid 18th century were Worcester, Bow, Lowestoft, the Liverpool factories and Caughley. Early Worcester wares were sophisticated, reflecting a combination of rococo and

◁ *DELFTWARE BOWL. This type of English delftware bowl provided the foundation for painters who were later to work on English blue and white porcelain. The two materials were used concurrently until the end of the 18th century. (The rim is chipped.) 1780; 3in wide.* **£250 – £300**

▽ *WORCESTER SAUCE BOAT with underglaze blue decoration enclosed within moulded scrolls. The subject matter was invariably based on Chinese originals made for export. 1755; 7¹/₂ in long.* **£800**

△ *WORCESTER TEAPOT painted in underglaze blue with a Chinese lady and boy in a garden. Both the lid and the pot bear a painter's mark. 1755; 3¹/₂ in high.* **£1,800**

▷ *PEARLWARE PLATE made in Staffordshire or Liverpool, transfer-printed with a design from a Chinese original. The name 'Pearlware' derives from the blue-tinged glaze over a cream-coloured body. Plates with pierced borders are known as 'ribbon plates'. 1795; 7¹/₂ in.* **£120**

◁ *PICKLE DISH from Limehouse in London's East End. Until 1989 such pieces were thought to have been made by William Reid of Liverpool. Excavations, however, revealed Limehouse to be the site of the first English factory to make blue and white porcelain. 1748; 4¹/₄ in.* **£1,000**

chinoiserie styles. The factory was successful, and more pieces of Worcester porcelain have survived than from any other factory.

Bow, founded by Thomas Frye in 1744, exported large quantities of blue and white porcelain. The style of painting on Bow pieces is unusually bold, and the earlier designs are in a bright, inky blue. The Caughley factory (pronounced calf-lea) was founded in 1772 near Worcester. Its wares, largely underglaze blue, were often direct copies of Worcester, and one of its marks, a 'C', looked very like Worcester's crescent. The Liverpool factories date from the mid 1750s, and there is still some confusion about who did what there. Certainly, however, pieces from the Christian, Gilbody, Chaffers and Pennington Brothers factories were mostly blue and white.

18TH CENTURY COLOURED PORCELAIN

The first English factories in the 18th century to produce porcelain were Chelsea and Bow, founded in 1744. Chelsea, under the guidance of silversmith Nicholas Sprimont, aimed mainly at the top end of the market and produced great quantities of coloured figures and finely enamelled pieces, but very little blue and white.

The Bow factory was founded by Thomas Frye. Its wares were aimed at a mass market, while occasionally aspiring higher with Chelsea-type figures. The factory's special bone-ash formula enabled it to produce large plates and dishes more easily than other factories, such as Worcester. The potting in such pieces is heavy, however, and the translucency is poor, with a straw-coloured hue.

Worcester is the only English factory from this period to have survived until today. Founded in 1751 by Dr John Wall, the factory joined forces with Benjamin Lund's Bristol factory in 1752. The resulting wares were sophisticated from very early on, reflecting the combined rococo and chinoiserie tastes popular at the time. Worcester had a considerable advantage over other factories: a clay mix containing soapstone which was easy to work, stable and impervious to temperature shock. An identifying feature of Worcester is that pieces often exhibit a green tinge when held to the light.

Lowestoft (founded in 1757), on the Suffolk coast, also used a bone-ash formula, but its wares were 'lighter' than Bow's. The influence was Chinese and the factory specialized in dated and dedicated pieces, particularly birth plaques, which were made by no other factories. Like Bow, Lowestoft pieces display a straw-coloured translucency: chips and cracks turn brown and the unglazed foot rims are often brown-tinged.

Two other London factories, Vauxhall and Limehouse, have recently been identified; their wares had previously been attributed to Liverpool. Neither factory lasted for more than a few years, however, and their pieces are rare.

The Derby factory, established in 1750, concentrated on decorative wares such as figures and vases. The factory switched to making practical objects in about 1756 and eventually amalgamated with the Chelsea factory in 1770.

The first factory to manufacture porcelain in Staffordshire was Longton Hall, near Stoke on Trent, which was founded in the same year as Derby. The general quality of its figures and practical wares tends to be somewhat naive, and the colouring can be harsh.

▽ *BOW CANARY, somewhat naively modelled. Bow figures are rarer than Chelsea figures and bolder in colour. Because the leaves and branches, known as 'bocage', are so fragile, these figures are often damaged. This piece is in good condition. (it is one of a pair). 1760; 3in high.*
The pair **£1,000 – £1,500**

◁ *PAIR OF BOW FIGURES entitled 'Matrimony' and 'Freedom'. The high scroll base is a common Bow feature, as is the purple colouring on the garments. 18th century English figures are a somewhat erratic market at present and prices are unpredictable. 1760; 8½ in high.* **£2,500**

△ *Derby Butter Tub* (one of a pair) in excellent condition. The shape is unusual and the painting in bright enamels is of a high standard. 1760 – 65; 5in wide. The pair **£4,000**

▽ *Worcester Plate* which is a copy of a Japanese Imari original dating from about 1710. In the late 18th century the Imari style was still highly regarded in England and was considered worth reproducing. 1765; 8¼ in. **£900**

△ *Rare Liverpool Teapot* The painting of a Chinese scene, 'The Stag Hunt', was copied by many other factories. 1765; 4in high. **£2,000**

◁ *Lowestoft Tea Bowl* There is some evidence of Chinese influence in the decoration of this bowl. The flowers are painted in underglaze blue, iron red and gilding. 1770; 3in across. **£80**

CHELSEA PLATE

A Chelsea plate is translucent when held to the light, but the straw-coloured hue and 'moons' of paler colour can be clearly seen. Both features are common in Chelsea ware made between 1752 and 1760, and help with attribution.

19TH CENTURY CERAMICS

British society probably saw more rapid changes in the 19th century than in any other period of its history. The Industrial Revolution was in full swing and Britain ruled the largest empire the world has ever seen.

In the early 1800s the English ceramics industry began experimenting with a new material – bone china. Containing up to 50% burnt bones, it proved more satisfactory than any of the alternative materials previously tested. Pottery continued to be used for cheap exports and decorative domestic items in England, such as mass-produced Staffordshire figures.

Some of the great names of the 18th century, including Worcester, Derby and Minton, continued production into the 20th century, building on past successes and introducing new styles and techniques. The neo-classical style survived into the 19th century but was soon overtaken by

Regency interest in Chinese and Indian motifs. This, in turn, gave way to a rococo revival. In the middle of the century the Great Exhibition at Crystal Palace featured renaissance-style wares, and by 1860 Limoges-style enamels made by Worcester had come back into fashion.

After Japan had been opened up to the West in 1853, and had begun showing at international exhibitions, a heady Eastern exoticism swept through the English potteries. As a result, superb quality cloisonné wares were made by Minton, and Japanese figures by Worcester and Brownfields. Worcester, at the same time, was producing fine quality figures by James Hadley with sprinkled gold coloration, and Minton had achieved perfection in the pâte-sur-pâte technique of white figures on a dark background. Fine hand-painted services were made throughout the century, but few are marked with anything other than a pattern number. It is almost always a mistake to split such a service.

◁ *MINTONS MOON FLASK A fine example of imitation cloisonné ware, a popular decorative style in the 1870s. The cloisonné technique was expensive, since laborious hand-painting was involved. Prices are lower than would be expected, considering how rarely pieces come up for sale. 1874; 12in high.*
£800 – £1,200

△ *ENGLISH BONE CHINA VASES made for a mantelpiece, in the ornamental style of antique Greek vessels. The maker is Bates, Brown, Westhead & Moore of Stoke-on-Trent. 1860; 6in high.* The pair **£150**

▷ *ROYAL WORCESTER ELEPHANT, well cast and coloured, after a model by James Hadley. Worcester of this period, though far more interesting than the later, more famous, Highland cattle, remains underpriced. 1880; 9in long.*
£600 – £800

▽ *COALPORT VASE in typically elaborate neo-rococo style, with scrolled handles and flower-encrusted body. 1840; 10in high.* **£100 – £500**

△ *A BELLEEK BASKET The Belleek factory in Northern Ireland specialized in woven parian porcelain. It was usually given a shiny glaze, but a few rare examples, as here, were coloured. Uncoloured examples fetch between £2,000 and £3,000. 1885; 10in wide.* **£3,000 – £4,000**

▽ *MINTON VASE decorated by Marc Louis Solon in the laborious pâte-sur-pâte technique. His work is rare and highly collectable. 15in high.* **£2,000 – £3,000**

△ *STAFFORDSHIRE BONE CHINA PASTILLE BURNER in the shape of a Regency cottage. Spices and resins were burned inside to help banish household odours. These pieces are much sought after, and forgeries abound. 1825; 6in high.* **£350 – £500**

THE ENGLISH JUG

In the 19th century, water, milk and even ale were fetched in jugs, and poor families were likely to have had more jugs than they had forks. It is hardly suprising, then, that jugs are among the most common 19th century ceramics – and also among the cheapest.

Apart from earthenware, two other materials were predominantly used for making jugs: stoneware in various colours and, in the 1840s, parian. Both of these can be moulded to create finely detailed figures, and floral or geometric designs. Of particular interest to the collector, they frequently bear makers' marks, dates, registration of design marks and even the title of the jug. Most can be bought for between £30 and £100, or less if the jug is damaged. It should be noted that the matt surface and subdued colouring of these jugs makes it difficult to detect restoration.

Less sophisticated earthenware jugs covered in copper-lustre and enamelled with flowers and leaves were commonly seen in the homes of country folk throughout Britain in the 19th century. These jugs have great charm, and are popular with a wide variety of collectors. Prices range from £30 to £200, and for earlier silver lustre or canary-yellow pieces, they can be as high as £800.

Wedgwood's famous blue and white jasper ware continued in popularity throughout the 19th century and into the 20th, and his great rival Adams produced similar pieces. Poorer families could only afford earthenwares with underglaze-blue transfer prints of flowers, or the ever-popular 'Willow Pattern'. Majolica ewers and jugs were made, complementing the teapot designs. Some of the best are the simplest, and these tend to cost over £150, although jugs from factories such as Holdcroft are about £40 upward.

▽ *STAFFORDSHIRE EARTHENWARE JUG This is a poor example of its type – it is badly moulded, muddy-coloured and thick glazed. It was probably made by Holdcroft. 1870 – 80; 5in tall.* **£30 – £40**

△ *STAFFORDSHIRE OR WELSH EARTHENWARE LUSTRE JUG; often seen in labourers' cottages, particularly in Wales. 1850; 7in high.* **£60 – £80**

▷ *MOCHAWARE JUG, used by the owner's mother to carry beer from the cellar to the bar in which she worked. The wording reads 'The Population of Kent in the year 1841 was 54861'. It would fetch more if it were sold in Kent. 9½ in high.* **£200 – £500**

STAFFORDSHIRE FIGURES

In the 18th century Staffordshire became the centre of the ceramics industry in Britain and produced pottery figures by the thousand. Horses, deer and sheep were cast, as well as shepherds and shepherdesses – echoing their more expensive porcelain cousins – soldiers, sportsmen, the seasons and literary or classical figures.

In the 19th century, mass production gave a huge boost to the industry and the Stoke-on-Trent potters turned out a vast number of figures, often reflecting contemporary events. Coronations and royalty, politicians, entertainers, battle scenes and even murderers were depicted. The early figures were modelled in the round, with almost as much detail at the back as on the front. Later, the figures evolved into 'flatbacks' which, since they were for mantlepieces, were flat and plain at the back. The best known of these are the Staffordshire spaniels.

▷ SIR ROBERT PEEL A rare figure commemorating the death of Sir Robert Peel, founder of the police force, in a riding accident. There are two versions of this figure; one with a cloak over the right arm, and the other without. 1850; 6in high. **£1,000 – £1,500**

△ FIGURE OF ANDROMACHE, probably by Ralph or Enoch Wood. Classical subjects were fashionable at the end of the 18th century. Andromache, the wife of Hector, was captured by the Greeks at the fall of Troy. 1790; 9in high. **£180**

△ OZZY THE OWL This simple pottery owl – now a celebrity – was used as a flower pot by the owners for many years. When their daughter took Ozzy along to the Roadshow, however, he was identified as a rare Staffordshire slipware jug with a detachable head that forms a cup. Ozzy would probably have been used in a 17th century inn. 7½ in high. **£20,000**

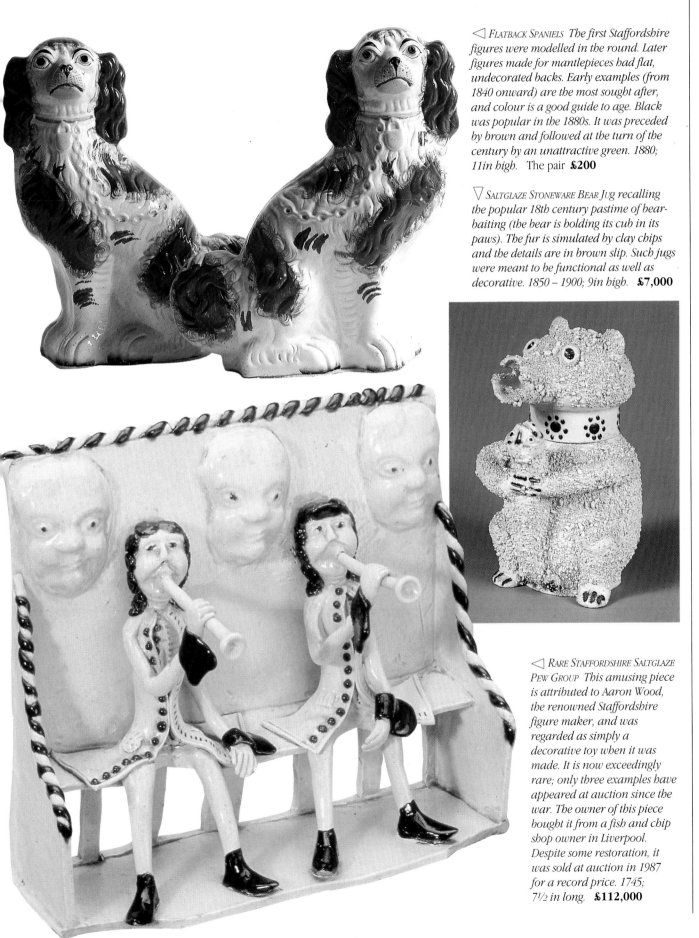

◁ *FLATBACK SPANIELS The first Staffordshire figures were modelled in the round. Later figures made for mantlepieces had flat, undecorated backs. Early examples (from 1840 onward) are the most sought after, and colour is a good guide to age. Black was popular in the 1880s. It was preceded by brown and followed at the turn of the century by an unattractive green. 1880; 11in high.* The pair **£200**

▽ *SALTGLAZE STONEWARE BEAR JUG recalling the popular 18th century pastime of bear-baiting (the bear is holding its cub in its paws). The fur is simulated by clay chips and the details are in brown slip. Such jugs were meant to be functional as well as decorative. 1850 – 1900; 9in high.* **£7,000**

◁ *RARE STAFFORDSHIRE SALTGLAZE PEW GROUP This amusing piece is attributed to Aaron Wood, the renowned Staffordshire figure maker, and was regarded as simply a decorative toy when it was made. It is now exceedingly rare; only three examples have appeared at auction since the war. The owner of this piece bought it from a fish and chip shop owner in Liverpool. Despite some restoration, it was sold at auction in 1987 for a record price. 1745; 7½ in long.* **£112,000**

DOULTON

Henry Doulton, whose surname is inscribed on much of the nation's sanitary ware, expanded the family business to coincide with the installation of London's new drainage system in the 1860s. Having made his fortune, Doulton started a factory at Lambeth making art-pottery from stoneware. Here, he employed young artists, many of them women, from the local art school. For the first time in the pottery industry, artists at Doulton's Lambeth factory were treated as such and were even permitted to sign their work. Pieces made by artists such as sisters Hannah and Florence Barlow now sell for between £300 and £2,000. The best-known male artist is George Tinworth, who often decorated pots with scrolling gothic foliage and modelled reliefs, frequently in terracotta and usually of a religious nature.

Doulton also started a factory in Stoke-on-Trent for the production of bone china and earthenware.

△ *EARTHENWARE PLATE, printed by lithographic transfer in stylized designs. Many plates were issued in this series, dating from after World War I. At this time, Doulton used an impressed date code giving the last two numbers of the year; for example, code 29 = 1929. 10in.* **£20 – £40**

▽ *ROYAL DOULTON STONEWARE JARDINIERE This colourful piece by an un-named Doulton artist is made from ordinary drain-pipe clay. Doulton ware did not become 'Royal' until 1902. 1910; 10in high.* **£250**

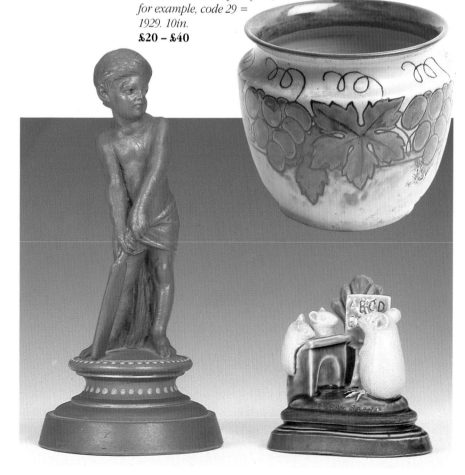

△ *PANTELLETTES, designed by Leslie Harradine. This Royal Doulton figure was in production between 1929 and 1938. Three miniature versions were introduced in 1932 and withdrawn in 1945. Three other versions, all in the same size, were withdrawn in 1949. 4½ in high; HN No. 1362.* **£150 – £200**

▷ *STONEWARE by George Tinworth, dating from around 1885. The trio of mice, called 'School Board', is a menu-holder. Cricketer, 8½ in high.* **£1,950** *Mice, 4in high.* **£700**

MAJOLICA

Brightly coloured majolica is generally regarded as the 'jewel in the crown' of 19th century British pottery. The first Victorian art books printed in colour made the arts and crafts of different cultures widely accessible. Inspired by the colourful ceramic dishes and vases of the Italian Renaissance, Staffordshire potters and designers attempted imitations, which they called 'majolica' (taken from the name Majorca). The first pieces were fairly straightforward copies, but once potters realized the true potential of the earthenware and brilliant glazes, they began working on a series of wildly inventive ceramic masterpieces. The three principal makers of majolica were Minton, George Jones and Wedgwood. Although Minton (later Mintons) was perhaps the best quality maker, Jones was more inventive. Design influences came from as far afield as Persia, France and the Orient, and even included the Gothic revival. Majolica has never been cheap, and prices have recently increased, but collectors will often find pieces with a few chips or cracks greatly discounted.

△ MAJOLICA SARDINE DISH, COVER AND STAND by George Jones and Sons. The base displays the typical mottled green-yellow-brown colouring of the factory. 1874; stand 9in across. £400 – £500

▽ GEORGE JONES MAJOLICA CAMEL This wonderfully exotic piece is possibly a sweetmeat or flower holder. 1870s; 9in high. £2,000 – £3,000

△ MINTONS MAJOLICA TEASET
Each piece is marked with the maker's name (an 's' was added to Minton in 1872), the pattern and mould number, the potter's mark and the date code. A set may have pieces with date codes that vary by a few years; this does not indicate that it has been made up of pieces from several sets. 1872 – 74; tray 12in wide. £3,000

◁ MINTONS MAJOLICA TEAPOT in the shape of a monkey clutching a coconut. The handle is broken and the rim chipped, but this amusing piece is a splendid example of the japonaiserie manufactured following the London Exhibition of 1867. If it were in perfect condition it would be worth at least twice as much. 1890; 5in high x 8in wide. £350

COMMEMORATIVE WARE

Since the 17th century, England has produced pottery which provides a clear picture of the loyalty and affection felt by the nation for its monarchs. Even disliked figures such as George IV were deemed worthy of a dignified ceramic memorial. The popularity of Queen Victoria was unparalleled. Millions of plates and jugs commemorating both her Golden and Diamond Jubilees were given out, often at parties held for children of the poor. These pieces were regarded as family heirlooms and handed down generation after generation.

As well as royal celebrations, other events were recorded on pottery and porcelain. Some were of local, or even family interest; others were more general, such as those celebrating a wartime victory. The earliest pieces, from the 17th century, were made of tin-glazed earthenware, or delft, and most frequently commemorated a marriage.

In the late 18th century, the enormous interest in hot-air and gas ballooning was reflected on a number of delft plates. In the early 19th century, Staffordshire potters produced slip-cast jugs, often with coloured designs, relating to the Napoleonic wars. The Duke of Wellington and General Hill, famous in the Peninsular War of 1808, were both depicted on a Prattware jug of about 1810, as was Nelson. Politics was as exciting a subject then as it is today, and Charles Fox, Burdett, Disraeli, Chamberlain and Churchill have all appeared on Staffordshire jugs.

▷ *A Paragon China Plate This design was originally made for the coronation of Edward VIII. After his abdication, the design was adapted for his brother George VI. It is one of the better designs of the period. 1931; 8in diameter.* **£150 – £200**

▽ *Staffordshire Earthenware Plate made to commemorate the coronation of George V and Queen Mary. Coloured transfers were used on much commemorative ware, but the inaccurate representation of an ox roasting was drawn for this particular plate. 1911; 9in diameter.* **£60**

▷ *Staffordshire Pottery Jug made for the Golden Jubilee of Queen Victoria, to celebrate the 50th year of her reign. The black transfer print has been coloured and gilded by hand. 1887; 9in high.* **£35 – £50**

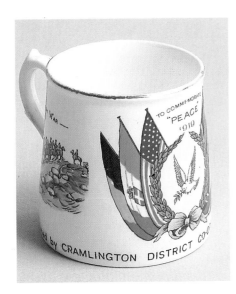

△ STAFFORDSHIRE MUG with coloured transfer, made for the Cramlington District Co-op to commemorate the signing of the Treaty of Versailles after World War I. 1919; 3½ in high. **£15 – £18**

△ ENGLISH DELFT PLATE, probably Lambeth, showing Lunardi ascending in his hot air balloon. Some devotees of ballooning material would compete with collectors of English delft for a plate such as this. 1785; 9in diameter. **£800 – £1,000**

◁ POOLE POTTERY PLATE Only four such plates are known to exist. One was given to Harry Hopkins, the American who negotiated Lease Lend for Britain during the war and who landed at Poole Harbour in a flying boat. (The inscription on the base is shown below.) 1940; 5in. **£1,000**

DRINKING GLASSES

In spite of their apparent fragility, glasses over 200 years old are not uncommon, nor are they even particularly expensive. A wine glass made in 1770 with an attractive knopped (bulged) stem can be bought for under £100, while a plain-stemmed glass costs between £50 and £60.

More ornate examples typically feature some sort of wheel engraving, usually flowers or swags, but once the decoration becomes historically significant the price rapidly rises. An engraving of a simple spray of roses, for example, may be interpreted as support for the Jacobite cause, while a rosebud stands for the Young Pretender.

Most 18th century glasses were made by a process of gathering, blowing and joining the parts together. A rough

patch in the centre of the foot of a glass, called a pontil mark, was made by the glass rod, or pontil, which was used to remove the finished vessel from the blow pipe. After the 1830s the pontil mark was usually ground smooth.

In the late 18th century, large-bowled, short-stemmed glasses known as rummers became popular. They were commonly used in taverns for ale or cider, and many good examples have survived today. Rummers can be bought for between £30 and £50, or with fluted bowls for £40 to £70. Engraving on these, as on other glasses, adds to the price. Rummers are ideal for serving water, beer or wine: Georgian custard or jelly-glasses also make unusual glasses for aperitifs, and cost beween £5 and £10 each at antique shops.

▷ *'JAGDHUMPEN' These large glasses were very popular in Germany and Bohemia (now Czechoslovakia) in the 16th and 17th centuries. They were passed around the company after the hunt. Late 16th century; 11½ in tall.* **£10,000**

▽ *ENAMELLED BEAKER German spa towns were developed at the turn of the 19th century and, as in England, it became fashionable to 'take the waters'. To commemorate a visit, a sufferer could buy a glass which was enamelled or engraved with a local view. The best artists signed and dated their work. This beaker, showing a Dresden or Leipzig scene, is dated and signed 'S. Mohn'. Such glasses are now much sought after, especially in Germany. 1812; 4in tall.* **£10,000**

△ *RUMMER with a lemon-squeezer base. It is well engraved with a sailing ship and a message of friendship. An example without engraving would be worth only £70 to £100. Late 18th century; 5in high.* **£350 – £500**

TYPES OF DRINKING GLASS

Dram glass | Rummer | Beaker | Stemmed glass | Ale glass | Goblet

126

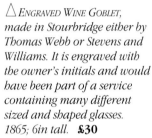

△ ENGRAVED WINE GOBLET, made in Stourbridge either by Thomas Webb or Stevens and Williams. It is engraved with the owner's initials and would have been part of a service containing many different sized and shaped glasses. 1865; 6in tall. **£30**

▽ JACOBITE GLASS with air-twist stem, of the type used by supporters of the descendants of King James II. The symbols of the Jacobite cause are engraved on the bowl: a rose represents James II of England, and the two buds stand for the Old and Young Pretenders. Late 18th century; 7½ in tall. **£150 – £200**

▽ 'FACON DE VENISE' GLASSES Glasses with serpent stems in plain or coloured glass were made of soda-glass which lends itself well to complex forms. Made in Italy, and elsewhere in Europe, such glasses are evidence of the glass-blower's artistry. Despite their fragility, they have survived in fair numbers, probably because they were intended more for display than for use. Mid 17th century; 9½ – 12in tall. Each **£2,000 – £3,000**

▷ CORDIAL GLASS with colour-twist stem and enamel decoration, probably made by William Beilby of Newcastle. Colour-twist stems are rare, and even without enamel decoration similar glasses are worth around £1,000. 1760 – 70; 6in tall. **£2,000**

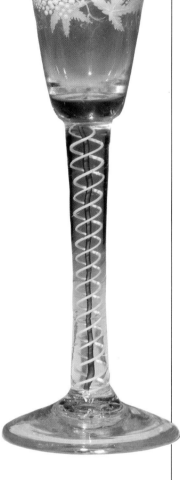

▽ AIR-TWIST STEMMED WINE GLASSES engraved with swags and tassles. The price of glasses that are part of a set of 6, 8 or 12, increases to £100 – £200 each. Late 18th century; 7in tall. Each **£70 – £100**

▽ ENGLISH GOBLET with a Silesian stem and a domed and folded foot. Big, solid English goblets in such good condition are rare. 1730; 8in tall. **£600 – £800**

DECANTERS

The English have always been highly appreciative of fine French wines, and this is borne out by the huge number of antique wine decanters available today. Modern methods of wine-making have all but cured the problem of wine throwing a sediment, but until recently it was necessary to decant all wine before it was served. Once this need was eliminated, it became fashionable to serve wine in the bottle, so that the importance of the label could impress guests. Now, however, the trend is changing, and decanters are back in vogue.

In the past, large country houses kept enormous stocks of decanters. At a Georgian dinner party, a dozen or more decanters were needed for the wine, and that is apart from those needed for sherry, port, spirits and liqueurs. Most of these sets have now been split up, and individual decanters can be found in many antique shops. They range from thin-walled mallet-form examples dating from the late 18th century, through early 19th century decanters in heavily cut lead glass, to mass-produced examples from the late Victorian period. Prices, too, vary widely, ranging from £10 for a poor, moulded example with the wrong stopper, to several thousand pounds for an enamelled decanter by William Beilby of Newcastle, who produced some of the finest mid 18th century enamelled glass.

A stopper should not only be in the same style as the decanter, it should also fit tightly. Sometimes a number is engraved on the bottom of the stopper, which should match a number engraved on the neck of the decanter.

△ *ENAMELLED GLASS SPIRIT FLASKS made in Bohemia. These are typical examples of flasks used for gin and other spirits. Such pieces are frequently dated and inscribed and, as here, have male and female portraits. They were often given as marriage gifts. Mid 18th century; 9in high.*
The pair **£600 – £800**

▷ *ENGLISH LIQUEUR SET, containing four decanters and 14 glasses with acid-etched geometric patterns. The cabinet is made of burr walnut. 1880; 12in high.*
£800 – £1,200

◁ RUBY OVERLAY DECANTER
The 'onion form', clear
glass body has been over-
laid in red and cut with
windows and lozenges.
The decanter could have
been made in England or
Bohemia – it is often
impossible to distinguish
between pieces made in
these countries. It may
originally have been one
of a harlequin set of
matching decanters in
different colours. 1850;
9in high. **£160**

▷ BOHEMIAN OVERLAY
'SHIP'S DECANTER' This type
of decanter is known
traditionally as a ship's
decanter because, with
its wide, flat bottom, it
is unlikely to tip over in
a stormy sea. This is a
very late piece made for
landlubbers' use. The
cutting is somewhat
uninspired. 1920;
9in high. **£40**

▷ GILT LIQUEUR SET, probably
Bohemian, in Art Deco style.
The geometric gilt network
pattern is typical of the period.
Such sets are quite inexpensive
even if, as here, they are of
reasonable quality. 1930;
decanter 9in high. **£80**

◁ CLARET DECANTERS
These plain glass wine
decanters have attractive
rococo-style silver mounts
in the form of shells and
coral. They are marked
with the initials of the
retailer, Walter Thornhill,
and the maker, Edward
Stockwell. 1882; 10in high.
£2,000 – £3,000

△ ENGLISH DECANTERS with their
original box. These unusual
pieces have pouring lips, so
perhaps they were meant for
use whilst riding in a carriage.
The mahogany box has
an ivory keyhole. 1800;
decanters 8in high. **£400**

ART GLASS

The term 'art glass' embraces all types of decorative glass, particularly that produced at the end of the 19th and beginning of the 20th centuries. For the greater part of the 19th century the most popular type of glass was highly decorative cut glass, sometimes described as 'fussy cut' or 'brilliant cut' glass, and produced mainly by English manufacturers.

Towards the end of the century, a break with traditional styles in art and a move towards nature and natural 'organic' forms brought about a change in glass design that culminated in Art Nouveau glassware. By the 1880s Japanese influence, too, had become evident in pieces produced in Great Britain and in America.

The most famous maker of art glass in America was Louis Comfort Tiffany, whose work was at its peak between 1890 and 1920. Tiffany is best known for leaded glass lampshades and iridescent glass pieces.

Two eminent French makers, Emile Gallé and Daum Frères, had glassworks in Nancy and are best known for their cameo glass. Cameo pieces are made up of two or more layers of different coloured glass, the outer layer of which is carved to create a design in relief. Most Gallé and Daum glass was produced industrially, and their rarer, studio-crafted pieces are much sought after by collectors.

The renowned French designer René Lalique, who began as an Art Nouveau jeweller, worked in Paris at around the turn of the century. It is estimated that over eight million pieces of Lalique glass were produced in his lifetime: those signed 'R. Lalique' were made while he was alive, and those signed simply 'Lalique' were made after his death.

◁ *LALIQUE FROSTED GLASS FIGURE OF 'SUZANNE', reputedly modelled on Lalique's daughter. She stands on a bronze illuminated base, the light from which accentuates the subtle form and precision moulding. The piece is marked 'R. Lalique' in moulded relief; if it were opalescent with a little colour, it would be worth twice as much. It is in perfect condition. 1928; 9in high.* **£6,000 – £7,000**

LALIQUE SCENT BOTTLES
1 *A rare Lalique bottle, Le Jade, the colour of which is solid jade. 1930; 4½ in high.* **£3,000**
2 *A Bouchon Cassis enamelled scent bottle with vertical ribs. The 'tiara' stopper is moulded in the shape of blackcurrants. Tiara stopper bottles are the most rare and valuable. 1932; 3½ in high.* **£25,000**

▽ *IRIDESCENT ART GLASS VASE* A typical piece of handblown iridescent art glass by Loetz of Austria. The vase is unsigned: the factory never signed pieces made for the home market. 1905; 9in high. **£1,000**

△ *CAMEO GLASS VASE signed by the French glassmaker, Barg. The design theme is decidedly Arabic. Arabia became popular in the early 1920s thanks to films such as* The Sheik *starring Rudolf Valentino. 1920; 15in high.* **£600 – £900**

◁ *IRIDESCENT GLASS VASE* An elegant Art Nouveau vase with pewter mounts, probably made in Austria. It is in the style of the German metalware company, WMF, who produced many pieces combining pewter and glass. 1905; 16in high. **£80 – £120**

△ *LOETZ VASE* An Art Nouveau gooseneck vase made of cobalt papillon iridescent art glass (purely decorative, rather than utility, glass). It may have been designed by Max von Spaun. 1900; 10in high. **£3,500**

◁ *PEACOCK BLUE IRIDESCENT CANDLESTICK signed by Tiffany, who so admired the acid-worn appearance of excavated Roman glass that he invented a technique to reproduce a similar effect by chemical means. 1910; 3in high.* **£800**

CLOCKS, WATCHES & PRECISION INSTRUMENTS

SIMON BULL

For the 1991 series of the *Antiques Roadshow*, the BBC has made a long overdue change – there is a new photograph of me to be displayed in the hall during recordings. Portrait painters have always flattered their subjects, but it is said that the camera never lies, and so when a visitor to the show politely enquired: 'Excuse me, but are you the gentleman in the photograph over there?', I knew that it was time for an update. I should add that this only happened once, and also that the mendacious picture was taken after the very first 'pilot' Roadshow, recorded at Hereford in 1978.

Those who watched that first programme will recall the late and much lamented Arthur Negus – the lynchpin around which the series was initially planned and a gentleman whose totally natural manner in dealing with the public, both on and off the screen, was an impossible act to follow. Having discovered a technically interesting and reasonably valuable watch belonging to a local collector, I asked Arthur for advice on how to approach a live recording. 'No problem' was the answer. 'If you know what you're talking about, and do so enthusiastically, then it will come across to the owner and the viewers.' No problem at all! I knew exactly what I was talking about on this occasion, and even though the recording was to be made in one live take with no previous discussion with the owner (as they still are), I was ready to go.

When the cameras began to roll, I tore into the subject with gusto – first the dial, then the case, a tour around the movement and then back to the maker's marks. I made another quick comment about the insides, and lastly gave a valuation. The owner seemed happy enough; indeed, he produced a second watch from the folds of his overcoat, followed by at least another half dozen. I talked on for another five minutes, before realizing that the cameras were still filming what I thought was an informal chat!

Twelve years on, and I am trying to reflect on what I might have learnt. I think that if I could start all over again I would choose another subject – pictures, for instance, which repose calmly on an easel, or pots, perhaps, which are nice and round with no insides to worry about. One thing I did discover on that first day was the importance of doing a little sneaky homework when no-one is looking – it is often wise to make sure in advance that a watch case does not need a ten pound hammer to open it, or to check that the

18ct gold gentleman's lever watch. 1877; 1¼ in wide.   £250

extremely heavy hood door of that nine foot grandfather clock is not going to come crashing down on top of your head when it is removed.

So spare a thought for we mechanics if we sometimes appear a little distracted; it is probably just the strain of trying to demonstrate and talk about a treasured but recalcitrant timepiece that refuses to open, despite all the earlier practises, and which unaccountably stops working just five seconds after recording begins.

It is impossible to cover even the barest outline of the many areas of horology in just a few words, but there are several basic pros and cons to consider when starting to form a collection of clocks and watches. Any collection will be incomplete unless at least some of the pieces actually work. This may sound facetious, but it is meant as a serious word of warning. Regrettably, the days of the village clockmaker who could fix anything and every-thing are past, and the majority of the larger chain stores no longer find it economically viable to take on anything that is not of recent manufacture (that is, with available spares)

English lacquer dial clock, 1850. £400

or relatively straightforward. The situation is improving gradually as more young people take up the trade, but working on old clocks is time-consuming, and the final bill for repairs can easily compare with that for a major service on the car. However, much of what is readily available on the market can be over-hauled by the amateur 'mechanic', although it must be said that a plan or set of instructions is rarely included when one buys an antique watch. Fortunately, books on the subject are available, so the amateur should not be left completely without help, and basic tools are unlikely to be overly expensive. You could even turn a hobby into a part-time business.

Putting aside the truly rare and important collectors' items, which cost several hundred and even many thousands of pounds, the majority of clocks from the 19th century were mass produced in very large numbers, and are therefore of relatively little value. In this context, little value means items worth less than £100, with a potential for doubling their price over the next few years, but not for multiplying tenfold as has happened in other areas of the antiques business. Although mass-produced clocks may not increase in value particularly rapidly, one bonus is that they nevertheless compare favourably with what is available new on the market today. Another hidden benefit of mass-produced clocks is that the beginner can be reasonably free from worries about his intended purchase being a fake. Few, if any, of the clocks in the lower price range can be copied successfully.

Pocket watches are an entirely different matter. Again, the quantities made at certain times during the last hundred years sometimes ran into millions, and so many have survived as treasured family heirlooms. Such timepieces could not be recreated today for any price, and a collection of outstanding interest can be built up for little cost providing the intricate and often highly decorative details of the movements are appealing.

Wristwatches should be treated as yet another subject, quite distinct from anything that would normally be labelled 'antique'. Firstly, wristwatches in good, working order are eminently usable, and older models bear direct comparison with their modern equivalents, in terms of both price and quality. Secondly, despite the comparatively high prices that they can command, there is one advantage with wristwatches in that they can be repaired and maintained with relative ease.

If you are considering horology as the field for your collection, it may be worth bearing in mind the following points. Before buying a clock or pocket watch, try to ascertain the condition of the movement. This may prove difficult at an auction, but any dealer should give you an opinion, even if he is not a specialist. Always get a quote for repair work, preferably together with an estimation of the piece's value to help you decide whether it is indeed worth having the repair work done.

Remember that the maintenance of clocks and watches usually involves two different crafts – clockmaking and cabinet or case work. You may be able to do some of the repairs yourself, but the necessity for both skills should be considered when buying. For wristwatches, casework is difficult and potentially expensive, and the condition of the case can dramatically affect the value of the piece.

Finally, if you wish to attempt to carry out any repairs yourself, do go ahead, but be sure to make notes and drawings of how your latest acquisition comes to pieces. It will be very frustrating if you cannot remember where to replace all those nicely cleaned parts, especially if you have taken a great deal of time and trouble over them.

MY FAVOURITE ITEMS

1991 was a very good year for clocks, watches and precision instruments, but for me the highlight was the Gubelin watch from Stowmarket. When I opened the box and saw it there, the sensation was akin to being plugged into the National Grid! It was difficult to keep a suitable poker face while being filmed, but the ensuing gasp from the owner when the piece was valued made my effort well worthwhile.

△ *This is the magnificent white gold wristwatch with minute repeating, signed by Gubelin. Although in recent years classic wristwatches have risen from virtual obscurity and become a major field for collectors, very few command the sort of value placed on this example. Three different features combined were the reasons for such a high price; first, wristwatches with minute repeating (a mechanism wound by a small slide which enables the watch to repeat the time on steel gongs to the nearest minute) are extremely rare; second, the case was square and made of white gold; and third, although signed by Gubelin, the retailer, the watch was in fact made by Audemars Piguet, a leading manufacturer –this was not mentioned on the recording as it had to be confirmed by research in the company's record. The watch was subsequently sold for an astonishing £67,000.*

◁ *Carriage clocks are regular visitors to the Antiques Roadshow, but because they were produced without break from the mid 19th century onward, and indeed are still being made today, few are of significant value. When this exceptional example by Le Roy was first shown to me I had no particular reason to believe that it would be anything but run of the mill. However, the complexity of the movement which enabled the clock to strike both the hours and quarters at every quarter hour (known as 'grand sonnerie'), and a very high quality escapement, meant that it was something special. Made in 1885, the clock was valued at between £4,000 and £5,000, proving just how wrong first impressions can be.*

ALL ABOUT CLOCKS

The history of the mechanical clock goes back some 700 years, but it is only in the last 150 years that clocks have become an intrinsic feature in most households.

The oldest working clock in Britain belongs to Salisbury Cathedral. A huge contraption with wheels and ropes, it was made in around 1386. Over the following centuries there developed a multiplicity of clock designs whose sizes, shapes and colours were influenced by changing room sizes, prevailing fashions, technical innovations and the availability of decorative materials.

The trade of the clockmaker was originally allied to that of the blacksmith, but from the 17th century it developed into a powerful guild. The celebrated clockmakers Thomas Tompion and George Graham achieved such great fame in their lifetime that they were honoured with burial in Westminster Abbey.

Mass production dispelled much of the mystery surrounding the clockmaker's art, and today many people own clocks from the Victorian age, when production techniques enabled the industry to produce accurate, attractive and affordable timepieces.

THE FACE

Many of the elements common to all clock faces can be seen in this classic 18th century longcase clock face.

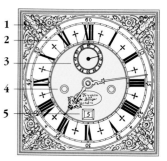

1 Cast and chased brass spandrels.
2 Chapter ring with numerals.
3 Seconds ring.
4 Key aperture.
5 Date aperture.

CLOCK SHAPES

Clocks come in a wide variety of shapes, depending on their intended location and function.
1 A dial clock of the type that could be seen in every 'age of steam' railway station from the mid 19th century onward.
2 A bronze wall clock. This grand 18th century French style remained popular throughout the 19th century.

3 An 18th century tavern, or 'Act of Parliament', clock, so named because of a tax imposed on privately owned clocks in 1780.
4 A classic English longcase or 'grandfather' clock of imposing 18th century design.
5 An elegant 19th century French skeleton clock.
6 A lantern clock – the earliest English household clock; first made in around 1600.

7 A classic French carriage clock.

1   2   3   4   5   6   7

HOW CLOCKS ARE DRIVEN

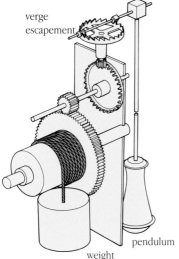

verge escapement

From the 16th century until the late 18th century, clocks were driven by weights and regulated by a verge escapement (left). An escapement in a clock or watch is the part of the mechanism that allows the power stored (either by a weight or a spring) to literally 'escape' at regular intervals. The anchor escapement (right) was used in longcase clocks from about 1670. Later, the spring provided an alternative motive force for clock movement. Spring-driven bracket clocks of good quality were usually fitted with a fusee (a cone-shaped device) attached by a cord or fine chain to the spring barrel, which equalized the tension of the spring as the clock ran down (right). When combined with the anchor escapement it was capable of exceptional accuracy.

pendulum
weight

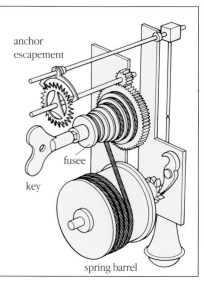

anchor escapement

fusee

key

spring barrel

LONGCASE CLOCKS

The development of the longcase or 'grandfather' clock is directly linked to the invention of the long pendulum in around 1672. The long pendulum, together with the anchor escapement, enabled domestic clocks to keep accurate time. Since pendulums measuring almost three feet long were vulnerable to being knocked or even stopped, long protective cases were introduced. Initially, longcase clocks were owned solely by the wealthy, and cases were made of an expensive wood like ebony and finished with ornate decoration such as walnut marquetry.

The period from 1670 to 1720 was the heyday of the English longcase clock, and during this time some of the greatest clockmakers practised their craft. The 18th century saw the manufacture of longcase clocks spread to the provinces. Cases were simple, and often painted or stained to simulate valuable and exotic timbers. Towards the end of the century such clocks were usually built to order, and their manufacture became essentially a cottage industry. The movements were made in industrial centres such as Birmingham, while the cases were made by local cabinet-makers.

◁ *WALNUT LONGCASE CLOCK signed by Daniel Smith; probably made for a wealthy country family. The case, decorated with floral marquetry, has been rebuilt. 1720; 8ft 2in high.* **£3,000**

▷ *VICTORIAN GOTHIC LONGCASE CLOCK The signature on the circular silvered regulator dial of this light oak clock reads 'Gaze Ebrors, London'. Decorative features include 'Father Time' depicted on a partly gold ground, and roundels flanked by cluster columns. The trunk door is glazed, revealing the pendulum. Victorian; 8ft 2in high.* **£1,000**

△ *CARVED OAK CLOCK A late 18th century oak longcase clock 'improved' by Victorian carving. The Victorians were very keen on adding decoration to earlier pieces of furniture. The crudeness of the carving was an attempt to age the piece, but in reality 17th and 18th century carving was always of a high standard. 1780s; 8ft 2in high.* **£650**

MANTEL & BRACKET CLOCKS

The invention of the spring balance and pendulum in the 17th century, and the subsequent appearance of the longcase clock, set the scene for the development of the clock-making industry. Clocks became smaller and more accurate over the centuries, but no further technical advances were made.

The Industrial Revolution led to a great increase in the production of clocks. Large longcase clocks went out of fashion in the 19th century and were replaced in popularity by mantel and bracket clocks ('bracket' is the name given to spring-driven clocks made to stand on a table or bracket).

The Victorian imagination knew no bounds, and this is demonstrated in the wide variety of shapes and decorative elements in clocks from this period. Yet despite great differences in design, virtually all clocks share the same technology, with movements differing only in small details.

◁ *ORMULU AND MARBLE STRIKING MANTEL CLOCK in Louis XVI style. This clock is of unusually high quality – the mountings are almost as well finished as those on the original clocks. The dial is white enamel with blue numerals. Mid 19th century; 12in high.* **£1,000**

▽ *FRENCH MYSTERY CLOCK made of bronzed soft metal. Mystery clocks (so named because the power source is often barely discernible) were made in several different designs. The clock section swings to and fro and is worked by a tiny pendulum at the top. 1900 – 10; 12in high.* **£150**

▽ *PORCELAIN MANTEL CLOCK Although hand-made in Dresden, it bears a fake late 18th century Meissen mark. The two Grecian figures represent 'Music' and 'Painting'. Late 19th century; 15in high.* **£1,500**

△ *MAHOGANY BRACKET CLOCK with gilt metal mounts and a sophisticated chiming mechanism of bells and gongs. This clock is an example of the Victorian revival of interest in 18th century styles. Although it was made in Germany, similar clocks were also made in Birmingham. Late 19th century; 20in high.* **£2,500**

CARRIAGE CLOCKS

The carriage clock made its debut in the late 18th century. Its heyday was from 1850 to1925, and during this period hundreds of thousands of clocks were made, mostly in France. The popularity of this type of clock was due to the fact that most families could not afford to buy more than one clock for the home, and therefore required a clock that could be carried from room to room. The carriage clock, being small and light, proved ideal for such a purpose. Although carriage clocks were not made primarily for use in carriages, people generally took one along on their travels. Initially all such clocks were sold with a travelling case, but over the years most of these have been lost. The variety of carriage clocks is enormous. Values vary, depending on size, the decoration of the case, the complication of the striking mechanism, and whether or not the clock has additional calendar dials.

△ MINIATURE FRENCH CARRIAGE CLOCK, *made of ivory. The dial and hands are in good condition, but the case is cracked and the handle is a poor replacement. Late 19th century; 2½ in high.* **£300 – £400**

◁ OVAL CARRIAGE CLOCK *A rare early clock, complete with fitted case, by the French clockmaker A. Dumas. 'Half size' clocks such as this are very desirable and are generally more valuable than standard sized clocks of the same quality. 1870; 4in high.* **£400**

▷ FRENCH FULL-CALENDAR CLOCK *This very elaborate clock is signed 'Dent à Paris'. Dent was an English retailer, many of whose clocks were made in Paris. It has three calendar dials and an early original lever platform. The cast case, with masks, fruit and scrollwork, is ornate for the period. 1860; 6in high.* **£1,200 – £1,500**

◁ ROSEWOOD CARRIAGE CLOCK *This English clock has the double fusee movement typical of such clocks. Because the case has been repolished and the dial repainted, a little of the clock's charm has been lost . 1850; 9in high.* **£800 – £1,000**

POCKET WATCHES

I n the 16th and early 17th centuries, pockets in clothes were not universal and 'pocket' watches were often worn around the neck on a leather or velvet thong. Late 17th century watches were fairly large in size – French examples were nicknamed 'oignons' – but they became smaller and more elaborately decorated over the next century. No major technological advances were made, however, until the development of the lever escapement at the end of the 18th century. Watches gradually became more affordable, and after the Industrial Revolution, which transformed production methods, ordinary people were able to buy pocket watches for the first time. From the 1860s Swiss makers dominated the industry, and by 1900 the production of pocket watches had reached its peak. They declined in popularity after World War II, and the few examples made today are virtually hand-crafted.

▷ *18CT GOLD FULL PLATE ENGLISH LEVER WATCH in immaculate condition. It is presented in a red tooled-leather box bearing the Royal Warrant and the name of the watchmaker, George Edward & Sons, Buchanan Street, Glasgow. 1870; 1½ in.* **£350**

▽ *AMERICAN GOLD WATCH with chain, fob and protective 'hunter' case. Although it is of no great interest as a collector's item because of the numbers made for the English market, the weight of the gold makes it valuable. 1890; 2¼ in.* **£600**

△ *CYLINDER WATCH in a silver open face case. It is signed James Scrymgeour, Glasgow, and hallmarked London. 1889; 2¼ in.* **£550**

◁ *EARLY ENGLISH WATCH with verge escapement. The protective silver case is covered in leather and decorated with silver pinwork. The stylized tulips and other flower engravings on the case are in excellent condition, as are the dial and the engraved silver centre. A calendar ring with a tiny blued-steel hand, rotating anti-clockwise, can be seen around the outside of the chapter ring. The movement is signed by Richard Riccard, who worked in London in 1675. 1660; 2in.* **£10,000**

WRISTWATCHES

The earliest wristwatches, many of which were converted pocket watches, were made in the last quarter of the 19th century. Custom-made wristwatches first appeared in the early 20th century, but they did not really capture the public's imagination until World War I. Between the wars both pocket watches and wristwatches were popular, but by World War II pocket watches had almost disappeared.

In the 1940s and '50s wristwatches were fairly costly to buy, and it was not until the development of the quartz movement that they became universal and cheaply available. Ten years ago the collecting of old wristwatches was confined to a few enthusiasts, but in the last five years the market has expanded enormously, due in part to a revival of interest in the watch mechanisms themselves.

▷ *18CT GOLD WRIST CHRONOGRAPH by Patek Philippe & Co., combining a watch and stopwatch. It has a tacheometer scale and a perpetual calendar with apertures for the day, month and phases of the moon. The bracelet is 14ct gold. 1945.*
£60,000 – £75,000

▽ *GOLD WRISTWATCH with partly enamelled case. It would have been worn as a piece of jewellery. The case and dial are similar to late 19th century fob watches. 1920.* **£250 – £300**

▽ *PLATINUM AND DIAMOND LADIES' WRISTWATCH by Léon Hatot, with the designer's sketch. It has a silvered dial and nickel-finished lever movement by Lecoultre. 1930.*
£3,500 – £5,000

▷ *PATEK PHILIPPE WRISTWATCHES*
1 *Rare 18ct gold universal time zone watch. At the press of a button the time in a different zone is displayed. This function has to be preset. 1960.* **£20,000 – £25,000**
2 *Fine curved watch with 18ct gold case. 1911.* **£4,000 – £5,000**

1   2

MICROSCOPES

The effectiveness of the earliest microscopes in the 17th century was limited, but over the centuries the quality of lenses improved greatly, leading to the discovery of all sorts of startling phenomena in the fields of both pure and natural science.

Early microscopes were made from lignum vitae – a South American hardwood – and covered with embossed vellum (fine parchment) or fish skin. From the early 18th century brass was used in the construction of microscopes and, with the exception of a very few silver instruments, continued to be used well into the 20th century.

There are two basic types of microscope – simple and compound. Simple microscopes have only one lens and provide limited magnification of the object under scrutiny, while compound microscopes have two or more lenses held apart from each other in a tube, and provide far more powerful magnification. Microscope accessories are also of value, and it is advisable to buy instruments that are as complete as possible, preferably in their original wooden case.

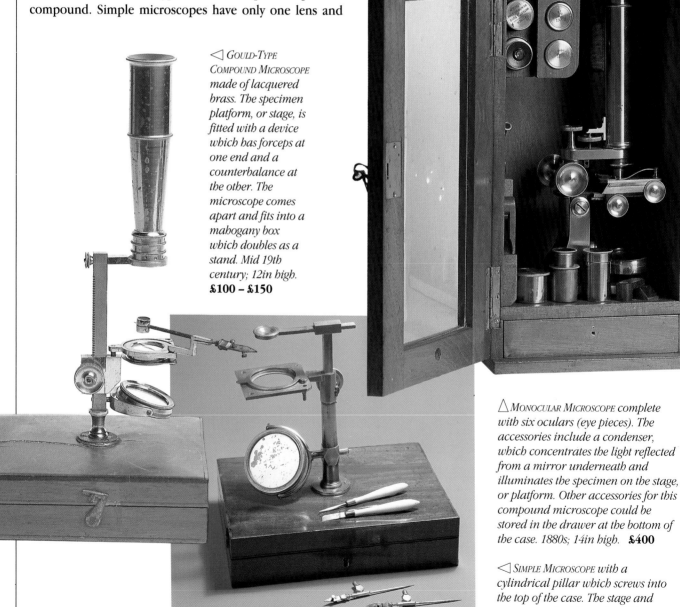

◁ *GOULD-TYPE COMPOUND MICROSCOPE made of lacquered brass. The specimen platform, or stage, is fitted with a device which has forceps at one end and a counterbalance at the other. The microscope comes apart and fits into a mahogany box which doubles as a stand. Mid 19th century; 12in high.* **£100 – £150**

△ *MONOCULAR MICROSCOPE complete with six oculars (eye pieces). The accessories include a condenser, which concentrates the light reflected from a mirror underneath and illuminates the specimen on the stage, or platform. Other accessories for this compound microscope could be stored in the drawer at the bottom of the case. 1880s; 14in high.* **£400**

◁ *SIMPLE MICROSCOPE with a cylindrical pillar which screws into the top of the case. The stage and mirror can be taken apart for packing. 1830s; 6½ in high.* **£400**

BAROMETERS

The earliest barometers, from the 17th century, used mercury, and their 'stick' design was necessitated by the fact that a height of at least 30 inches of mercury was required to measure a change in atmospheric pressure. Initially their use was purely scientific, but gradually they found their way into the homes of the wealthy.

Simple barometers have a silvered ivory or paper scale, usually showing inches on one side and expected weather conditions on the other. With the invention of the aneroid barometer in the 19th century, a wide range of barometers, from pocket-sized to elaborate wall instruments, became generally affordable. Early 18th century barometers are usually valuable, but they should be of good quality and ideally have an elaborately decorated case.

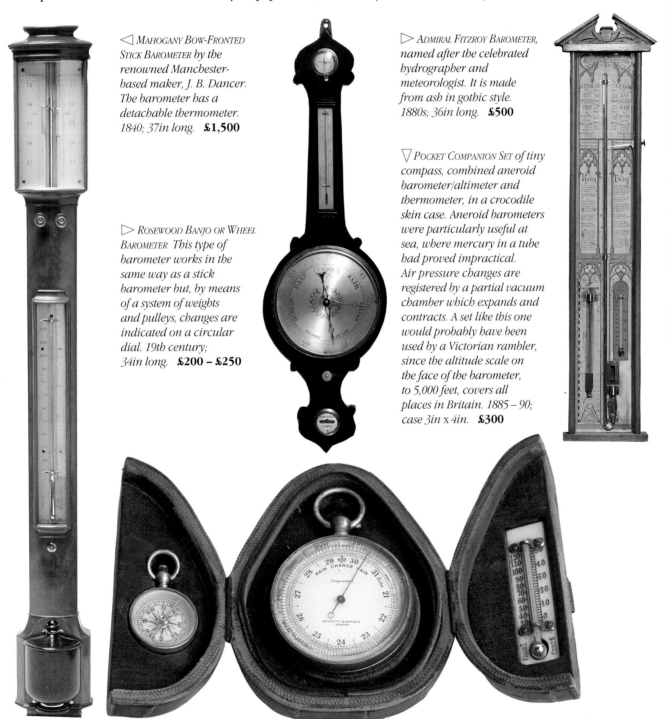

◁ *MAHOGANY BOW-FRONTED STICK BAROMETER by the renowned Manchester-based maker, J. B. Dancer. The barometer has a detachable thermometer. 1840; 37in long.* **£1,500**

▷ *ROSEWOOD BANJO OR WHEEL BAROMETER This type of barometer works in the same way as a stick barometer but, by means of a system of weights and pulleys, changes are indicated on a circular dial. 19th century; 34in long.* **£200 – £250**

▷ *ADMIRAL FITZROY BAROMETER, named after the celebrated hydrographer and meteorologist. It is made from ash in gothic style. 1880s; 36in long.* **£500**

▽ *POCKET COMPANION SET of tiny compass, combined aneroid barometer/altimeter and thermometer, in a crocodile skin case. Aneroid barometers were particularly useful at sea, where mercury in a tube had proved impractical. Air pressure changes are registered by a partial vacuum chamber which expands and contracts. A set like this one would probably have been used by a Victorian rambler, since the altitude scale on the face of the barometer, to 5,000 feet, covers all places in Britain. 1885 – 90; case 3in x 4in.* **£300**

Silver, Gold & Jewellery

Ian Pickford

I will always remember my first *Antique's Roadshow*, at Worthing, recorded back in 1986. 'Will anything turn up?', I wondered. The odd piece of pre-17th century silver would certainly be welcome. I spent the morning discussing many a set of coffee spoons and Britannia Metal teapots, until the lady in the green hat arrived, that is. She produced from her pocket a small bundle, inside which was concealed a box. It was not pre-17th century – in fact, it was not even made of silver, but of Old Sheffield Plate and tortoiseshell. That did not matter, however – it became my first recorded item of silver on the

Antiques Roadshow, and as such was sheer joy.

Although I have worked on many of the programmes, that wonderful feeling of anticipation which I experienced at my first recording has never diminished, and to date has always been rewarded at each new location. I was lucky enough to be part of the team that went on the Roadshow's first excursion abroad to Denmark and Sweden. In Elsinor, Denmark, we were inundated with silver, and in Malmo, Sweden, I found a marvellous 16th century spoon. Back in Britain I have also made many memorable discoveries. In Harrow, for example, I came upon a superb pair of Russian candlesticks, and in Bournemouth a delightful, though tiny, silver pig.

My most exciting and unusual find was undoubtedly the boxing belt that was brought to the Birmingham Roadshow. The owner set an old leather case down on my table with the declaration: 'There is over a hundred ounces of silver in there'. I have heard such statements many times before, and the item in question frequently turns out to be rather disappointing and not very old. But in this instance, it was a very important mid 19th century world championship boxing belt which I valued at between £15,000 and £20,000, and for which the owner had already been offered (and had fortunately turned down) £1,000.

The most extraordinary things can happen at Roadshows. While recording the Islington show, for example, I had to discuss a Russian beaker with the owner while she was lying flat out on a stretcher. She had collapsed while waiting in the queue, and refused to be taken to hospital until her beaker had been seen by me. On another amusing occasion a lady with a bent spoon simply refused to believe that it had been damaged. It was a typical Scandinavian spoon of about 1900 with a twisted stem and ball finial. At some stage in its

Silver sugar bowl and tongs.

life someone had obviously sat on it and bent the stem in the middle to a right angle. All this I explained, and suggested that it would be a good idea for her to have it restored. 'Oh no!' she replied, 'that is how it should be and that is why I have brought it in. It must be for a special purpose', and she demanded to know what this special purpose was. Despite independent confirmation from my colleagues of what I had already told her, off she went declaring that we really did not know what we were talking about.

Most of the items we see at the Roadshows are individual pieces, but when collections are brought in, they can be of great interest. It is always intriguing to know how they were started and how long they have taken to build up. More fascinating, however, are the stories that are so often attached to each piece, and which the owners love to tell with relish – stories of how they 'found that one in a junk shop' or 'paid too much at the time but I fell in love with it and just had to have it'.

How then should you go about collecting silver? Most importantly, you should collect pieces you enjoy, then go for pieces of the finest quality and in the best possible condition. If you follow these three basic rules you should end up with a really fine collection. People do sometimes start off with the intention of 'investing', which some purists find abhorrent. My experience of this over the years is that, almost without fail, those who start in this way end up as true collectors with a great love of the subject.

Maltese gold bangle, 1870. £1,000

Most new collectors tend to suffer from a 'magpie complex'. Lacking knowledge and experience, they acquire a number of second-rate examples 'because they were very cheap'. When asked to examine a collection, I often recommend that early acquisitions be weeded out. Patience is a virtue, and never more so than when you are searching out new items. The best collections I have seen have always taken years to put together. The total number of objects is often not great, but each has been carefully selected as the finest that could be acquired of its type. In most cases the owner will have been paying over the marked price for the standard items in order to get the best, and, in my experience, never regrets having done so.

'Doing your homework' is required before embarking on a collection. Having thought of a theme, can you afford the very best examples? If the answer is no, then perhaps you should think again, because you may only be frustrated by never being able to form a truly fine collection.

Availability is a most important consideration. You may have a passion for medieval standing cups, but even with the finest bank balance there will be no possibility of forming a collection of these.

The most popular collecting areas for silver must be boxes, spoons, jewellery and cameos. One advantage to the collector of these items is that information about them is readily available. A disadvantage, however, is that competition can be fierce, particularly for the best pieces, so forming a good collection can be quite difficult.

If you can find a theme you enjoy where few others are collecting, and where good pieces are available in your price range, you should do well.

At the moment, for example, it is possible to find very cheap cigarette cases. This is because they are no longer fashionable and, on a practical note, the older ones will not hold modern-sized cigarettes. The exceptions, as far as prices go, are the enamelled cases, particularly if the enamels are of women. The general rule here is that the fewer clothes they have on, the more expensive they will be. If something particularly naughty is going on then they will be very expensive indeed!

Collecting themes can vary widely from type of object to maker or period. One approach to collecting silver is to acquire pieces of tableware which can be both used and enjoyed – this can be fun and rewarding. Choose a pattern, period and maker, and then build up a table service. It is probably best to start with the dessert forks, as they are hardest to find, and then match the other pieces to them.

What better way to finish a meal than with coffee served from a fine silver vessel? However, do you really need a coffee pot? Why not a coffee jug? They are usually significantly less expensive than pots, and at the same time they are really far more practical. Jugs may be used for other drinks too, whereas pouring anything other than coffee from a coffee pot looks rather odd.

One of the bonuses of precious metals is that they can usually be dated precisely by the hallmarks. Hallmarking in itself can be an area of great interest for the collector. Not only are there the different official assay offices with their many cycles of marks, but also various minor provincial centres, each with their, often rather quirky, labels.

Enamel and gold pendant watch, 1875. £500 – £750

MY FAVOURITE ITEMS

What a marvellous year we had in 1991! The series produced some of the most important silver ever seen at the Roadshow, and an extremely wide range of pieces, both in date and type of object. The items shown here are my favourites from all the shows – we can only hope for a comparable hoard next year!

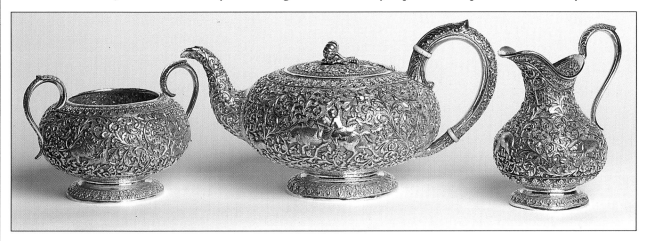

△ *Before our visit to Stowmarket, had anyone suggested to me that I would ever get excited by an Indian silver teaset I would have been sceptical, to say the least. I have seen hundreds over the years – nearly all with fairly standard, and generally not very well executed, chased decoration. Here, though, was something way above the norm, a set which was superbly chased with elephants and other animals within foliage. It came as no surprise when it was revealed that it had been presented to the owner's great-grandfather by a Maharajah. The set was valued at £1,200.*

▽ *Rarely on the Roadshow do we see any silver made before the mid 18th century. However, amongst a vast array of silver and jewels, Malta produced an important late 17th century ewer and dish, very similar in form to those made in England by the great Huguenot goldsmiths. These were certainly the most important early pieces from the 1991 series, and they were valued together at £70,000.*

◁ *A wonderful set of early George III table knives and forks was brought to Hexham. The set was remarkable for three reasons: it was still in its original case, it was in superb condition, and it was complete except for one odd knife of the same date. Most cases of this type have been gutted and converted into stationery holders. The set was made in Sheffield in around 1775, and it was valued at £2,000 – £3,000.*

TEA SERVICES

Although tea was a luxury item in the 17th century, costing around £2 per pound, it was nevertheless enjoyed by a great many people. Even so, no-one really knew the proper way to make it, and at one time it was promoted as a medicinal cure-all. This lack of general knowledge about tea led to the development of all kinds of curious teapots – the earliest looking something like modern day coffee pots.

By the early 18th century, the familiar teapot shape as we know it today had evolved. Pots were silver and fairly plain in style. Wealthy families built up complete silver services bit by bit, comprising tea, coffee and chocolate pots, milk jugs, sugar basins and caddies. A silver kettle, which was also considered an essential part of a tea service, would have been placed on a stand by the tea table, while teaspoons were placed on a silver spoon tray. By the end of the 18th century, tea had become cheaper to buy and was consumed by more people than ever before. The increasing demand for tea and tea services led to the manufacture of many more complete silver services.

The Victorians favoured highly ornate, expensive-looking sets for use on special occasions. Similar 'showy' versions were produced for the cheaper end of the market using silver plate (EPNS) and Britannia metal instead of silver.

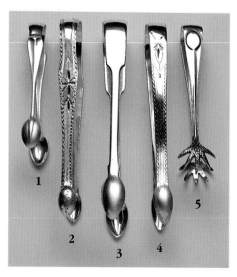

◁ *Sugar Tongs The spring-style handles indicate that they were made after 1775.*
1 *'Rat tail' design along the back of the bowl.*
2 *and* **4** *both feature a bright-cut pattern which reflects the light.*
3 *Fiddle pattern.*
5 *Art Nouveau, claw-type design, 1885 – 1914.*
Each **£25 – £60**

△ *Electroplated Teapot (left) and Milk Jug (right) This pair is part of a French tea or coffee service. Both bear the maker's mark, Frenais, and display mask faces at the top of each foot. 1880; teapot 8in high, milk jug 6in high.* The pair **£170**

▽ *PUMP-ACTION TEAPOT made of electroplated Britannia metal, by James Dickson and Sons of Sheffield. When the lid is pumped up and down the tea flows into the cup. (The lid here is in the 'up' position.) 1885; 12in high.* **£50**

△ *SILVER TEAPOT AND KETTLE with wooden handles. Although Queen Anne-style fluting is visible on the lower halves of both pieces, they were in fact made in the 20th century. The kettle is heated by means of a methylated spirit burner. Two hinges attach the kettle to its stand, and by removing the back hinge the kettle can be tipped and poured without leaving the stand. 1930s; teapot 7in high.* The set **£900 – 1,200**

▽ *SILVER TEASET This four-piece set displays typical Edwardian chasing. Both the teapot and the water jug have blackened carved wood handles. 1900 – 10; 6½ in high.* **£600**

△ *SCOTTISH BULLET TEAPOT It has a characteristic silver handle and pedestal foot, but the curved spout makes it rather unusual. Made in Glasgow, its spherical shape differs from that of an English bullet teapot. (The handle sockets and foot have been repaired.) 1730; 7in high.* **£2,000**

▷ *TEA STRAINER This flamboyant rococo style was much admired by the Victorians. 3½ in long.* **£175**

▷ *TEA STRAINER with an ebony handle, made in Sheffield by William Hutton and Sons. 1907; 4½ in long.* **£30**

TABLEWARE

Salt, that apparently humble condiment, has in fact played a substantial role throughout history. In Roman times it was one of the staple payments made to Imperial soldiers (hence the word 'salary'). In the Middle Ages it was used to preserve food, and it has also served as a valuable commodity with which to trade. It comes as no surprise, then, that special vessels to contain such an important condiment were made in both gold and silver.

From medieval times until about the last quarter of the 17th century much thought was given to the design and workmanship of the salt cellar. Although many interesting early examples can still be found, few 'Great Salts' – large standing salts – have survived (the tallest Great Salt in existence today measures 22 inches).

Other condiments needed different types of container. From the late 16th century through to the 18th, pepper and nutmeg became popular, and shakers were required to hold them. Mustard, which was used in dry powder form until the mid 18th century, required a similar sort of container.

In past centuries sugar was far coarser than it is today, and required a large shaker. In the late 17th and early 18th centuries sugar shakers, or casters, were made as part of a set of three. The sugar caster was the largest piece in the set, and there were two smaller shakers – one without piercing for dry mustard, and the other for pepper. After the mid 18th century such pieces were usually made individually to suit the requirements of the household. The Victorians continued to produce salt cellars, mustard pots and casters in a wide range of designs, often reviving or borrowing from past styles.

The earliest cruets, dating from about 1715, were simply two glass bottles in a silver frame – one for oil and the other for vinegar. The larger sets that followed were named 'Warwick' cruets, after the Earl of Warwick, and generally contained three silver casters as well as two glass bottles for oil and vinegar. The casters came in a variety of sizes and, as with earlier sets, were used for mustard, spice, pepper and sugar. Cruets with five containers were

△ SILVER SUGAR CASTER *or shaker, made in London. The style, but not the decoration, mimics the style of the 1740s. Such items were commonplace in the average middle class Victorian household. 1898; 7in high.* **£250**

△ WILLIAM AND MARY CYLINDRICAL CASTER SET, *made of silver, for sugar, mustard and a spice. Each stands on a fluted circular base and has a partly fluted pierced domed cover. 1694; sugar caster 6¾ in high; others 5½ in high.* **£12,000 – £18,000**

◁ SILVER SPICE CONTAINER *This decorative piece would have been used for storing spice. Made in Scandinavia, it has no hallmark. 19th century; 3½ in high.* **£40 – £60**

commonplace in the late 18th and early 19th centuries. They were used for spices, sauces, oil and vinegar. In the Victorian period cruets containing six or even eight pieces were not unknown – the more condiments that were required the more complicated the cruet became.

In the second half of the 18th century many cruets were made from Old Sheffield plate – the newly invented and cheaper alternative to silver. From the 1840s, the introduction of electroplating (silver plating by electrolysis) led to the mass production of cruets which were relatively inexpensive to buy. The most common cruets brought to the Roadshow are the mass-produced variety, mostly dating

from the early 1900s. Unfortunately, many of the moulded glass bottles are poorly cut.

In addition to cruets, silver baskets for bread or fruit were commonly used in Victorian dining rooms. Many have pierced decoration and, since they were probably used every day, are likely to show signs of wear and tear.

When buying an antique cruet it is important to ensure that the bottles and stand are from the same period. The same applies to silver and silver-plated cruet sets, although with these it is also important to check for worn or damaged handles and hinges, and also for soldering, which indicates that repair work has been carried out.

△ SILVER MUSTARD POT AND SALTS, set with cabochon amethysts, made by C. R. Ashbee's Guild of Handicraft. The Guild, inspired by William Morris, was set up in 1888 in an attempt to counteract the industrialization of crafts, and C. R. Ashbee put Morris's ideas into effect in his own work. Although the glass salt containers are missing, the value of the set has not been affected significantly. 1902; mustard pot 3in high. The set £1,000

◁ SILVER MUSTARD POTS made in London. Handles on pots were introduced in around 1760 when the tradition of serving dry mustard, to be made up on a diner's plate, had died out and been replaced with a fashion for serving made-up mustard.
1 1798; 2¼ in high. £650
2 1798; 2¼ in high. £600
3 1843; 2in high. £350
4 1783; 2¼ in high. £650
5 1794; 2in high. £750

▽ SILVER CONDIMENT SET A complete silver salt, pepper and mustard set of typical form. It was made in Birmingham and retailed by Mappin & Webb. Sets in this style are still made today. 1919; pepper pot 2½ in. **£140 – £150**

◁ ELECTROPLATED CRUET A mass-produced example, typical of those brought to Roadshows around the country. It has been very cheaply stamped out and has a crimped base. 1920s; 10in high. **£80 – £120**

▽ CRUET by Charles Thomas and George Fox, comprising three bottles and two casters in a silver frame with silver mounts. The cruet would originally have been one of a pair or one of a set of four. 1855; 10in high. **£1,500**

▷ ELECTROPLATED CRUET by James Dixon & Son, one of the top 19th century makers. Such a piece would have graced the dining table of every middle class home in the country. They are now much harder to find because many have been exported to the United States. This example has a guilloche handle with a lotus motif at the bottom, and a pierced gallery. The cut glass bottles are original, and in good condition. 1880; 11in high. **£120 – £160**

◁ SILVER-PLATED CRUET BY CHRISTOPHER DRESSER, *a designer born in the 1830s who achieved renown for work that was far ahead of its time. The angular lines of this cruet, for example, would not look dated even in this century. Dresser visited Japan in 1876 and was greatly influenced by the simplicity of Japanese design. He was most prolific in the 1870s and '80s, and designed for major manufacturers such as James Dixon, Hukin & Heath, and Elkington. 1880s; 10in high.* **£4,000 – £6,000**

▷ ELECTROPLATED CRUET *This pierced design was commonplace about 100 years before the cruet was made. Early 20th century; 11in high.* **£100 – £120**

△ WILLIAM IV SILVER BASKET *embossed with fruit and pheasants. 1830 – 36; 10in long.* **£900 – £1,000**

◁ PIERCED SILVER SWING-HANDLED BASKET *The design is based on mid 18th century Rococo style. Victorian; 9in long.* **£900 – £1,000**

CUTLERY

Since medieval times cutlery has played an essential role in everyday life, but until the late 17th century spoons and knives were the only items of cutlery used at table, and dinner guests were expected to bring their own.

When Charles II returned from exile in France in 1660, he brought with him many French habits, including that of eating with a fork. Under the restored monarchy, fashion dictated that a table be pre-set with implements for eating, and services of cutlery began to be made. Antique services usually comprise 12 tablespoons, 12 forks, 12 dessert spoons, 12 dessert forks and 12 teaspoons. Knives are not usually included, since few have survived, and now it is considered acceptable to add modern knives to old services. In addition, extras such as serving spoons, gravy ladles and

soup ladles may be found, and some American services include a fascinating range of ancillary items such as ice-cream 'eaters', oyster forks and lobster picks.

The four main styles of British flatware are Hanoverian, Old English, Fiddle, and King's, made from around 1710, 1760, 1800 and 1810 respectively. These four basic shapes have been reproduced in almost all flatware services since, and are still used today with a variety of decorative patterns. Consequently, shapes and patterns are of little help when trying to date flatware.

Collectors generally opt for one of the following: a service of the same date and maker; the same maker but mixed dates; or mixed dates and makers. The first option is the most expensive to collect, but it is also the most

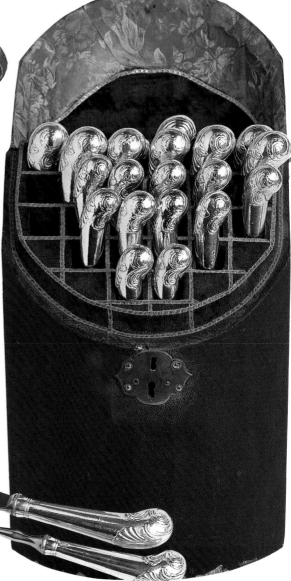

△ SILVER SERVICE These pieces are from a rare silver service comprising 12 tablespoons, 12 table forks and a serving spoon. The service was made by Etienne Castelbon, a noted French silversmith, except for the serving spoon, which was made by Joseph Talon. The pattern corresponds to the English Fiddle, Thread and Shell design, but the pattern on the back of the spoons is typically French. The pieces are also decorated with a contemporary armorial engraving. The full service comes in a brown leather case. 1724. £12,000 – £20,000

▷ CUTLERY BOX This Sheffield-made piece is remarkable in that it is complete: many such boxes have been gutted and converted into stationery holders. The knives have steel blades and the forks have two, rather than three, steel prongs. 1770 – 80. £2,000 – £3,000

valuable. Least desirable of all is the mixed cutlery service.

Although spoons were first made in Roman times, they had virtually disappeared by the time the Roman Empire had fallen, and they were not produced again in Europe in significant quantities until the 12th or 13th century. Spoon collectors today should consider themselves lucky if they find any silver examples dating from before 1500.

Sets of spoons were not made regularly until the late 17th and early 18th centuries, although before that sets of apostle spoons were occasionally produced, the earliest of which date back to the beginning of the 16th century. Early spoons were unlike those we know today; the stems were thinner and the bowls fig-shaped. The familiar

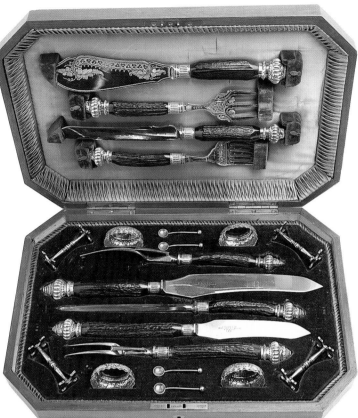

△ CARVING SET in a velvet and satin-lined box. This fine quality set, with horn handles and electroplated mounts, includes carving and serving implements, knife rests, four salts and salt spoons. Early 1900s; 18in long. **£500 – £600**

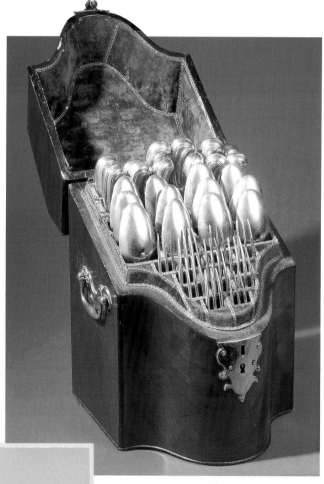

▷ SILVER GILT DESSERT SERVICE in Hanoverian pattern, comprising 12 spoons, 12 forks and 12 knives. Each implement is engraved with the royal crest and garter. 1790. **£3,000 – £5,000**

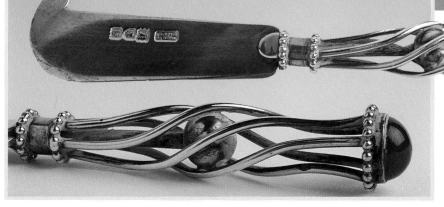

△ SILVER BUTTER KNIFE, with gemstone inset. It is marked 'G of H Limited', which stands for The Guild of Handicraft, a group that promoted a return to 'natural forms'. Confusingly, a Guild member, G. Hart, used a very similar mark after the Guild failed, but his pieces are less valuable. 1900; 6in long. **£250**

form did not develop until the early 18th century when various types of spoon began to emerge, among them straining spoons, serving spoons, toddy and punch ladles, dessert spoons and teaspoons. Not until the 19th century were spoons made as commemorative items, and towards the end of the century the Victorians began making replicas of earlier examples.

Certain spoons fetch remarkably high prices. A set of 13 Henry VIII apostle spoons (each spoon has a finial in the shape of one of the 12 apostles), with a figure of the Virgin Mary as the master spoon, fetched £120,000 in 1981. It is nevertheless possible to collect spoons on a fairly modest budget. There is a huge variety available, from small spoons such as salt, mustard and teaspoons, to the bigger basting spoons and soup ladles. The most common spoons brought to the Roadshow are sets of teaspoons and tablespoons. Tablespoons look superficially like serving spoons, but they were in fact used for soup.

1 *SILVER FRUIT SPOON for serving compotes. It has a gilded bowl embossed with fruit and foliage. 1800 (the decoration was added in the 1860s); 9in long.* **£55**

2 *SILVER PRESERVE SPOON This was an innovation of the style-conscious Victorians. 1870s; 5in long.* **£35**

3 *SILVER SUGAR SPOON for sifting sugar on to fruit. 1900; 6in long.* **£90**

4 *GEORGE III MARROW SCOOP made by Smith and Crossley of London. The wide end was used for beef marrow, and the narrow end for leg of lamb marrow. 1775; 7in long.* **£120**

5 *SCOTTISH SILVER BASTING SPOON in Hanoverian pattern with rat tail design along the back of the bowl. It was made in Edinburgh by Harry Bethune. The spoon bears the initials EP, for Edward Penman, the Assay Master. In mint condition it would have been worth twice as much. 1716; 18in long.* **£500 – £600**

6 *SILVER STRAINING SPOON This attractively pierced spoon has an unusual, slightly square bowl. The maker's mark, George Smith of London, is barely decipherable, and although the date letter is also faint, it can be made out as 1778. 10in long.* **£150**

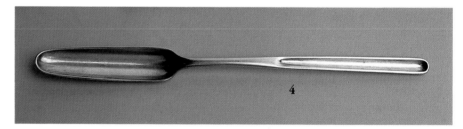

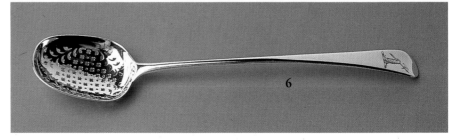

▷ SOUP LADLE *The rare pattern of this ladle is known as 'Onslow', after Arthur Onslow, an 18th century politician renowned for his speech-making in Parliament. The bowl has been repaired, halving the ladle's value. 1770; 14in long.* **£250**

◁ SILVER GILT SPOONS *made in Cologne. The smaller example bears the silversmith's mark of Peter Kaff (sometimes known as Petrus Kaft). Spoons such as these were not meant to be used, but to be given as christening presents or as tokens of appreciation. 1650 – 70; 7in and 7¼ in long.* Each **£600 – £800**

▷ SIX SILVER SPOONS *bearing the maker's mark of Francis Higgins of London. These must have been egg spoons because the bowl interiors are gilded to prevent tarnishing. The handles are shaped as Lewis Carroll-type fantasy figures. Items with novelty value such as these often sell for high prices. 1890; 4½ in long.* Each **£200 – £300**

CANDLESTICKS

Most antique candlesticks today date from after the mid 17th century. Much of the silver made before this period was melted down during the English Civil War (1642–51) to make coins to pay for troops and to buy arms. Some fine examples from later in the 17th century have survived, however, and although they look fairly chunky, they actually weigh far less than the cast and loaded sheet metal candlesticks that were made later on.

The casting of candlesticks began at the end of the 17th century. More silver was used in this process, and consequently cast pieces have a solid feel. Casting continued until the late 18th century, after which candlesticks were made from sheet metal (fine rolled silver) and filled with pitch to make them more stable. Later, plaster of Paris was sometimes added to give extra weight. Because the silver used in these pieces was so thin, such candlesticks are prone to wear, particularly at the base and the narrowest part of the stem.

Cast candlesticks, on the other hand, contained ample silver to cope with generations of polishing and handling.

Sheffield plate, invented in the early 1740s, was also used for candlesticks, and provided a cheaper alternative to silver. It was made by fusing a sheet of sterling silver to an ingot of copper, which was then reduced to a sheet of metal. From the 1840s, electroplated silver gradually replaced Sheffield plate.

Throughout the 17th century candlestick bases were mostly angular. Round bases, sometimes gadrooned but more often with shell decoration, came into fashion in the 18th century, and stems continued to be knopped and more varied than the traditional fluted cylindrical columns of the previous century. Around 1770, lighter, neo-classical styles became popular, followed by delicate Adam designs. Heavier styles were fashionable in the 1820s, and at the end of the century popular classical styles were revived.

SILVER CANDLESTICKS of typically 18th century design. A silver-plated pair in this highly desirable pattern would fetch between £80 and £120. 18th century; 10in high. **£2,000 – £3,000**

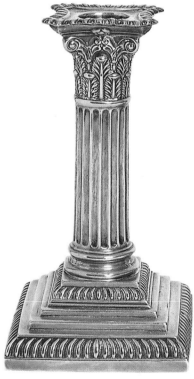

△ *SILVER NEO-CLASSICAL STYLE CANDLESTICK with a Corinthian column on a stepped square base. Such pieces range from 6 to 12 inches high. Electroplated examples are worth £30 – £50. 1910; 6in high.* **£120 – £150**

▷ *SPIRIT LAMP shaped like a candlestick. This silver-plated piece would probably once have had a glass shade and a chimney. Many such pieces have been converted to electricity. Candlesticks, too, have often suffered the same fate. Holes have been drilled through their pedestals, and cables passed up through their columns. This reduces their value, and is not advisable. Late 19th century; 22in high.* **£150 – £200**

▽ *SHEFFIELD PLATE CANDLESTICKS The glow of the copper base 'bleeds' attractively through the worn silver plate of this pair of telescopic candlesticks, the height of which can be adjusted. 1810; 8in extending to 11in high.* The pair **£250 – £350**

▽ *CORINTHIAN COLUMN SILVER CANDLESTICK Swag decoration is incorporated around the base. 1895 – 1910; 9in high.* **£200 – £300**

◁ *SNUFFER SCISSORS, made of Sheffield plate, for snuffing out lighted candles and trimming the wicks. This pair has attractive foliate decoration and original turned feet. 1835; 7in long.* **£85**

INKSTANDS

Some of the most impressive silver inkstands date from the mid 17th century. Shaped like silver caskets, they were originally known as 'standishes', and most had specific placements for a variety of boxes, bottles and containers. Many also included a position for a bell which could be rung to summon a servant.

The bottles and compartments contained ink, wafers (adhesive discs for sealing letters), sealing wax and sometimes a small taper stick. There were also pots with pierced lids for sand or sandarac gum, and since the purpose of these items is not immediately apparent, they are likely to be something of a mystery to those unfamiliar with inkstands from this period. A sand shaker may indeed seem a curious requirement when writing a letter, but pure sand was rubbed on parchment before writing to remove the fibres and create a smooth surface on which to write, and sandarac gum, which has an absorbent quality, was shaken on to parchment to act as 'blotting paper' for the ink.

Early inkstands are extremely rare because so few people were able to read or write in the 17th century. In the 18th century, a greater section of society than ever before was made up of artisans and professional people who required writing equipment for their businesses, and desktop inkstands became more widespread. It was only towards the end of the 19th century, when education had become widely available, that inkstands became popular throughout the country. To meet the increased demand for writing implements and accessories, great numbers of basic, yet extremely attractive, inkstands were manufactured both in silver and Sheffield plate.

Inkstands were made in a vast range of styles, according to the tastes and fashions of the day. In the Regency period, ormolu-mounted cabinet work was used for very large pieces, while Tunbridgeware was popular for miniature versions. Victorian inkstands in particular were often unusual and occasionally bizarre. They were made in the shape of globes, sphinxes, dogs, boats, emus, and even desert islands complete with palm trees.

▽ *ROCOCO REVIVAL INKSTAND This silver inkstand was made by Henry Wilkinson and Company of Sheffield, and sold by the retailer Joseph Mayer of Liverpool. There is an inscription on the front of the piece. 1850; 14in long x 9in wide.*
£1,800 – £2,500

◁ *ELKINGTON INKSTAND* The maker is G. R. Elkington, regarded by many as 'the father of electroplating'. 1841; 6in long. **£500**

▽ *OBLONG INKSTAND* set on separately cast, leaf-capped lion's paw feet. The sides are chased with rosettes and foliage, and the inkwells and covers are detachable. The piece was made by Paul Storr. 1821; 10in long. **£5,000 – £8,000**

◁ *OLD SHEFFIELD PLATE INKSTAND* It has a pierced gallery and three pierced containers holding two glass inkwells and a pot for sand. 1780; 9in long. **£1,200**

▽ *GEORGE II-PERIOD SILVER INKSTAND* with a pounce pot (sand pot), inkwell and central bell. It has a heavy cast gadroon border and scroll feet. It bears the hallmark of Anne Tanqueray, London. 1750; 12in long. **£15,000**

▷ *SILVER CONTINENTAL INKWELL* in Renaissance revival-style. Such highly ornate pieces were much favoured by the Victorians. Late 19th century; 4in high. **£125**

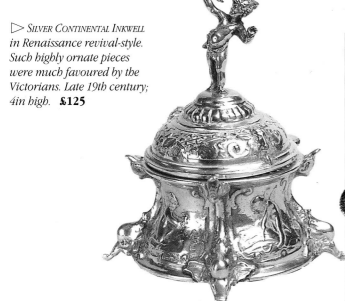

SILVER HALLMARKS

The marking of silver to indicate quality began in England in 1300, but even before this date the standard of purity of both gold and silver was strictly regulated. Silver was tested for purity by 'Touch Wardens', who carried out their duties at goldsmiths' shop premises. Some wardens were corrupt, however, and gave official marks to sub-standard wares. To combat corruption, and to facilitate stricter controls, all testing moved into the Goldsmiths' Hall in the City of London in 1478.

In the United Kingdom and the Republic of Ireland today most silver must carry four official marks from an assay office: the town mark, the standard mark, the maker's mark and the date letter. The town mark is often a symbol, such as an anchor or a rose; the standard mark is usually the familiar sterling lion, or 'lion passant'

(varied occasionally); the maker's mark comprises the maker's initials and the date letter is a letter of the alphabet to denote the year in which a piece was made.

Between 1697 and 1719 the standard of silver was raised from 92.5% silver (sterling) to 95.8% silver. To indicate the new standard, the sterling lion was replaced with a figure of Britannia, and London's town mark, a leopard's head, was replaced with a lion's head in profile. This mark was called 'the lion's head erased'. A leopard's head was also used by many other assay offices in addition to their own marks. In 1720 the sterling standard (lion passant) was reintroduced, and the Britannia mark continued to be used for higher quality silver. From 1784 to 1890 the Sovereign's head – a duty mark – was also stamped on silver, with the exception of 19th century watch cases.

Lion's Head Erased
(for Britannia standard)

Britannia

Sovereign's
Head

A typical silver hallmark.

LONDON'S HALLMARKS

The four London marks were established by the mid 16th century. The town mark was the leopard's head, introduced in 1300. The maker's mark, required by law after 1363, was usually represented by the maker's initials, although symbols were used on early silver. From 1478 the date was indicated by a letter of the alphabet. Other assay offices started this practice later, using different styles of letter. The standard mark – the lion passant – shows the sterling lion walking towards the left. This mark was introduced in 1544 to show royal control of the assay office. Although these marks have been used together in London for 400 years, it is often quite easy to identify a particular year from various alterations to their character, usually most obvious in the date letter. The style changed (from Roman script to gothic script, for example) at the end of every 20-year cycle. The examples on the far right show the changing styles of the date letter, leopard's head and maker's mark. In cycle I, symbols were used for the maker's mark; by cycle V, initials had been introduced, and by cycle VIII, initials alone were generally used. The changes to the leopard's head are shown more clearly on the right. The most significant modification came in 1821, when the leopard lost his crown. A complete set of hallmarks would also include the lion passant.

THE CHANGING
STYLE OF THE
LEOPARD'S
HEAD

1475

1592

1727

1832

LONDON CYCLES

Cycle I	Town Mark	Date Letter	Maker's Mark
1479 – 80			
1480 – 81			
1481 – 82			
Cycle V			
1559 – 60			
May 1560 – Jan 61			
Jan 1561 – May 61			
Cycle VIII			
1619 – 62			
1620 – 21			
1621 – 22			

OTHER ENGLISH HALLMARKS

Many other assay offices operated in England besides London, each distinguished by its own town mark. The Birmingham and Sheffield offices are still operating today, and both resulted from petitions to Parliament in 1773. Their marks, a crown for Sheffield and an anchor for Birmingham, were inspired by meetings of the petitioners at the Crown and Anchor public house in Westminster. Now defunct, but important in their day, were assay offices in Chester (closed 1962), Newcastle (closed 1884), Exeter (closed 1882) and York (closed 1858). Several other towns and cities also had their own marks – Norwich, Bristol and Hull, for example, though few items bearing their marks have survived. Similarly, several small towns had silversmiths who, in the 17th century and earlier, struck their own marks on pieces. In general, from 1701 all towns and cities used systems similar to London's, adding their own town mark to the four 'London-style' marks.

| Chester 1686 – 1962 | Birmingham 1773 – present | Sheffield 1773 – 1975 | Newcastle 1423 – 1884 | York 1423 – 1700 | York 1701 – 1858 | Exeter 1701 – 1882 |

SCOTTISH HALLMARKS

Edinburgh is the only Scottish city still marking today. Some of its early marks, however, are difficult to decipher. The town mark, a castle, is straightforward, as are the date letters from 1681 onward. But before then silver was struck with the marks of the town, the maker and the deacon, so pieces can, confusingly, appear to have two maker's marks. The deacon's mark was replaced by the assay master's mark in 1681, which was in turn replaced by the thistle (1759) and then the lion rampant (1975). Edinburgh added the mark of the Sovereign's head at the same time as London (1784), but Glasgow did not use this mark until the official foundation of its own assay office in 1819 (it closed in 1963). Glasgow's town mark was a tree, bird, fish and bell symbol, and from 1819 until 1914 the complete hallmark included the tree symbol, the lion rampant, the date letter and the maker's mark. The thistle was added in 1914 and used, with the town mark, until 1963.

Provincial Scottish marking makes a fascinating study, particularly since craftsmen in numerous centres struck their own marks. In addition to the maker's mark, a town mark, often an abbreviation of the town's name, was used; for example, ABD for Aberdeen, or INV for Inverness.

| Edinburgh 1485 – present | Glasgow 1819 – 1914 | Thistle (used with mark, left, 1914 – 63) |

Aberdeen (Typical abbreviation of a town's name)

Lion Rampant

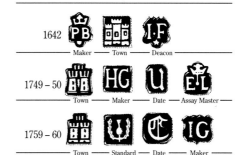

1642	Maker	Town	Deacon
1749 – 50	Town	Maker	Date	Assay Master
1759 – 60	Town	Standard	Date	Maker

IRISH HALLMARKS

Ireland's only official assay office is Dublin. Marking began in the 17th century: three marks were used officially between 1638 and 1730 – the crowned harp (the town mark), the date letter and the maker's mark. In 1731 Hibernia was added as a fourth mark, and in 1807 the Sovereign's head was used for the first time in Dublin, and continued to be used as in the rest of Britain until 1890. Irish provincial marks can also be found from Cork and Limerick. Both used the word 'sterling', albeit with various spellings and abbreviations, together with makers' marks.

Dublin 1638 – present

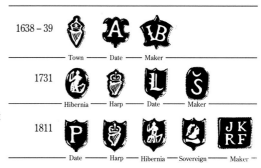

1638 – 39	Town	Date	Maker
1731	Hibernia	Harp	Date	Maker
1811	Date	Harp	Hibernia	Sovereign	Maker

DATE CHARTS

Since most of the silver brought to the Roadshow is of 19th and early 20th century dates, the following charts have been selected to cover this period. In addition to the marks shown, many pieces will also have a maker's mark. Up to 1890 a sovereign's head mark will also be found on most pieces. Should the piece be made of gold, then the style of date letter will be the same for each assay office, but the shape of the marks may differ.

LONDON

Year	Letter
1799-1800	D
1800-1	E
1801-2	F
1802-3	G
1803-4	H
1804-5	I
1805-6	K
1806-7	L
1807-8	M
1808-9	N
1809-10	O
1810-11	P
1811-12	Q
1812-13	R
1813-14	S
1814-15	T
1815,16	U
1816-17	a
1817-18	b
1818-19	C
1819-20	d
GEO.IV 1820-21	e
1821-22	f
1822-23	g
1823-24	h
1824-25	i
1825-26	k
1826-27	l
1827-28	m
1828-29	n
1829-30	o
WM.IV 1830-31	p
1831-32	q
1832-33	r
1833-34	s
1834-35	t
1835-36	u
1836-37	A
VICT. 1837 38	B
1838-39	C
1839-40	D
1840-41	E
1841-42	F
1842-43	G
1843-44	H
1844-45	J
1845-46	K
1846-47	L
1847-48	M
1848-49	N
1849-50	O
1850-51	P
1851-52	Q
1852-53	R
1853-54	S
1854-55	T
1855-56	U
1856-57	a
1857-58	b
1858-59	c
1859-60	d
1860-61	e
1861-62	f
1862-63	g
1863-64	h
1864-65	i
1865-66	k
1866-67	l
1867-68	m
1868-69	n
1869-70	o
1870-71	p
1871-72	q
1872-73	r
1873-74	s
1874-75	t
1875-76	U
1876-77	A
1877-78	B
1878-79	C
1879-80	D
1880-81	E
1881-82	F
1882-83	G
1883-84	H
1884-85	I
1885-86	K
1886-87	L
1887-88	M
1888-89	N
1889-90	O
1890-91	P
1891-92	Q
1892-93	R
1893-94	S
1894-95	T
1895-96	U
1896-97	a
1897-98	b
1898-99	c
1899-1900	d
1900-1	e
EDW.VII 1901-2	f
1902-3	g
1903-4	h
1904-5	i
1905-6	k
1906-7	l
1907-8	m
1908-9	n
1909-10	o
GEO.V 1910-11	p
1911-12	q
1912-13	r
1913-14	S
1914-15	t
1915-16	u
1916-17	a
1917-18	b
1918-19	c
1919-20	d
1920-21	e
1921-22	f
1922-23	g
1923-24	h
1924-25	i
1925-26	k
1926-27	l
1927-28	m
1928-29	n
1929-30	o
1930-31	p
1931-32	q
1932-33	r
1933-34	s
1934-35	t
1935-36	u
EDW.VII 1936-37	A
GEO.VI 1937-38	B
1938-39	C
1939-40	D
1940-41	E
1941-42	F
1942-43	G
1943-44	H

BIRMINGHAM

Year	Letter
1798-99	a
1799-1800	b
1800-1	c
1801-2	d
1802-3	e
1803-4	f
1804-5	g
1805-6	h
1806-7	i
1807-8	j
1808-9	k
1809-10	l
1810-11	m
1811-12	n
1812-13	o
1813-14	p
1814-15	q
1815-16	r
1816-17	s
1817-18	t
1818-19	u
1819-20	v
GEO.IV 1820-21	w
1821-22	X
1822-23	Y
1823-24	Z
1824-25	A
1825-26	B
1826-27	C
1827-28	D
1828-29	E
1829-30	F
WM.IV 1830-31	G
1831-32	H
1832-33	J
1833-34	K
1834-35	L
1835-36	M
1836-37	N
VICT. 1837-38	O
1838-39	P
1839-40	Q
1840-41	R
1841-42	S
1842-43	T
1843-44	U
1844-45	V
1845-46	W
1846-47	X
1847-48	Y
1848-49	Z
1849-50	A
1850-51	B
1851-52	C
1852-53	D
1853-54	E
1854-55	F
1855-56	G
1856-57	H
1857-58	I
1858-59	J
1859-60	K
1860-61	L
1861-62	M
1862-63	N
1863-64	O
1864-65	P

The Lion Passant can clearly be seen.

Pierced spoon with Continental marks.

Birmingham (continued)

Year	Letter	Year	Letter	Year	Letter
1865-66	Q	1892-93	s	1919-20	u
1866-67	R	1893-94	t	1920-21	v
1867-68	S	1894-95	u	1921-22	w
1868-69	T	1895-96	v	1922-23	x
1869-70	U	1896-97	w	1923-24	y
1870-71	V	1897-98	x	1924-25	z
1871-72	W	1898-99	y		(anchor, lion)
1872-73	X	1899-1900	z	1925-26	A
1873-74	Y		(anchor, lion)	1926-27	B
1874-75	Z	1900-1	a	1927-28	C
	(lion, anchor)	EDW. VII 1901-2	b	1928-29	D
1875-76	a	1902-3	c	1929-30	E
1876-77	b	1903-4	d	1930-31	F
1877-78	c	1904-5	e	1931-32	G
1878-79	d	1905-6	f	1932-33	H
1879-80	e	1906-7	g	1933-34	J
1880-81	f	1907-8	h	1934-35	K
1881-82	g	1908-9	i	1935-36	L
1882-83	h	1909-10	k	EDW VIII 1936-37	M
1883-84	i	GEO V 1910-11	l	GEO VI 1937-38	N
1884-85	k	1911-12	m	1938-39	O
1885-86	l	1912-13	n	1939-40	P
1886-87	m	1913-14	o	1940-41	Q
1887-88	n	1914-15	p	1941-42	R
1888-89	o	1915-16	q	1942-43	S
1889-90	p	1916-17	r	1943-44	T
1890-91	q	1917-18	s	1944-45	U
1891-92	r	1918-19	t	1945-46	V

CHESTER

Period	Letter	Period	Letter	Year	Letter
5 July 1823 / 5 July 1824	E	5 July 1824-5 July 1825	F	1846-47	H
[20 July 1799-20 July 1800]	C	5 July 1825-5 July 1826	G	1847-48	J
[20 July 1800-20 July 1801]	D	5 July 1826-5 July 1827	H	1848-49	K
[20 July 1801-20 July 1802]	E	5 July 1827-5 July 1828	I	1849-50	L
1802-1803	F	5 July 1828-5 July 1829	K	1850-51	M
1803-1804	G	5 July 1829-5 July 1830	L	1851-52	N
1804-1805	H	5 July 1830-5 July 1831	M	1852-53	O
1805-1806	I	5 July 1831-5 July 1832	N	1853-54	P
1806-1807	K	5 July 1832-5 July 1833	O	1854-55	Q
1807-5 July 1808	L	5 July 1833-5 July 1834	P	1855-56	R
5 July 1808-5 July 1809	M	1859-60		1856-57	S
5 July 1809-1810	N	1860-61		1857-58	T
1810-5 July 1811	O	5 July 1834-5 July 1835	Q	1858-59	U
5 July 1811-1812	P	5 July 1835-5 July 1836	R	1859-60	V
1812-5 July 1813	Q	5 July 1836-5 July 1837	S	1860-61	W
5 July 1813-5 July 1814	R	5 July 1837-5 July 1838	T	1861-62	X
5 July 1814-1815	S	5 July 1838-5 July 1839	U	1862-63	Y
1815-1816	T	1864-65		1863-64	Z
1816-5 July 1817	U	1865-66		1864-65	A
5 July 1817-5 July 1818	V	1839-40	A	1865-66	B
5 July 1818-7 Sept. 1819	A	1840-41	B	1866-67	C
7 Sept. 1819-10 May 1820	B	1841-42	C	1867-68	D
10 May 1820-8 Nov. 1821	C	1842-43	D	1868-69	E
8 Nov. 1821-5 July 1823	D	1843-44	E	1869-70	F
		1844-45	F	1870-71	G
		1845-46	G	1871-72	F
				1872-73	I

Year	Letter	Year	Letter	Year	Letter
1873-74	k	1897-98	O	1920-21	U
1874-75	l	1898-99	P	1921-22	V
1875-76	m	1899-1900	Q	1922-23	W
1876-77	n	1900-1	R	1923-24	X
1877-78	o	(skull, shield)		1924-25	Y
1878-79	p	EDW. VII 1901-2	A	1925-26	Z
1879-80	q	1902-3	B	(symbols)	
1880-81	r	1903-4	C	1926-27	a
1881-82	s	1904-5	D	1927-28	b
1882-83	t	1905-6	E	1928-29	c
1883-84	u	1906-7	F	1929-30	d
(lion, shield)		1907-8	G	1930-31	e
1884-85	A	1908-9	H	1931-32	ff
1885-86	B	1909-10	I	1932-33	g
1886-87	C	GEO V 1910-11	K	1933-34	h
1887-88	D	1911-12	L	1934-35	i
1888-89	E	1912-13	M	1935-36	k
1889-90	F	1913-14	N	EDW VIII 1936-37	l
1890-91	G	1914-15	O	GEO VI 1937-38	m
1891-92	H	1915-16	P	1938-39	n
1892-93	I	1916-17	Q	1939-40	o
1893-94	K	1917-18	R	1940-41	p
1894-95	L	1918-19	S	1941-42	q
1895-96	M	1919-20	T	1942-43	r
1896-97	N				

The anchor hallmark indicates that this sugar bowl was made in Birmingham.

EXETER

Date	Letter	Date	Letter	Date	Letter
[marks]		1828-29	m	[marks]	
1800-1	D	1829-30	n	1857-58	A
1801-2	E	WM.IV 1830-31	o	1858-59	B
1802-3	F	[marks]		1859-60	C
1803-4	G	1831-32	p	1860-61	D
1804-5	H	1832-33	q	1861-62	E
[marks]		1833-34	r	1862-63	F
		1834-35	s	1863-64	G
1805-6	I	1835-36	t	1864-65	H
1806-7	K	1836-37	u	1865-66	I
1807-8	L	[marks]		1866-67	K
1808-9	M	VICT. 1837-38	A	1867-68	L
1809-10	N	1838-39	B	1868-69	M
1810-11	O	1839-40	C	1869-70	N
1811-12	P	1840-41	D	1870-71	O
1812-13	Q	1841-42	E	1871-72	P
1813-14	R	1842-43	F	1872-73	Q
1814-15	S	1843-44	G	1873-74	R
1815-16	T	1844-45	H	1874-75	S
1816-17	U	1845-46	J	1875-76	T
[marks]		1846-47	K	1876-77	U
1817-18	a	1847-48	L	[marks]	
1818-19	b	1848-49	M	1877-78	A
1819-20	c	1849-50	N	1878-79	B
GEO.IV 1820-21	d	1850-51	O	1879-80	C
1821-22	e	1851-52	P	1880-81	D
1822-23	f	1852-53	Q	1881-82	E
1823-24	g	1853-54	R	1882-83	F
1824-25	h	1854-55	S		
1825-26	i	1855-56	T		
1826-27	k				
1827-28	l				

SHEFFIELD

Close up of hallmarks on a tea strainer.

Date	Letter	Date	Letter	Date	Letter
[marks]		1827-28	d	1855-56	M
1799-1800	E	1828-29	e	1856-57	N
1800-1	N	1829-30	f	1857-58	O
1801-2	H	WM.IV 1830-31	g	1858-59	P
1802-3	M	1831-32	h	1859-60	R
1803-4	F	1832-33	k	1860-61	S
1804-5	G	1833-34	l	1861-62	T
1805-6	B	1834-35	m	1862-63	U
1806-7	A	1835-36	p	1863-64	V
1807-8	S	1836-37	q	1864-65	W
1808-9	P	VICT. 1837-38	r	1865-66	X
1809-10	K	1838-39	s	1866-67	Y
1810-11	L	1839-40	t	1867-68	Z
1811-12	C	1840-41	u	[marks]	
1812-13	D	1841-42	v	1868-69	A
1813-14	R	1842-43	x	1869-70	B
1814-15	W	1843-44	z	1870-71	C
1815-16	O	[marks]		1871-72	D
1816-17	T	1844-45	A	1872-73	E
1817-18	X	1845-46	B	1873-74	F
1818-19	I	1846-47	C	1874-75	G
1819-20	V	1847-48	D	1875-76	H
GEO.IV 1820-21	Q	1848-49	E	1876-77	J
1821-22	Y	1849-50	F	1877-78	K
1822-23	Z	1850-51	G	1878-79	L
1823-24	U	1851-52	H	1879-80	M
[marks]		1852-53	I	1880-81	N
1824-25	a	1853-54	K	1881-82	O
1825-26	b	1854-55	L	1882-83	P
1826-27	c				

Date	Letter	Date	Letter	Date	Letter
1883-84	Q	1894-95	b	1906-7	o
1884-85	R	1895-96	c	1907-8	p
1885-86	S	1896-97	d	1908-9	q
1886-87	T	1897-98	e	1909-10	r
1887-88	U	1898-99	f	GEO.V 1910-11	s
1888-89	V	1899-1900	g	1911-12	t
1889-90	W	1900-1	h	1912-13	u
1890-91	X	EDW.VII 1901-2	i	1913-14	v
1891-92	Y	1902-3	k	1914-15	w
1892-93	Z	1903-4	l	1915-16	x
[marks]		1904-5	m	1916-17	y
1893-94	a	1905-6	n	1917-18	z

19th century candlesticks made to a late 18th century design.

EDINBURGH

Date	Letter	Date	Letter	Date	Letter
[marks]		1807-8	b	1816-17	k
1799-1800	T	1808-9	c	1817-18	l
1800-1	U	1809-10	d	1818-19	m
1801-2	V	1810-11	e	1819-20	n
1802-3	W	1811-12	f	[marks]	
1803-4	X	1812-13	g	GEO.IV 1820-21	o
1804-5	Y	1813-14	h	1821-22	p
1805-6	Z	1814-15	i	1822-23	q
[marks]		1815-16	j	1823-24	r
1806-7	a				

Date	Mark	Date	Mark	Date	Mark
1824-25	S	1855-56	D	1884-85	c
1825-26	t	1856-57	Z	1885-86	d
1826-27	u	1857-58	A	1886-87	e
1827-28	V	1858-59	B	1887-88	f
1828-29	W	1859-60	C	1888-89	g
1829-30	X	1860-61	D	1889-90	h
WM IV 1830-31	y	1861-62	E	1890-91	i
1831-32	Z	1862-63	F	1891-92	k
1832-33	A	1863-64	G	1892-93	l
1833-34	B	1864-65	H	1893-94	m
1834-35	C	1865-66	I	1894-95	n
1835-36	D	1866-67	K	1895-96	o
1836-37	E	1867-68	L	1896-97	p
VICT. 1837-38	F	1868-69	M	1897-98	q
1838-39	G	1869-70	N	1898-99	r
1839-40	H	1870-71	O	1899-1900	s
1840-41	I	1871-72	P	1900-1	t
1841-42	K	1872-73	Q	EDW VII 1901-2	u
1842-43	L	1873-74	R	1902-3	v
1843-44	M	1874-75	S	1903-4	w
1844-45	N	1875-76	T	1904-5	y
1845-46	O	1876-77	U	1905-6	z
1846-47	P	1877-78	V	1906-7	A
1847-48	Q	1878-79	W	1907-8	B
1848-49	R	1879-80	X	1908-9	C
1849-50	S	1880-81	Y	1909-10	D
1850-51	T	1881-82	Z	GEO V 1910-11	E
1851-52	U	1882-83	a	1911-12	F
1852-53	U	1883-84	b	1912-13	G
1853-54	W			1913-14	H
1854-55	f			1914-15	I

Date	Mark	Date	Mark	Date	Mark
1915-16	K	1923-24	S	1931-32	A
1916-17	L	1924-25	T	1932-33	B
1917-18	M	1925-26	U	1933-34	C
1918-19	N	1926-27	V	1934-35	D
1919-20	O	1927-28	W	1935-36	E
1920-21	P	1928-29	X	EDW VIII 1936-37	F
1921-22	Q	1929-30	Y	GEO VI 1937-38	G
1922-23	R	1930-31	Z	1938-39	H

DUBLIN

Date	Mark	Date	Mark	Date	Mark
1800	D	1815	T	1831-32	L
1801	E	1816	U	1832-33	M
1802	F	1817	W	1833-34	NN
1803	G	1818	X	1834-35	OO
1804	H	1819	Y	1835-36	PP
1805	I	GEO IV 1820	Z	1836-37	QQ
1806	K	1821	A	VICT 1837-38	RR
1807	L	1822	B	1838-39	S
1808	M	1823	C	1839-40	T
1809	NN	1824	D	1840-41	UU
1810	OO	1825-26	Ee	1841-42	V
1811	P	1826-27	F	1842-43	W
1812	Q	1827-28	G	1843-44	X
1813	R	1828-29	H	1844-45	Y
1814	S	1829-30	II	1845-46	Z
		WM IV 1830-31	K		

Rococo-revival inkstand, made in 1841.

Date	Mark	Date	Mark	Date	Mark
1846-47	a	1878-79	H	1909-10	O
1847-48	b	1879-80	I	1910-11	P
1848-49	c	1880-81	K	1911-12	Q
1849-50	d	1881-82	L	1912-13	R
1850-51	e	1882-83	M	1913-14	S
1851-52	ff	1883-84	N	1914-15	T
1852-53	gg	1884-45	O	1915-16	U
1853-54	hh	1885-86	P	1916	a
1854-55	j	1886-87	Q	1917	b
1855-56	k	1887-88	R	1918	c
1856-57	l	1888-89	S	1919	e
1857-58	m	1889-90	T	1920	e
1858-59	n	1890-91	U	1921	f
1859-60	o	1891-92	V	1922	g
1860-61	p	1892-93	W	1923	h
1861-62	q	1893-94	X	1924	i
1862-63	r	1894-95	Y	1925	k
1863-64	s	1895-96	Z	1926	l
1864-65	t	1896-97	A	1927	m
1865-66	u	1897-98	B	1928	n
1866-67	v	1898-99	C	1929	o
1867-68	w	1899 1900	D	1930-31	p
1868-69	x	1901-1	C	1932	q
1869-70	y	EDW VII 1901-2	f	1933	r
1870-71	z	1902-3	G	1934	s
1871-72	A	1903-4	H	1935	t
1872-73	B	1904-5	K	1936	u
1873-74	C	1905-6	L	1937	v
1874-75	D	1906-7	M	1938	w
1875-76	E	1907-8	M	1939	x
1876-77	F	1908-9	N	1940	y
1877-88	G			1941	z

BROOCHES

Although brooches were used by the Romans, Celts and Vikings to fasten their clothing, they did not become popular as decorative wear until the late 17th century. Many of the larger pieces from this period, such as elaborate corsage ornaments and huge 'stomachers', have been split up and made into smaller items. Bows, ribbons, and flower sprays were perenially popular.

Mourning brooches, usually with black enamel and pearl borders and frequently containing a lock of a loved-one's hair, were popular in the late 18th century. In the 19th century, round or oval target and cluster brooches became fashionable, and by the end of the century all sorts of novelty brooches were in vogue – many inspired by items excavated from Assyrian, Egyptian, Greek and Roman sites. Bird and animal brooches were also popular in the 19th century, and there was a brief craze for japonaiserie between 1875 and 1885.

Art Deco, with its geometric outlines, daring use of colour, and unusual gem combinations, became fashionable after World War I and remained so until the outbreak of World War II. During this period, American designers introduced the 1940s, or 'retro', style. Brooches of this type, using more gold and fewer stones, are large and 'swirly' in shape.

◁ *GOLD BROOCH with sapphire centre and two rose diamonds. Such brooches were mass produced in the late 19th century. 1½ in long.* **£140**

△ *GOLD BAR BROOCH (top) set with a tiny faceted aquamarine gemstone. Late Edwardian; 2½ in long.* **£110**
GOLD AND DIAMOND BAR BROOCH (above) This type of brooch would have been given as a birthday or an anniversary present. 1920; 1½ in long. **£175**

▽ *DIAMOND AND OPAL BROOCH mounted in gold. The opals are full of 'fire' and are of good quality. 1900; 1½ in long.* **£400**

◁ *VICTORIAN BROOCH in the shape of a violin. The diamonds are inset in silver, and the remainder is gold. This type of novelty piece in the form of a musical instrument is very collectable. 1880; 1½ in.* **£400 – £600**

◁ RIBBON BROOCH with a large baroque pearl drop. It is set with cushion-cut diamonds – an early version of the brilliant-cut developed at the beginning of the 18th century. The bow or ribbon motif has been extremely popular since the late 17th century. 1769; 2in long. **£3,000**

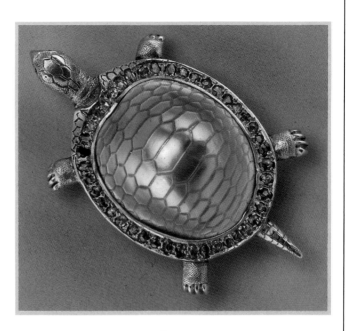

△ TORTOISE BROOCH mounted in gold with an engraved mother-of-pearl back. It is set with a border of rare green garnets. Such garnets can be found on jewellery made between 1880 and 1910; 2in long.   **£1,500**

△ FOUR-LEAF CLOVER BROOCH
This pretty, fine-quality gold brooch is decorated in green enamel and set with seed pearls. It was made in England. 1890s; 1in across.   **£500**

△ GOLD BUTTERFLY BROOCH decorated with opals and half pearls. The goldwork is in the style of early 19th century 'canetille' beaded scrollwork. Insect brooches of all types were very popular at the end of the 19th century. 1890; 1½ in across.   **£500**

CAMEOS

The art of crafting cameos can be traced back to ancient Egyptian times. The most common image portrayed on a cameo is that of a head in profile or a whole figure, often depicted in a classical manner. Although pastoral scenes are far rarer than profiles and figures, they too provided inspiration for carvers.

Cameos were incorporated into many different types of jewellery including bracelets, pendants, rings and brooches. The most popular material to use was shell; the Italian conch shell was most highly favoured because it was the easiest to work. Other much used materials included lava from Mount Vesuvius, rubies, sapphires, and more unusual gems such as labradorite, which flashes like opal. Semi-precious stones were also frequently used, agate being a particular favourite because, like shell, it could be pared away layer by layer to reveal different colours. Cameo mounts vary considerably; some have pearl or diamond borders, while others are set inside plain or decorative gold borders.

The heyday of the handcut cameo was probably from 1840 to the 1880s. After this date cameos were mostly cut by machine and hand-finished, and their quality is not nearly as good as that of crisp, handcut examples.

A good cameo can be bought for as little as sixty pounds, but a high quality piece may cost several hundred pounds.

◁ *SHELL CAMEO BROOCH with a gilt metal swivel mount. The central section can be turned around to reveal a locket at the back. The carving is a little blurred and is not of the highest quality. 1875 – 1900; 2½ in long.* **£80 – £100**

▽ *ITALIAN CAMEO BROOCH depicting a scene from Roman mythology. The gold cannetille mount is inset with turquoise. The piece was probably used originally as a hair ornament. 1830; 4½ in long.* **£1,250**

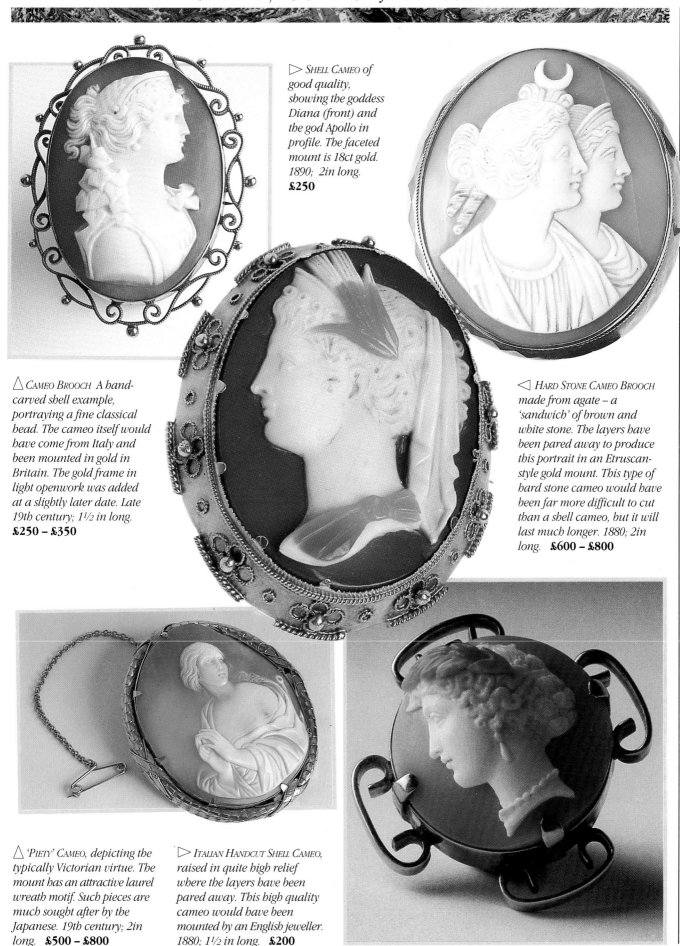

▷ SHELL CAMEO of
good quality,
showing the goddess
Diana (front) and
the god Apollo in
profile. The faceted
mount is 18ct gold.
1890; 2in long.
£250

△ CAMEO BROOCH A hand-
carved shell example,
portraying a fine classical
head. The cameo itself would
have come from Italy and
been mounted in gold in
Britain. The gold frame in
light openwork was added
at a slightly later date. Late
19th century; 1½ in long.
£250 – £350

◁ HARD STONE CAMEO BROOCH
made from agate – a
'sandwich' of brown and
white stone. The layers have
been pared away to produce
this portrait in an Etruscan-
style gold mount. This type of
hard stone cameo would have
been far more difficult to cut
than a shell cameo, but it will
last much longer. 1880; 2in
long. **£600 – £800**

△ 'PIETY' CAMEO, depicting the
typically Victorian virtue. The
mount has an attractive laurel
wreath motif. Such pieces are
much sought after by the
Japanese. 19th century; 2in
long. **£500 – £800**

▷ ITALIAN HANDCUT SHELL CAMEO,
raised in quite high relief
where the layers have been
pared away. This high quality
cameo would have been
mounted by an English jeweller.
1880; 1½ in long. **£200**

PENDANTS

The pendant was a natural development from the necklace, which had been worn since prehistoric times. Pendants were popular items of jewellery, but they became particularly fashionable during the Renaissance period. In a painting by the court painter, Holbein, King Henry VIII is portrayed wearing a massive necklace and pendant. Such large and weighty items were also favoured by fashionable men and women in the 19th century.

Archaeological discoveries during this period proved influential in many spheres. A revival of Etruscan styles in jewellery produced oval pendants in gold with wirework borders, and others set with the most fashionable stones of the day. Pearls, too, were favoured, either set in clusters or surrounding a gemstone, and enamelwork pendants proved especially popular in the 1850s and '60s.

The last decade of the 19th century and the first part of the 20th saw the decline of heavy, rather formal pendants and the development of lighter, openwork jewellery with flowing, delicate lines. But changing styles, particularly relating to the neckline, resulted in the pendant going out of fashion, and by the end of the Edwardian era it had virtually disappeared. Only recently has the pendant enjoyed a revival.

The locket originated early in the 17th century during the reign of Charles I. Many had an ornamental front and opened at the back, and a loved-one's lock of hair was generally enclosed inside. Following the advent of photography in the 1860s, small, portrait-type photographs were frequently placed inside lockets, sometimes together with a lock of hair. These proved immensely popular sentimental items, and many such lockets have been passed down through generations.

▷ *TWIN-HEART LOCKET with a green enamel border and raised diamond and pearl surround. 1900; 1in long.* **£800**

◁ *MALTESE GOLD LOCKET with a rose diamond flower spray. 1860s; 1¼ in long.* **£800 – £1,000**

▷ *JAPANESE DAMASCENE NECKLACE made from mixed base metal and inlaid with gold and silver. The designs include temples, flowers and Japanese good luck symbols. 1910; necklace 16in long, pendant 1in long.* **£60**

◁ *HEART-SHAPED PENDANT in 9ct gold. On one side there is an inset portrait miniature, and on the other a six-pointed star with a garnet in the centre and seed pearls at each point. A pretty piece of this type would have been given to a young girl as a love token. 1905; ⅝ in long.* **£85**

▽ *VICTORIAN FACETED AMETHYST PENDANT, inset with a diamond double horseshoe motif. The 60-inch guard-chain makes it very saleable. The chain was originally intended to go through a muff and hold a lorgnette on the end. 1880; pendant ⅝ in long.* **£400 – £600**

△ *TORTOISESHELL PIQUE PENDANT set with gold and mother-of-pearl. 1880; 1¼ in long.* **£50 – £60**

▷ *GOLD AND ENAMEL PENDANT made in France or Switzerland. 1890; 1¼ in long.* **£250 – £300**

▷ *BLUE ENAMEL AND DIAMOND-SET PENDANT with a locket back. Photography had just been introduced, so the locket may have contained a photograph instead of a lock of hair. 1860; ¾ in across.* **£600 – £800**

△ *FRENCH PENDANT set with diamonds in an attractive design. The bright, clean stones are of very high quality. 1850; 2in long.* **£300 – £400**

BRACELETS

Most of the bracelets brought to the Roadshows date from the 20th century – although a few are from the 19th – and almost all are made of gold. In the early 19th century single chain bracelets with fancy links and ornate clasps were popular, as were flat mesh bracelets with chunky clasps, and wide hinged bangles with chased designs. Archaeological discoveries in the 1830s and later had a profound effect on jewellery, and ancient designs were copied widely. Stones and pearls were popular in bracelets throughout the century. Coral was carved into bracelets and bangles during the 1850s and 1860s, and inlaid tortoiseshell was in fashion from about 1850 to 1880.

Silver went out of fashion toward the end of the 19th century, and at the turn of the century, under the influence of Art Nouveau, jewellery became more delicate, and solid, heavy metal was replaced by filigree. The discovery of Tutankhamen's tomb in 1922 prompted a revival of Egyptian-style jewellery, and the 1920s Art Deco movement gave rise to bracelets with angular lines, panels and geometric designs. Today, costume jewellery from the 1920s to the 1970s is very much in vogue.

▷ *HOLLOW LINK GOLD BRACELET with a tiny padlock, set with semi-precious stones. 1900s.*
£250 – £350

▽ *AMETHYST-SET BRACELET on a gold mesh band. This Victorian bracelet has an amethyst in the centre set with diamonds. 1830.* **£200**

△ *EXPANDING BRACELET in 9ct gold, featuring a pretty five-pointed star, set with a central garnet and seed pearls, surrounded by a crescent of seed pearls. 1900s.* **£150 – £250**

◁ *GOLD BRACELET inlaid with polished agates. One of the panels is in fact a locket containing a portrait. It comes in the original box from Drummonds of Perth in Scotland. 1860 – 80.*
£700 – £1,000

VINAIGRETTES

A vinaigrette is a small decorative container in which was kept a tiny sponge soaked in spiced, aromatic vinegar. First used at the end of the 17th century, vinaigrettes were held to the nose to ward off the foul stench of city streets. Early examples were flask shaped, but from the late 18th century the form changed to a small, gilt-lined box with a flip-up lid. Vinaigrettes went out of fashion in the mid 19th century and were replaced by a double-ended scent bottle with an ordinary opening at one end and a vinaigrette at the other. The bottles, fitted with a loop which could be hung from the belt of a gown, were a popular ladies' accessory from about 1860 to 1890.

Vinaigrettes by Nathaniel Mills, Samuel Pemberton and Thomas Shaw are the most sought after, and frequently command high prices, but attractive vinaigrettes can be bought for an average price of £60 to £80.

△ CASTLE-TOP VINAIGRETTE *depicting Windsor Castle, by the famous maker, Nathaniel Mills. Vinaigrettes with a castle top embossed or engraved on the lid were particularly popular. A plainer vinaigrette of this size would fetch £100. 1840; 1½ in long.* **£500 – £800**

△ RUBY GLASS AND SILVER GILT SCENT BOTTLE WITH VINAIGRETTE BASE *This is a fine example of an early flask-shaped vinaigrette. It has a hole in the top and a pierced grille in the bottom which allowed the aroma to waft out. It was made by Sampson Morden and is in very good condition. It is important to inspect the inside of a bottle neck for signs of damage, since the mount often conceals chips or cracks. 1871; 4½ in long.* **£200**

◁ RARE SILVER GILT NELSON VINAIGRETTE, *made in Birmingham by Matthew Linwood after the Battle of Trafalgar. A bust of Nelson is engraved on the lid, and the grille is cast and pierced inside with Nelson's ship, the 'Victory'. 1805; 1½ in long.* **£5,000**

ARMS & MILITARIA

BILL HARRIMAN

I was introduced to the *Antiques Roadshow* some five years ago by my friend and mentor, the late Douglas Nie. I had just taken over from him at the catalogue department of Weller & Dufty (auctioneers of firearms and militaria), and was still coming to terms with my new-found responsibilities. Doug suggested that I contact Robin Drake, the producer of the Roadshow at the time, and I arranged to meet him in Bristol for lunch. Two days before the meeting, disaster struck – I dislocated my shoulder and broke my wrist after parting company with my horse whilst going over a jump. The journey to Bristol was traumatic to say the least: the train was late, it was scorchingly hot, and

painkillers were making me very drowsy – hardly a good image to present at an interview. Robin gave me lunch in a bistro and, to cut a long story short, invited me to the Doncaster Roadshow as an observer.

The following year, 1986, I started in earnest with a recording at Bath. I was very nervous, but calmed myself with the thought that I would be able to watch the other experts and pick up a few 'pointers' as I went along. No such luck, however. Within half an hour I had been asked to discuss – in front of the cameras – a tiny pistol concealed in a poetry book. Supressing the urge to dash immediately from the room, I managed to recall a few of Eric Knowles' helpful hints about filming. Suddenly, there I was on-camera with the owner and her pistol. It was all over surprisingly quickly, and despite the tiny quaver in my voice during the recording, I was not displeased with my first effort for the Roadshow.

Much water has passed under the bridge since that recording; I have seen a vast number of items and a great many people, and throughout I have always been impressed by the patience and friendliness of our 'customers'.

I enjoy the companionship of the other Roadshow experts and the rest of the team very much, and look forward with great anticipation to each of the new season's venues. For me, the possibility of finding something important or unique always provides a great stimulus – perhaps that lost suit of 16th century Greenwich armour will turn up some-where. 'Such stuff as dreams are made on' indeed.

Anyone intending to start collecting arms and militaria should formulate a plan as to the content, theme, size and range that the collection is to encompass. Since the field is so large and varied, it is important to specialize early in order to gain a thorough

Pinfire revolver with ivory grips and gold plating. 1870; 7in long.   £250

knowledge of items that will form the collection. Another point to remember is that thematic, rather than eclectic, collections always have a greater resale value.

Once you have decided on an area in which to collect, try to avoid buying anything for at least six months. This may sound like odd advice, but it is important that the novice should not rush headlong into purchasing something that may be the cause of regret later. Instead, it is important for beginners to gain as much experience and knowledge of their subject as possible. You can gain practical experience of handling objects by attending auctions and arms fairs, by making contact with fellow collectors and by visiting dealers' premises. There is no substitute for actually picking up an item and carefully examining it, and if this is combined with visits to museum collections, the collector will soon develop an eye and a feel for his chosen field.

To complement this practical experience, it is essential to build up a good reference library of books and pamphlets. Reference books, whilst being a joy to own, are perhaps the most important 'weapons' that any collector can have in his 'arsenal'. The generalized coffee table style of book that concentrates on pretty pictures and little else should be avoided, and only well-written and scholarly volumes considered. These tend to be costly, but in terms of acquiring someone else's knowledge and experience, the expense is well worthwhile. In addition, the prices of books about guns and militaria have risen steadily over the last fifteen years, making them a sound investment for collectors.

As well as books, there is a plethora of periodical magazines that range from the excellent to the dreadful; it very much depends on individual taste as to which are taken. Learned societies and associations also produce their own specialized and well-written journals for distribution to members. First purchases are best made from reputable dealers, and you should always insist that the item is described on the sales invoice, with notes about its date and condition included in case of later dispute. If the dealer will not co-operate, it would be advisable to take your custom elsewhere.

Auction visiting is the next stage for collectors, but these should be treated with great caution as there are many pitfalls for the unwary. Always try to view before bidding, but if that is not possible, telephone the auctioneers for a condition report. Be aware that neither this nor the catalogue description is legally binding. Always read the conditions of sale (as printed in the catalogue) carefully, because by bidding you are deemed to have accepted them, and try to set a spending limit to avoid getting carried away. As a rule of thumb, buy objects that are in good condition, and be prepared to upgrade them when the opportunity arises. It is always better to have a small collection of pieces in fine condition than a large collection of mediocre items.

Arms or militaria that are purchased will often be dirty or damaged, and it is very satisfying to be able to restore these items. This not only makes them more aesthetically pleasing, it can also increase their value. It is important, however, not to overdo restoration work. A metal such as steel is best cleaned with fine steel wool soaked in a light oil; under no circumstances use emery cloth and do not overpolish. Brass is best left unpolished, but it may be cleaned gently with a little vinegar. Wood can be cleaned with fine steel wool and meths, and finished with boiled linseed oil or wax polish. French polish is an attractive finish if applied subtly. Leather should be saddle-soaped to clean it, then treated with a good quality hide food and finished with boot polish. Materials such as textiles or paper should be referred to specialist restorers, rather than worked on by the amateur. Never use chemicals such as acids or rust removers, and try to practise on unimportant items. Be patient and gentle – the accumulated dirt of a century will not come off in ten minutes.

As your collection begins to grow, you will inevitably wish to display it. Guns and rifles look well on wall racks; pistols can be mounted in glazed cabinets, and medals, badges and other small items look splendid framed. In all cases direct sunlight should be avoided, as it rots textiles, bleaches wood and causes colour-hardened steel to fade.

It is always a good idea to keep collections behind drawn curtains to discourage the opportunist thief, and it is well worth taking out an insurance policy for the replacement value of your collection. A detailed catalogue description of each item provides not only a clear record for insurance purposes, but also an interesting read over the years.

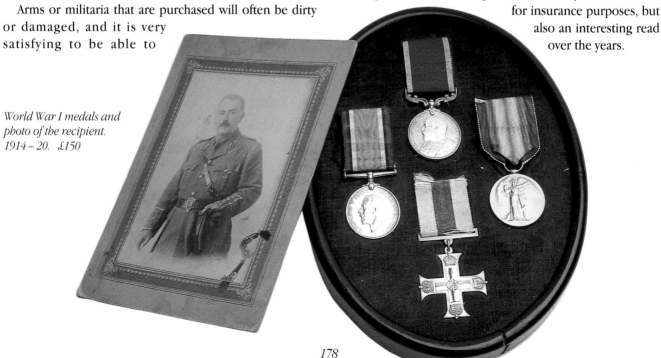

World War 1 medals and photo of the recipient. 1914 – 20. £150

MY FAVOURITE ITEMS

The 1991 Roadshow series was well up to par for arms and militaria. Whilst nothing of outstanding importance turned up, there was still a steady trickle of interesting objects that were a pleasure to see. On an international note, as the frontiers of Eastern Europe have crumbled, I hope to see an increase in arms and militaria from the East. We do not see a great deal of it in the West and I am sure that it is going to be a fascinating new field.

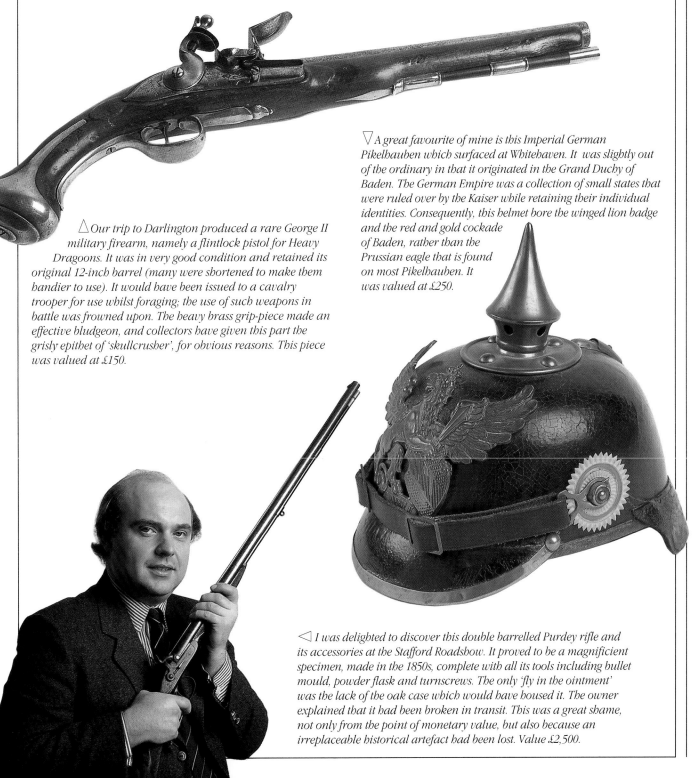

△ Our trip to Darlington produced a rare George II military firearm, namely a flintlock pistol for Heavy Dragoons. It was in very good condition and retained its original 12-inch barrel (many were shortened to make them handier to use). It would have been issued to a cavalry trooper for use whilst foraging; the use of such weapons in battle was frowned upon. The heavy brass grip-piece made an effective bludgeon, and collectors have given this part the grisly epithet of 'skullcrusher', for obvious reasons. This piece was valued at £150.

▽ A great favourite of mine is this Imperial German Pikelhauben which surfaced at Whitehaven. It was slightly out of the ordinary in that it originated in the Grand Duchy of Baden. The German Empire was a collection of small states that were ruled over by the Kaiser while retaining their individual identities. Consequently, this helmet bore the winged lion badge and the red and gold cockade of Baden, rather than the Prussian eagle that is found on most Pikelhauben. It was valued at £250.

◁ I was delighted to discover this double barrelled Purdey rifle and its accessories at the Stafford Roadshow. It proved to be a magnificent specimen, made in the 1850s, complete with all its tools including bullet mould, powder flask and turnscrews. The only 'fly in the ointment' was the lack of the oak case which would have housed it. The owner explained that it had been broken in transit. This was a great shame, not only from the point of monetary value, but also because an irreplaceable historical artefact had been lost. Value £2,500.

FLINTLOCK PISTOLS & FLASKS

The flintlock was developed in France in around 1600 as the means of igniting gunpowder. Flintlock pistols survived in common usage until well into the 19th century, and were still being made in Birmingham for use in Africa right up to the start of World War I.

Holster pistols, the largest of the flintlock pistols, were carried by mounted men on their saddlebows and often had bulbous knobs at the end of the stocks, so that once fired they could be used as a club. Smaller carriage pistols were kept in special pockets on coach doors as a defence against highwaymen, and pocket pistols were carried by anyone who needed an easily concealed weapon.

Perhaps the most desirable flintlock pistols are those made for duelling. Although vigorously condemned, duelling was popular from about 1780 to 1820. The classic English duelling pistol has a 10-inch barrel of ½-inch bore and a full length walnut stock with a butt like a hockey stick. They were always presented cased and in pairs, together with accessories. A pair of cased pistols is over three times more valuable than a single example.

Pistols were generally loaded by means of a ramrod. Screw-barrel, or 'turn off' pistols, however, were loaded by unscrewing the barrel and inserting the powder and ball into the chamber; the barrel was then replaced and the pan primed. These elegant weapons are very collectable and can command high prices. As a result, they have been extensively faked: if in doubt, seek a second opinion before buying.

In the days of muzzle-loading guns, a flask was used to carry gunpowder. Its main purpose was to keep the powder dry, but many flasks also incorporated a measuring device to ensure that the right amount was loaded. Animal horns were found to be the ideal material for flasks because they are sparkproof, waterproof and

△ *SCREW-BARREL POCKET PISTOLS*
This pair of poor quality pistols was made in Birmingham. The barrels unscrew, allowing the chambers to be loaded with powder and ball. 1825; 6in long.
Single pistol **£150**
The pair **£450**

△ *BRASS-BARRELLED BLUNDERBUSS PISTOLS, signed 'Joyner'. The flared muzzles were designed to intimidate and to ease loading. 1790; 12in long.*
Single pistol **£650**
The pair **£2,000**

▷ *QUEEN ANNE-STYLE SCREW-BARREL CARRIAGE PISTOLS with silver mounts. 1780; 10in long.*
Single pistol **£350**
The pair **£1,100**

relatively transparent, but the most commonly used materials were copper and gilded metal. Flasks were also made from nickel silver, zinc, tin plate and leather-covered steel; examples in wood and leather can also be found.

Flasks vary in size according to the firearm with which they were to be used. Those for use with sporting guns range between six and nine inches, while those for use with pistols are sized from three to five inches. Very small or unusually large flasks command higher prices than those of normal size because of their comparative rarity. The most common shape for flasks is that of a pear.

Most English flasks were made in Sheffield by one of the four major manufacturers – Dixon, Sykes, Bartram and Hawksley. Newly made flasks were finished with a coloured lacquer, and any flask that retains this should not be cleaned or polished.

△ 16-BORE ENGLISH HOLSTER PISTOL made by Ketland, London. Although it took the service cartridge, it does not bear a Board of Ordnances stamp, indicating a service-issue pistol. It probably belonged to a Yeomanry cavalry officer (similar to today's Territorial Army). 1790; 9in long. **£400**

▽ SAW-HANDLED DUELLING PISTOLS The unusually shaped butts provided a clear line of sight for fast, instinctive shooting. 1810; 13in long. Single pistol **£800** Cased pair **£4,500**

△ FLINTLOCK DUELLING PISTOLS AND '3-WAY' POWDER FLASK by Sykes, Oxford. The locks have French cocks, safety bolts, water-proof priming pans and anti-friction rollers. These fine pistols were made solely for duelling and come in a mahogany case. The flask is known as a '3-way' because it has separate compartments for powder, bullets and flints. On its own it would be worth £150. 1820; 12in long. Single pistol **£1,200**; cased pair **£4,000**

▷ ENGLISH FLASKS
1 Powder flask for a sporting gun. Plain but of good quality, it retains its original protective lacquer. 1860; 8in long. **£50**
2 3-way flask containing powder, bullets and percussion caps. It is of the type often found in a case with duelling pistols. 1840; 5in long. **£75**
3 Top quality shot flask for a sporting gun. The ring at the bottom of the leather body can be attached to a strap. 1860; 9in long. **£60**

RIFLES

The 19th century saw great technical advances in the design of firearms. At the start of the century, soldiers were still using large calibre flintlock muskets which were inaccurate above 90 yards. As the 20th century approached, high velocity rifles were being made, capable of accurate shooting at 900 yards.

The most exciting time during this period was from 1840 to 1880. Every major world power was running trial programmes that produced innumerable designs for breech-loading rifles. These were much easier and quicker to use than the earlier muzzle-loading models that used a ramrod to thrust home the bullet and powder. Consequently, many conversion systems were developed to modernize muzzle-loading weapons. The American Civil War of 1861, the Italian Campaign of 1867 and the Franco-Prussian War of 1870 provided actual combat conditions in which the new designs were put to the ultimate test.

The infantry have never had the characteristic glamour of the cavalry, nor have their weapons had the same following among collectors as cavalry carbines. This is changing, however, and rifles have risen steadily in value over the last ten years, unlike most other groups of firearms.

All the rifles shown here may be owned without a Firearms Certificate, provided that they are not fired.

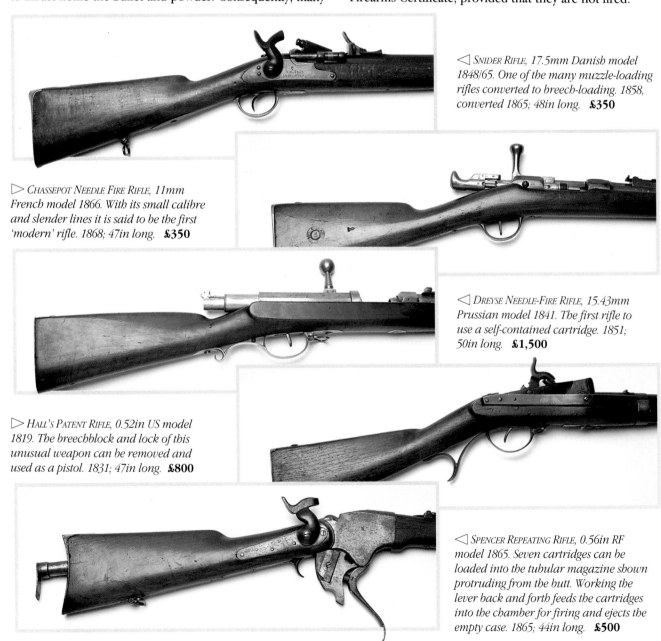

◁ *SNIDER RIFLE, 17.5mm Danish model 1848/65. One of the many muzzle-loading rifles converted to breech-loading. 1858, converted 1865; 48in long.* **£350**

▷ *CHASSEPOT NEEDLE FIRE RIFLE, 11mm French model 1866. With its small calibre and slender lines it is said to be the first 'modern' rifle. 1868; 47in long.* **£350**

◁ *DREYSE NEEDLE-FIRE RIFLE, 15.43mm Prussian model 1841. The first rifle to use a self-contained cartridge. 1851; 50in long.* **£1,500**

▷ *HALL'S PATENT RIFLE, 0.52in US model 1819. The breechblock and lock of this unusual weapon can be removed and used as a pistol. 1831; 47in long.* **£800**

◁ *SPENCER REPEATING RIFLE, 0.56in RF model 1865. Seven cartridges can be loaded into the tubular magazine shown protruding from the butt. Working the lever back and forth feeds the cartridges into the chamber for firing and ejects the empty case. 1865; 44in long.* **£500**

BAYONETS

A bayonet is essentially a knife which attaches to a rifle, making it a defensive weapon for close-quarter fighting. The earliest bayonets were used by European armies in 1680, and they are believed to have originated in Bayonne, France, hence their name. Early examples were simply knives stuck into weapon barrels, but this prevented the weapon from being fired, and so a separate socket to hold the bayonet was developed in about 1700. This weapon was used well into the 19th century.

There are over 2,000 different types of bayonet, ranging in price from £3 to £500. All kinds of collecting 'themes' are possible, such as sword bayonets, World War II weapons, or bayonets from a particular country.

Collectors should search out bayonets that come complete with a scabbard and 'frog' (belt hanger). The condition of a piece is all important, too. A weapon with its original finish is worth more than one which has been worked on, refinished or polished.

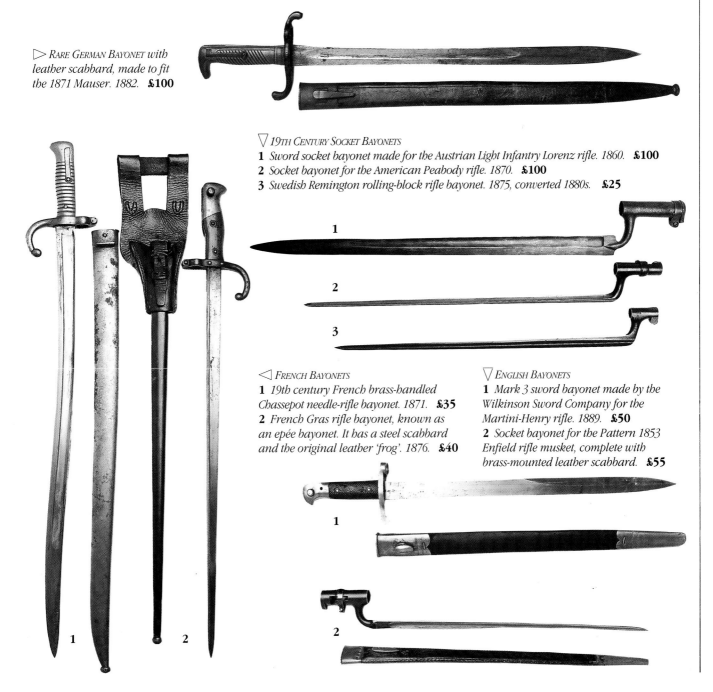

▷ *RARE GERMAN BAYONET with leather scabbard, made to fit the 1871 Mauser. 1882.* **£100**

▽ *19TH CENTURY SOCKET BAYONETS*
1 *Sword socket bayonet made for the Austrian Light Infantry Lorenz rifle. 1860.* **£100**
2 *Socket bayonet for the American Peabody rifle. 1870.* **£100**
3 *Swedish Remington rolling-block rifle bayonet. 1875, converted 1880s.* **£25**

◁ *FRENCH BAYONETS*
1 *19th century French brass-handled Chassepot needle-rifle bayonet. 1871.* **£35**
2 *French Gras rifle bayonet, known as an epée bayonet. It has a steel scabbard and the original leather 'frog'. 1876.* **£40**

▽ *ENGLISH BAYONETS*
1 *Mark 3 sword bayonet made by the Wilkinson Sword Company for the Martini-Henry rifle. 1889.* **£50**
2 *Socket bayonet for the Pattern 1853 Enfield rifle musket, complete with brass-mounted leather scabbard.* **£55**

ENGLISH PERCUSSION REVOLVERS

The name of Sam Colt is synonymous with the revolver, and most people assume that American designs have dominated the hand gun's development. This is not the case, however; revolver making also flourished in Britain from 1850 to 1920, and many excellent designs were produced.

The Birmingham gun trade was highly significant in the production of revolvers, and used a great number of craftsmen who performed specialized tasks such as polishing, hardening, engraving, lock-filing and stock-making. Most of the makers were sub-contracted by large companies, and they rented rooms or benches in workshops built around a main courtyard. The names and addresses engraved on the barrels of English revolvers are therefore those of the retailers, rather than the makers.

In general, English revolvers have a better standard of finish than their American counterparts, although tens of thousands of poor quality examples were also produced. They tend to be five rather than six shot, and many are self-cocking or double action, rather than single action, which is the norm with American types. Single action means the hammer has to be cocked for each shot. Self-cocking means a pull on the trigger cocks the lock, rotates the cylinder and fires the pistol in one action. In a double action gun, either function can be used.

English revolvers are often presented in oak or mahogany cases, complete with accessories for shooting and maintenance. Such guns are always much sought after, and their value has risen steadily since the mid 1970s.

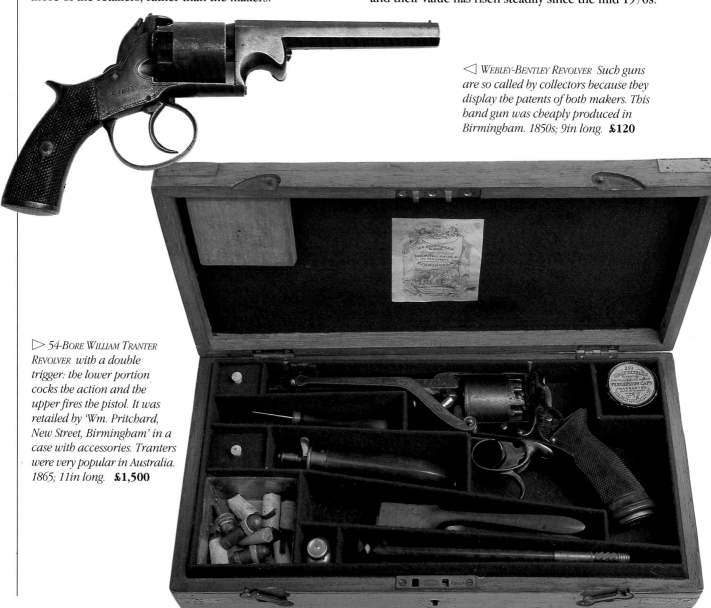

◁ *WEBLEY-BENTLEY REVOLVER* *Such guns are so called by collectors because they display the patents of both makers. This hand gun was cheaply produced in Birmingham. 1850s; 9in long.* **£120**

▷ *54-BORE WILLIAM TRANTER REVOLVER* *with a double trigger: the lower portion cocks the action and the upper fires the pistol. It was retailed by 'Wm. Pritchard, New Street, Birmingham' in a case with accessories. Tranters were very popular in Australia. 1865; 11in long.* **£1,500**

◁ BEAUMONT ADAMS REVOLVER which has a lock mechanism patented by a Lieutenant Beaumont in 1855. Beaumont's improvement meant that the five shots could be fired either by simply pulling the trigger for rapid action or by cocking the hammer each time for more deliberate fire. 1860; 12in long. **£250**

◁ 90-BORE PERCUSSION REVOLVER, known as a 'transitional' revolver by collectors because it bridges the gap between the pepperboxes of the 1840s and the true revolver. It was made in Birmingham. 1845; 13in long. **£150**

△ WEBLEY-BENTLEY REVOLVER Cheaply made weapons such as this were produced in great numbers. The gun can be fired only as a self-cocker; that is, by pulling the trigger to cock and fire the revolver in one action. This gives a rapid rate of fire but is not very accurate. 1860; 9in long. **£120**

△ 38-BORE ADAM'S PATENT REVOLVER This large-calibre pistol was popular with officers in both the Crimean War and the Indian Mutiny. Its action was designed so that all five shots could be discharged simply by pulling the trigger repeatedly. Its size and weight also made it an effective bludgeon when empty. This revolver has a case and accessories. 1853; 15in long. **£1,800**

▷ 'GAS SEAL' REVOLVER This high quality transitional type 90-bore revolver contains a device which pushes the cylinder forward to seal the gap between it and the barrel on firing. This prevents loss of the gas produced as the powder charge burns, giving higher velocity. Much controversy surrounds the origin of these revolvers, but they are known to collectors as 'Lang types' after Joseph Lang of Haymarket and Cockspur Street, London, who sold many such hand guns. This example comes in a case, complete with accessories. 1860; 10in long. **£1,800**

IMPERIAL GERMAN MILITARIA

Between 1871 and 1913 Germany was an empire, a federation of states, each one with its own individual characteristics. Its militaria has always been somewhat overshadowed by that from the Nazi era. However, as collectors become ever more disillusioned with the dubious authenticity of material from the Third Reich (there is much faking of Nazi items), the Imperial period is increasing in popularity. The most sought after items are 'Pikelhauben' or spiked helmets. These have been associated with the German soldier since Prussia's victory over France in 1871 and make a good focal point for a collection because of their numerous variations.

German industry produced a wide range of military souvenirs by which soldiers might remember their service; these include beer mugs, spirit flasks, pipes, custom-made bayonets and postcards. Many bear individual soldiers' names and regiments, making them unique. Imperial German militaria can be assembled on a broad basis or collectors can specialize in a particular state or item. Prices range from one pound to several thousand pounds.

◁ *STEEL HELMET The model 1916 steel helmet continued to be used into the 1930s. It has lugs for attaching a steel brow-piece to the front. The super-efficient design is based on that of a medieval helmet.* **£50**

▷ *PRUSSIAN SHAKO Although first made in 1871 for riflemen, this style of leather headgear was reissued in 1914 for soldiers in the Landsturm (3rd or 4th-line reservists).* **£350**

▽ *BELT BUCKLES indicating the state from which the wearer came (apart from (1), which is from Turkey – Germany's ally during World War I). 2 Telegraphist's buckle with carriers for reels of telephone wire. 3 Rare drum hanger. Telegraphist's buckle and drum hanger, each* **£50**; *the rest, each* **£10 – £30**

△ *EPAULETTES A selection of artillery, cavalry, naval and infantry shoulder straps. The grey straps are all post-1914: the poorer the quality, the later the date. The top left example has the crossed anchors and imperial crown of a naval infantry battalion. 1870 – 1919.* Each **£5 – £15**

◁ *CARTRIDGE POUCH made to hold 1871 Mauser rifle cartridges in varnished canvas loops. 1888; 8in long.* **£35**

CURIOSA

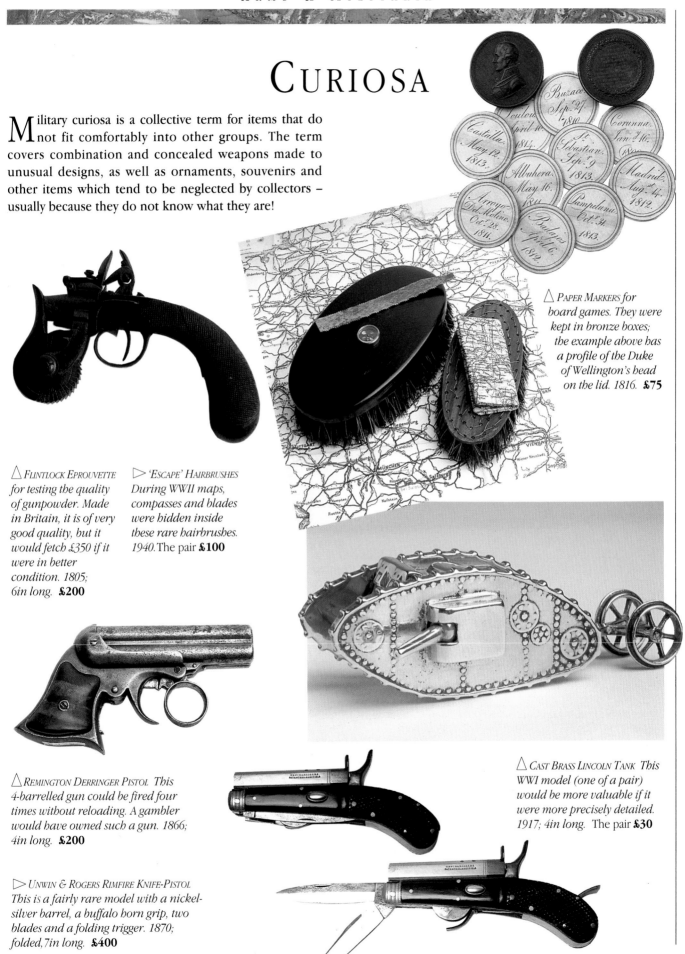

M ilitary curiosa is a collective term for items that do not fit comfortably into other groups. The term covers combination and concealed weapons made to unusual designs, as well as ornaments, souvenirs and other items which tend to be neglected by collectors – usually because they do not know what they are!

△ PAPER MARKERS *for board games. They were kept in bronze boxes; the example above has a profile of the Duke of Wellington's head on the lid. 1816.* £75

△ FLINTLOCK EPROUVETTE *for testing the quality of gunpowder. Made in Britain, it is of very good quality, but it would fetch £350 if it were in better condition. 1805; 6in long.* £200

▷ 'ESCAPE' HAIRBRUSHES *During WWII maps, compasses and blades were hidden inside these rare hairbrushes. 1940. The pair* £100

△ REMINGTON DERRINGER PISTOL *This 4-barrelled gun could be fired four times without reloading. A gambler would have owned such a gun. 1866; 4in long.* £200

▷ UNWIN & ROGERS RIMFIRE KNIFE-PISTOL *This is a fairly rare model with a nickel-silver barrel, a buffalo horn grip, two blades and a folding trigger. 1870; folded, 7in long.* £400

△ CAST BRASS LINCOLN TANK *This WWI model (one of a pair) would be more valuable if it were more precisely detailed. 1917; 4in long. The pair* £30

GLOSSARY

ACANTHUS A leaf pattern used extensively in classical antiquity and revived during the Renaissance as a popular decorative motif.

AIR TWIST A spiral pattern created in the stem of a glass by manipulating a trapped air bubble.

ART DECO A style of art and decoration that emerged between the two world wars, characterized by its elegant angularity.

ART GLASS An all-embracing term for glass which is principally decorative, particularly that produced during the late 19th and early 20th centuries.

ART NOUVEAU A style of art and decoration characterized by natural forms and sinuous lines; fashionable in the late 19th century.

ARTS AND CRAFTS MOVEMENT Formed in Britain in the late 19th century by a group of artists and craftsmen committed to hand-crafting, as opposed to machine-production. William Morris and John Ruskin were influential at the start of the movement.

BALLOON BACK CHAIR Back with an open 'O' shape and nipped waist. Popular style for sets of dining chairs 1820 – 1900.

BANDING Narrow strips of contrasting decorative veneer. Straight banding – cut with the grain; cross banding – cut directly across the grain; feather banding – cut diagonally across the grain.

BARLEY SUGAR TWIST Turned sections of wood in a spiral shape.

BAROQUE STYLE Continental style (principally Italian) characterized by very florid and heavy ornamentation. Fashionable in England 1660 – 1730.

BISQUE *see* Biscuit Pottery.

BISCUIT POTTERY A general term describing wares that have been fired once but not glazed. Originated in France in the mid 18th century.

BLANC DE CHINE An unpainted, highly translucent porcelain from China, characterized by a thick glaze; much copied by European factories.

BONE CHINA A hard, stable porcelain, invented in England in the 1790s, made with bone ash and kaolin.

BOCAGE Flowers or foliage surrounding or supporting a figure.

BOMBE French term for the swollen or bulging shapes in commodes or chests.

BRACKET FOOT Furniture foot resembling a bracket: straight bracket – straight from the corner edge; ogee bracket – an S-shaped curve on the inner edge; French foot or splay bracket – a slight curve outward on the outer edge.

BRITANNIA METAL Silver-white metal alloy made of tin, antimony and copper, sometimes with zinc added.

BURR WALNUT A highly decorative type of veneer cut from a cross-section of the gnarled grain at the base of a walnut tree.

CABOCHON A polished, unfaceted gemstone, cut with a domed face. The term also describes a convex oval ornament with a plain surface, carved on furniture. Popular in England 1740 – 60.

CABRIOLE LEG Furniture leg with a double curve – outward at the knee and inward above the foot.

CAMEO A low-relief carving on shell or stone, made up of two or more layers of different colours.

CAMEO GLASS A sandwich of coloured glass, carved to expose the under layer in much the same way as cameos. The top layer is frequently opaque white.

CARCASE The main structure of a piece of furniture, excluding drawers, doors, etc.

CARVER CHAIR Dining chair with arms; also known as an elbow chair.

CHASING A technique for decorating silver whereby a blunt punch is used to depress the background, leaving a raised design.

CHINOISERIE European imitations of Chinese decoration and design. Not to be confused with Chinese articles exported to Europe.

CHIPPENDALE, THOMAS (1718 – 79) English cabinet-maker and designer. Most of the 160 designs in his book, *The Gentleman and Cabinet Maker's Director* (published in 1754), are in Chinese, Gothic or French Rococo style.

CLOISONNE A decorative technique whereby a pattern made up of wires, or thin strips of metal soldered to a base, is filled with vitreous enamels.

CLUSTER COLUMNS Several small-diameter columns apparently clustered together to form a composite whole, used on furniture.

COBALT BLUE The colour resulting from cobalt oxide, and the blue used on early porcelain. It was the only colour that could withstand high temperature firing.

COCKBEADING A bead moulding decoration that projects from the surface of a piece of furniture; usually seen around drawer edges.

COMMODE A chest of drawers or cabinet, often in a highly decorated French style.

COQUILLAGE Decoration incorporating a shell-like motif.

CRACKLE Network of fine lines or cracks in a glazed surface; caused by differing expansion rates in the body and glaze.

CREAMWARE Cream-coloured earthenware with a transparent glaze. It was developed in the 1760s by Josiah Wedgwood, and became the standard domestic pottery used in Britain. Also known as Queen's ware.

DAVENPORT A small writing desk with a sloping top and case of drawers. It was popular from the late 18th century and throughout the 19th century.

DELFT WARE Tin-glazed pottery made in the Netherlands and England during the 17th and 18th centuries. The name is taken from the Dutch town of Delft, which was a key centre of production. Delft ware items usually serve a practical purpose.

DOVETAIL A series of close-fitting joints with interlocking tenons used in the construction of high quality furniture.

DRY POINT The technique of print engraving a copper plate using a hard steel needle. (Acid is not required.)

DUMB WAITER A dining room stand with two or three revolving tiers. It was used to hold condiments, sauce boats and after-dinner cheese and port.

EARTHENWARE Pottery made with porous clay which is fired at about 1200°C. The colour of the clays and the iron content produce a varied range of colours in the pottery. Most common clays are suitable for earthenware. *See* Stoneware.

EGG AND DART Carved or moulded ornamentation featuring a series of ovals with intervening arrow-heads, found particularly on cabinets.

ELECTROPLATED SILVER An electro-chemical process, developed in the 1840s, in which base metal is covered with a thin layer of pure silver.

EMBOSSING Decoration added to metalware by punching and hammering.

ENTABLATURE An architectural term adopted by cabinet-makers, referring to the architrave, frieze and cornice which surmount columns.

ESCAPEMENT Regulating mechanism of a clock which allows the stored power to be released at regular intervals.

ESCRITOIRE A cabinet with a pull-down writing table; a forerunner of the bureau.

ESCUTCHEON A decorative plate around a keyhole or edge of keyhole lining.

FAIENCE Tin-glazed earthenware, originally from Italy, which was introduced to the rest of Europe by migrant Italian potters.

FAMILLE-NOIRE 'Black family'; a transparent green enamel applied over a dull black pigment. This background can been seen on some Chinese ceramics.

FAMILLE-ROSE 'Pink family'; opaque enamels used 1723 – 35, the most conspicuous colours being rose-pinks (derived from gold).

FAMILLE-VERTE 'Green family'; transparent enamels, particularly brilliant green, decorating Chinese Kangxi-period porcelain.

FIDDLE BACK Violin-shaped splat found particulary in 18th century chairs.

FILIGREE Delicate ornamental lacy design made with threads of gold, silver or other precious metals.

FLATWARE In silverware, includes all flat pieces, particularly sets of forks and spoons. In porcelain, refers to plates and dishes.

FLUTING Vertical cuts or grooves made lengthways on a cylindrical object, such as a pillar or wine glass stem.

FUSEE A cone-shaped spool in a clock around which the chain is wound, and which evens out the pull of the mainspring to ensure constant timekeeping.

GADROON BORDER A carved or moulded decorative border made up of fluting or rounded beadings.

GATE LEG A pivoting leg on the frame of a table which supports a hinged leaf or flap.

GESSO (plaster of Paris) A surface finish, usually on wood, that gives a smooth base for painting or gilding; for example, on a doll's face.

GRAND SONNERIE Striking system in a clock which strikes the quarter hour and the hour on the quarters.

GUILLOCHE Decoration with a repeating pattern of intertwined ribbons, resulting in a series of small circles. Can be worked in single, double or triple bands.

HALLMARK Marks issued by British Assay Offices to authenticate the quality of gold, silver and platinum. First introduced in the 14th century by the Goldsmiths' company: stamping took place at their hall, hence the name 'hallmark'. A hallmark consists of four, or sometimes five, markings.

IMPRESSED MARK A pottery mark whereby a row of letters or marks is stamped into soft, unfired clay.

INCISED MARK Earliest method of marking pottery. The mark was scratched into the soft clay before firing.

INTAGLIO A design etched or engraved in metal or cut into stone etc; in letter seals and signet rings, for example.

JAPONAISERIE Small Japanese-style knick-knacks or ornaments.

JARDINIERE A large container, usually pottery, used for holding flowers and often masses of greenery.

JASPER WARE Type of dense unglazed stoneware made by Wedgwood. It is still produced in a variety of colours, and is also used as a base for applied relief decoration.

KAKIEMON WARE 17th century Japanese porcelain, vividly coloured and decorated with plants and birds. Widely imitated by European factories in the 18th century.

KNOP An ornamental knob or bulge, on the stem of a glass, for example.

LALIQUE, RENE (1860 – 1945) French glass-maker renowned for his decorative moulding, pressing and wheel-engraving techniques. Most of his early wares were small in size (scent bottles, for instance), but he later made larger pieces, such as vases and bowls.

LUSTRE WARE Pottery or porcelain to which a metallic glaze containing silver, copper, gold or platinum has been applied in order to produce a glistening sheen.

MAIOLICA Style of ceramics brought from Majorca to Italy. Inferior clay produced a soft, red or grey earthenware which was richly painted on a tin-enamelled base. Not to be confused with English majolica.

MAJOLICA Vividly decorated porcelain, moulded or pressed to produce sharp relief; developed in the mid 19th century by Herbert Minton.

MARQUETRY Decorative surface patterns on wood, made up of veneers and inlays.

MEERSCHAUM A mineral resembling white clay that can be carved when wet; used chiefly for making pipes.

NEO-CLASSICISM A revival style inspired by the art and architecture of ancient Greece and Rome. Developed in the late 18th century.

OPALINE A white, opalescent and opaque glass popular from the mid 19th century. Later examples, coloured green, pink and turquoise, were often painted or gilded.

ORMOLU The powdered gold used to gild furniture mounts. The term was later used to describe a gold coloured alloy of copper, zinc and tin.

PAPIER-MACHE Mixture of paper pulp, glue and chalk, sometimes with sand added, which is pressed and moulded into a shape and baked, then painted or lacquered.

PARIAN A hard paste porcelain with a semi-transparent body resembling marble; developed in the 19th century.

PATE-SUR-PATE ('paste-on-paste') A type of decoration in which layers of white slip are slowly built up over a dark background to create a cameo effect. The design appears pure white at the thickest point and shadowy at the thinnest. Developed in the mid 19th century at the Sèvres porcelain factory in France.

PEARL WARE Very hard, white creamware (or Queen's ware) developed in the late 18th century by Josiah Wedgwood; ideal for blue transfer printing.

PETITE SONNERIE Striking system in a clock which ting-tangs on the quarter hour and strikes a single ring on the hour.

PILASTER Partial column on a wall or piece of furniture, often rectangular in section.

PONTIL A solid iron rod used to remove the glass from the blow pipe after it has been blown. When cooled and removed, the pontil mark remains on the foot of the vessel.

PRATTWARE Relief carvings of figures, fruit and other motifs on earthenware, decorated in vivid underglaze blue, orange and green. Usually without a maker's mark, it was produced by a Staffordshire pottery family.

PURL WIRE Copper wire used for embroidery. Short lengths are wound round a needle, then threaded and sewn on to a base.

QUEEN'S WARE *see* Creamware.

'RAT TAIL' Decorative elongation of a spoon handle on to the bowl to give added strength. Developed during the late 17th century.

REEDING Similar to fluting. Instead of carved grooves, however, parallel convex decorative strips are added.

ROCOCO A highly decorative and elaborate architectural style that originated in France in the early 18th century. Its influence spread to other art forms, notably painting, sculpture and furnishings.

SALT GLAZE Technique involving the opening of the glazing kiln when it is at maximum temperature and throwing in salt, which is vitrified by the heat and produces a hard, glassy glaze.

SCRIMSHAW Handicrafts made by sailors from the bones and tusks of marine creatures. Items include carvings and incised scenes.

SHEFFIELD PLATE A thin layer of silver is fused to copper, which can then be worked as a single metal. The process was developed by Thomas Boulsover, a Sheffield cutler, in 1740.

SHELLWORK Mainly English decoration worked with small shells, sometimes with paper filigree.

SHERATON, THOMAS (1751 – 1806) English cabinet-maker. The refined elegance and balance of his designs can be seen in his book, *The Cabinetmaker and Upholsterer's Drawingbook* (1791 – 94).

SKELETON CLOCK A clock encased in glass, often with the plates cut away, so exposing the mechanism. Developed in France, this type of clock came to England in 1830.

SLIP Potter's clay reduced to a creamy consistency; used to coat pottery, or as an adhesive for external decoration.

SPANDREL Decorative triangular corner piece that fills or 'spans' the angles on furniture and clock dials.

STRINGING Fine lines of metal or contrasting wood inlaid on doors, drawers and other items of furniture

STUMPWORK A type of embroidery in which sections are padded out in order to create a raised effect.

STONEWARE An object made from clay fired at over 1250°C (almost as high as the firing temperature for porcelain); the resulting hard body is impervious to liquid.

TRANSFER PRINTING A technique perfected in the 18th century for applying decoration to mass-produced ceramics. Paper is printed with patterns in metallic oxides and then wrapped around the porcelain. It is burnt away during firing, leaving the pattern behind on the glaze.

TUNBRIDGE WARE Wooden articles, traditionally made in Royal Tunbridge Wells, decorated with different woods which had been glued together in thin strips to form one large block, and then cut into about fifteen smaller sections. The pattern was exactly duplicated throughout the block, as in a stick of rock. Also called 'English Mosaics', and popular from the mid 17th to late 19th century.

UNDERGLAZE BLUE *see* Cobalt Blue.

UNDERGLAZE COLOUR Decoration painted or printed on ceramics before final glazing and firing.

VENEER Thin sheets or bands of highly decorative wood such as walnut or mahogany, used to inlay or cover a base material. Veneers first became popular in England at the end of the 17th century.

VINAIGRETTE Small ornamental container, usually silver, with a compartment for a sponge soaked in aromatic vinegar; used to ward off unpleasant smells.

WHAT-NOT A multi-purpose mobile display stand which first became popular at the turn of the 19th century.

WHEEL ENGRAVING Method of cutting a design in glass using a revolving wheel and abrasive powder.

INDEX

Page numbers in **bold** refer to specific sections, and those in *italics* refer to illustrations.

Picture credits:TR=top right; TL=top left;
C=centre; CR= centre right; CL=centre
left; B=bottom; BL=bottom left;
BR=bottom right
Sotheby's 92T; 100L, 101C, BL, BR; 102BL,
BR; 103TR, C, BR; 106C, B; 107C, BR;
108L, R; 109TB; 110T, B, CL, CR; 114T;
115TL, TR, CL; 116L; 117TR, L, R; 118L, R;
120CL; 121C, B; 122B; 123TR, BR; 126C,
BL; 127TR, C; 128B.
Jerry Young 23TL, TR, BR; 28L; 29C, BL, BR;
30TL, TR; 32BR; 33BR; 53BL, BR; 54L, R;
55C, BR; 60BL; 84B; 85T; 92BR; 107TL,
BL; 113CL, BL, BR; 124BR; 137C; 142C;
143C, R; 167CL; 168T, B.
Bridgeman Art Library 21TL, TR; 22BR;
24CL; 69TR, BL; 161BR; 169TL, TR, BR.
John Bly 17BL; 23BL
Michael Holford 156T; 162T.
Victoria & Albert Museum 24CL
Christie's Colour Library 15T, C, B; 19T;
36T; 37CL, B; 62CL, 141L, TR, BR; 154CL,
155CR; 161CL, CR

Thanks to the following for loan of items
for front cover photograph
Antique picture frames: Lacy Gallery,
38 Ledbury Rd, W11; George II silver
candlestick: Asprey, 165-9 New Bond St,
W1; Doll: Steve Clark, Unit N1 Chenil
Galleries, 181-3 King's Rd, SW3;
Tortoiseshell necklace, Pinchbeck chain
and shell cameo: Trevor Allen, Unit E9-
E10, Chenil Galleries, 181-3 King's Rd,
SW3; Flintlock pistol: Holland & Holland,
31 & 33 Bruton St, W1; Chinese bowl,
microscope, clock, decanter, snuff
bottle, lowboy: Marshall Gallery,
67 Masboro Rd, W14

Photographer (front): Peter Rauter
Front cover stylist: Marion Price
Photographer (back): Clive Corless

With thanks also to: Aytac Antiques, Final
Whistle, Peter McAskie, Risky Business,
Donay Antiques, Antiquarius, Goldsmith
& Perris, Diane Harby